The Plain Language Guide to the World Summit on Sustainable Development

Janet R Strachan
Georgina Ayre
Jan McHarry
and
Rosalie Callway

COMMONWEALTH
SECRETARIAT

Routledge
Taylor & Francis Group

LONDON AND NEW YORK

from Routledge

First published by Earthscan in the UK and USA in 2005

For a full list of publications please contact:

Earthscan
2 Park Square, Milton Park, Abingdon, Oxon OX14 4RN
711 Third Avenue, New York, NY 10017

First issued in hardback 2017

Earthscan is an imprint of the Taylor & Francis Group, an informa business

Copyright © The Commonwealth Secretariat, 2005. Published by Taylor & Francis.

ISBN 13: 978-1-138-47149-8 (hbk)
ISBN 13: 978-1-85383-928-3 (pbk)

Typesetting by MapSet Ltd, Gateshead, UK
Cover design by Susanne Harris
Cover illustration: Mandala of the Elements © Lucy Hawkes 2004. The design is based
on the mandala – the Buddhist symbol of balance and integration. The animals in the
circles (from the right, clockwise) are influenced by Native American Indian art, and
represent earth, water, fire, and air, and the sun at the centre is energy or space. The
design represents balancing and harmony between the elements – the raw materials of
life – necessary for a healthy and sustainable planet and its peoples.
22883 Quicksilver Drive, Sterling, VA 20166-2012, USA

A catalogue record for this book is available from the British Library

Library of Congress Cataloging-in-Publication Data
The plain language guide to the world summit on sustainable development /
Jan McHarry ... [et al].
     p. cm.
   Includes bibliographical references and index.
   1. Sustainable development. 2. World Summit on Sustainable Development (2002 :
Johannesburg, South Africa) I. McHarry, Jan.
HC79.E5W6723 2005
338.9'27–dc22
                                                                2004019979

Contents

Part II: Implementing the Johannesburg Plan of Implementation

Annexes
(Source texts)

Foreword by the Commonwealth Secretary-General

The Commonwealth is a unique association, whose strength lies in the diversity of its membership and its ability to network and exchange best practices based on similar political, legal, administrative and education systems, and a shared language. The countries that make up its membership account for almost one third of the world's population and encompass many faiths, races, languages and cultures. Commonwealth countries are spread over every continent. They range from some of the largest in the world to small and micro-states; from the poorest to some of the wealthiest; and from natural resource-based economies to highly industrialized and knowledge-based ones. The Commonwealth's principles and the equal participation and voice of its member states have much to offer the international community as it works towards implementing the World Summit on Sustainable Development's (WSSD's) outcomes.

We all want the WSSD to be a landmark in the way we implement sustainable development policies, not a footnote in the history of false hopes that the last decades have seen. Its success will be measured by the real change it generates in the lives of people throughout the world. For this to happen, sustainable development must become a day-to-day reality for everyone – one of clean air and water; affordable shelter; access to health services; thriving ecosystems; peace and stability; the opportunity to develop fully as individuals and communities; equitable and democratic participation; the rule of law; and, most of all, freedom from the terrible shadow of disease, famine and poverty.

The poorest people in the world may know very little about the outcomes of the WSSD. What they know is that their lives will only be improved by decisive action. This is why all stakeholders – governments, civil society and the business sector – have a responsibility to live up to the commitments made at the summit.

One of the great assets of the Commonwealth in the pursuit of sustainable development is this diversity, and the equal participation, of its member states within the framework of shared fundamental principles. The Commonwealth is also a network of local governments, businesses, and professional and civil society organizations that will be an asset in implementing the outcomes from the WSSD. A deep commitment is needed to long-term partnerships, based on equity and collaboration that shows a spirit of generosity in their approach.

The Commonwealth has played an active role in three key international negotiations that have set the development agenda for the next decade by addressing critical concerns on trade, finance and sustainable development: the World Trade Organization (WTO) Doha Ministerial Meeting (December 2001); the Financing for Development Summit in Monterrey (March 2002); and the World Summit on Sustainable Development (September 2002). Together with the Millennium Development Goals (MDGs) – which have mobilized governments, international institutions and civil society to reduce poverty with renewed vigour and commitment – these processes must be brought more closely together to ensure that practical steps are taken, in a true spirit of international collaboration, to create prosperity and equity for all, and to reverse the continuing loss of environmental resources and quality that underpin the social, cultural, spiritual and economic foundations of our societies.

In February 2003, Commonwealth environment ministers considered the key challenges that they, as policy-makers, face in implementing the Johannesburg agreements. They sought greater dialogue on, and engagement with, partnerships for sustainable development that were announced in conjunction with the WSSD. In particular, they saw the need for ongoing efforts to promote awareness and understanding of the outcomes from WSSD amongst groups in society, business and government, in order to promote their full engagement in such partnerships. Commonwealth Heads of Government, at their meeting in Abuja in December 2003, welcomed the outcomes of the WSSD and pledged to work towards the full and effective implementation of Agenda 21 and the Johannesburg Plan of Implementation (JPOI).

This guide is a Commonwealth contribution towards these objectives. I am particularly pleased that the Commonwealth has developed it in close collaboration with Stakeholder Forum, and hope that the guide will be widely used in the Commonwealth and beyond to promote understanding and engagement in the WSSD process at all levels.

Don McKinnon
October 2004

Preface

The Plain Language Guide was inspired by a publication, in 1993, by the Centre for Our Common Future called *The Earth Summit's Agenda for Change*. Here, we have reprinted the original Preface by Warren (Chip) Lindner, which expressed the vision that sprang from Rio and was embedded in the Johannesburg summit. Chip was the then director of the Centre for Our Common Future and had been the secretary to the Brundtland Commission. He went on to be the political adviser to the chair of the 1998 World AIDS Conference and successfully campaigned for the conference to have its next conference, its first in a developing country, in South Africa. Chip died of an AIDS-related illness in November 2000. He felt that we had all, particularly developed countries, failed to live up to our commitments made at Rio. It was his hope that the legacy of Johannesburg would be different.

Felix Dodds
Executive Director
Stakeholder Forum for Our Common Future
October 2004

The Lindner Preface

The Earth Summit was an unprecedented event. It brought together more heads of government than any meeting in history. It effectively focused the world's attention on the most critical issues we face as a global community. And it adopted a global plan of action, Agenda 21, to address those issues. For all of these achievements history will, no doubt, accord it an honoured place.

In retrospect, however, history may, and I believe should, recognize that its most significant contribution was the process that it adopted to achieve its objectives. By attempting, at times more successfully than at others, to bring all sectors of society into its deliberative and decision-making functions, it became the first international experiment in democratizing intergovernmental decision-making.

Given the nature of the problems that confront us as a community of nations and peoples, we are now more than ever bound together by a common destiny. And solutions to those problems will have to be found both nationally and internationally. That means that international institutions and national governments must become increasingly more accountable and responsive to the views and expectations of the world's people as a whole. Indeed, it means that as we approach the next century we must move even further in the direction of a global democracy.

In preparing for the Earth Summit, the first tentative steps in this direction were taken. Never before have so many representatives of peoples' organizations from so many countries directly participated in the formulation of national and international policies. Never before have so many senior representatives of governments met in open debate with citizens from countries other than their own, as they did in the ECO 1992 public forums held throughout the world in preparation for the summit. Never before have so many representatives of civil society gathered together to address their own responsibilities in respect of environment and development issues as they did at the 1992 Global Forum in Rio.

These epoch-making first attempts at global democracy must be repeated, and they must be strengthened.

But to play a meaningful role in governance, people in all societies need the information necessary to prepare them for responsible participation. By making Agenda 21 and other Rio agreements accessible to people in an easy and understandable format, this book will help to provide some of that information.

In publishing *The Earth Summit's Agenda for Change*, we would like it to be a testament, and a tribute, to the thousands of individuals throughout the world – women, youth, journalists, citizen activists, teachers, business people, religious leaders, local authorities, trade unionists, representatives of indigenous people, scientists and researchers – who participated in framing the thinking of governments at the Earth Summit and contributed to the evolution of Agenda 21. The global momentum to achieve sustainable development and to implement the principles of Agenda 21 will only succeed with their continued participation in decisions that affect their lives, both nationally and internationally.

Establishing the precedent of broad public participation was the real hallmark of the Earth Summit. The Centre for Our Common Future is pleased to have played a part in helping to make that happen and remains committed to working with all groups and sectors of society in building the 'global partnership' called for in Rio.

W H Lindner
Executive Director
Centre for our Common Future
1993

Acknowledgements

We would like to give special thanks to the following individuals for peer reviewing specific chapters of the book: Dorothy Gordon; Jeffery Barber; Ruth Mubiru; Nora Ourbah; Berbalk Dagamara; Joanna Phillips; Harold Goodwin; Janet Stephenson; Claudia Strauss; Russell Howorth; Richard Ballhorn; Michael Massey; Thais Corral, Lars Goran Engfeldt, Pieter van der Gaag; Fanny Calder; Alice Palmer; Maria Onestini; Irene Dankelman; Jack Jeffery; Peter Warren; Maria Luiza; Mirian Vilela; Sian Pullen; and Yasmin von Schirndingy. Their expertise, pithy comments, time and knowledge greatly enhanced the guide. Any shortcomings that remain lie entirely at the door of the authors of the guide.

Thanks also go to colleagues in the Economic Affairs Division of the Commonwealth Secretariat for their advice and support: Indrajit Coomaraswamy; Eliawony Kisanga; Linda Chu; Ivan Mbirimi; Bridget Chilala; Bishaka Mukerjee; and Andreas Antoniou. Thanks go to Felix Dodds for being – Felix Dodds, and to Stakeholder Forum for their vision and drive in encouraging the hosting of the World Summit. Our personal thanks go to Simon Webb, Charles and Anne, Chris Church and Faith Ayre for all their support.

List of Acronyms and Abbreviations

ACC	United Nations Administrative Committee on Coordination
ACP	Africa, Caribbean and Pacific group of countries
AIDS	Acquired Immunodeficiency Syndrome
ANPED	Northern Alliance for Sustainability
AOSIS	Alliance of Small Island States
APEC	Asian Pacific Economic Cooperation
BOD	biological oxygen demand
BPoA	Barbados Programme of Action on the Sustainable Development of Small Island Developing States
Caricad	Caribbean Centre for Development Administration
Caricom	Caribbean Community Secretariat
CBD	United Nations Convention on Biological Diversity
CBTF	Capacity-Building Task Force on Trade, Environment and Development
CCCCC	Caribbean Community Climate Change Centre
CCD	United Nations Convention to Combat Desertification
CDB	Caribbean Development Bank
CDERA	Caribbean Disaster Emergency Response Agency
CEHI	Caribbean Environmental Health Institute
CFC	chlorofluorocarbon
CIS	Commonwealth of Independent States
CITES	United Nations Convention on International Trade in Endangered Species of Wild Fauna and Flora
COP	Convention of the Parties
CPF	Collaborative Partnership on Forests
CROP	Council of Regional Organizations in the Pacific
CSD	United Nations Commission on Sustainable Development
DAC	Development Assistance Committee (OECD)
DDAGTF	Doha Development Agenda Global Trust Fund
DESA	United Nations Department of Economic and Social Affairs
DFID	UK Department for International Development
DMD	Doha Ministerial Declaration
DOALOS	United Nations Division for Ocean Affairs and the Law of the Sea
DTIE	Division of Technology, Industry and Economics (UNEP)
EC	European Commission
EC	European Community
ECCB	Eastern Caribbean Central Bank

ECE	United Nations Economic Commission for Europe
ECLAC	United Nations Economic Commission for Latin America and the Caribbean
ECOSOC	United Nations Economic and Social Council
EEA	European Environment Agency
EEZ	Exclusive Economic Zone
ESCAP	United Nations Economic and Social Commission for Asia and the Pacific
ESCWA	United Nations Economic and Social Commission for Western Asia
EST	environmentally sound technology
EU	European Union
FAO	United Nations Food and Agriculture Organization
FDI	foreign direct investment
FFA	South Pacific Forum Fisheries Agency
FSM	Fiji School of Medicine
G8	Group of 8 industrialized nations: Canada, France, Germany, Italy, Japan, Russia, the UK and the US
GATS	General Agreement on Trade in Services
GATT	General Agreement on Tariffs and Trade
GDP	gross domestic product
GEENET	Global Environmental Epidemiology Network
GEF	Global Environment Facility
GEO	Global Environment Outlook (UNEP)
GESAMP	Joint Group of Experts on the Scientific Aspects of Marine Environmental Protection (United Nations agencies)
GIS	Geographical Information Systems
GMO	genetically modified organism
GNESD	Global Network on Energy for Sustainable Development
GNI	gross national income
GNP	gross national product
GPA	Global Programme of Action for the Protection of the Marine Environment from Land-based Activities
GRI	Global Reporting Initiative
GTI	Global Taxonomy Initiative
HECA	Healthy Environments for Children Alliance
HIPC	Heavily Indebted Poor Countries
HIV	Human Immunodeficiency Virus
HLSOC	High-level Summit Organizing Committee for the WSIS
IAEA	International Atomic Energy Agency
IATF	United Nations Inter-agency Task Force on Disaster Reduction
ICAO	International Civil Aviation Organization
ICLEI	International Council for Local Environment Initiatives
ICPD	International Conference on Population and Development
ICRI	International Coral Reef Initiative
ICSPAC	International Coalition on Sustainable Consumption and Production
ICT	information and communication technology
IEA	International Energy Agency

IFAD	International Fund for Agricultural Development
IFAP	International Federation of Agricultural Producers
IFC	International Finance Corporation
IFCS	Intergovernmental Forum on Chemical Safety
IFF	Intergovernmental Forum on Forests
IFI	International Financial Institution
IIED	International Institute for Environment and Development
IIF	Institute of International Finance
ILO	International Labour Organization
IMO	International Maritime Organization
IOC	Indian Ocean Commission Secretariat
IOC	Intergovernmental Oceanographic Commission of UNESCO
IMF	International Monetary Fund
INFORSE	International Network for Sustainable Energy
IPCC	Intergovernmental Panel on Climate Change
IPEC	International Programme on the Elimination of Child Labour
IPF	Intergovernmental Panel on Forests
IRPTC	International Register of Potentially Toxic Chemicals
ISDR	International Strategy for Disaster Reduction
ISO	International Organization for Standardization
ITC	International Trade Centre
ITPGR	International Treaty on Plant Genetic Resources for Food and Agriculture
ITU	International Telecommunication Union
IUCN	World Conservation Union
JPOI	Johannesburg Plan of Implementation
LA21	Local Agenda 21
LDCs	least developed countries
LMO	living modified organism
MARPOL	International Convention for the Prevention of Pollution from Ships
MDG	Millennium Development Goal
MEA	Multilateral Environmental Agreement
mm	millimetres
MMSD	Mining, Minerals and Sustainable Development
NAAEC	North American Agreement on Environmental Cooperation
NCSD	National Councils for Sustainable Development
NEPAD	New Partnership for African Development
NGO	non-governmental organization
ODA	Official Development Assistance
ODP	ozone depleting potential
ODS	ozone-depleting substance
OECD	Organisation for Economic Co-operation and Development
OECS	Organization of Eastern Caribbean States
OHRLLS	United Nations Office of the High Representative for the Least Developed Countries, Landlocked Developing Countries and Small Island Developing States
PIDP	Pacific Islands Development Programme

PIFS	Pacific Islands Forum Secretariat
POP	persistent organic pollutant
PP10	Partnership for Principle 10
PRTR	Pollutant Release and Transfer Register
R&D	research and development
RONA	United Nations Environment Programme Regional Office for North America
ROWA	United Nations Environment Programme Regional Office for West Asia
SADC	Southern African Development Community
SARD	Sustainable Agriculture and Rural Development
SEI	Singapore Environment Institute
SIDS	Small Island Developing States
SISEI	Système de Circulation d'Information et de Suivi de l'Environnement sur Internet en Afrique
SME	small- and medium-sized enterprises
SOCA	Sub-committee on Oceans and Coastal Areas (ACC)
SOPAC	South Pacific Applied Geoscience Commission
SPAC	sustainable production and consumption
SPBEA	South Pacific Board for Educational Assessment
SPC	Secretariat for the Pacific Community
SPREP	South Pacific Regional Environment Programme
SPTO	South Pacific Tourism Organization
TB	tuberculosis
TICAD	Tokyo International Conference on African Development
TNC	transnational corporation
TRIPS	Trade-Related Aspects of Intellectual Property Rights
UK	United Kingdom
UN	United Nations
UNAIDS	Joint United Nations Programme on HIV/AIDS
UNCED	United Nations Conference on Environment and Development
UNCHR	United Nations Commission on Human Rights
UNCHS	United Nations Centre for Human Settlements (now UN-Habitat)
UNCLOS	United Nations Convention on the Law of the Sea
UNCTAD	United Nations Conference on Trade and Development
UNDP	United Nations Development Programme
UNDPI	United Nations Department of Public Information
UNECE	United Nations Economic Commission for Europe
UNECLAC	United Nations Economic Commission for Latin America and the Caribbean
UNEP	United Nations Environment Programme
UNEP-ROLAC	United Nations Environment Programme – Regional Office for Latin America and Caribbean
UNESCO	United Nations Educational, Scientific and Cultural Organization
UNFCCC	United Nations Framework Convention on Climate Change
UNFF	United Nations Forum on Forests
UNFPA	United Nations Population Fund
UNGA	United Nations General Assembly

UNGASS	United Nations General Assembly Special Session
UN-Habitat	United Nations Human Settlements Programme
UNHCHR	United Nations High Commissioner on Human Rights
UNHCR	United Nations High Commissioner for Refugees
UNICEF	United Nations Children's Fund
UNIFEM	United Nations Development Fund for Women
UNIDO	United Nations Industrial Development Organization
UNITAR	United Nations Institute for Training and Research
UNPD	United Nations Population Division
UNRISD	United Nations Research Institute for Social Development
UPU	Universal Postal Union
US	United States
USP	University of the South Pacific
UWI	University of the West Indies
WBCSD	World Business Council on Sustainable Development
WEHAB	water and sanitation, energy, health, agriculture and biological diversity
WFP	World Food Programme
WHO	World Health Organization
WIPO	World Intellectual Property Organization
WMO	World Meteorological Organization
WRI	World Resources Institute
WSIS	World Summit on the Information Society
WSSCC	Water Supply and Sanitation Collaborative Council
WSSD	World Summit on Sustainable Development
WTO	World Trade Organization
WTO	World Tourism Organization
WTTC	World Travel and Tourism Council
WWF	World Wide Fund for Nature

Background

 The World Summit on Sustainable Development (WSSD)

The World Summit on Sustainable Development (WSSD) took place in Johannesburg from 26 August to 4 September 2002. It involved over 21,000 participants, including representatives of 191 governments and 104 heads of state or government. The aim of the summit was to complete a ten-year review of implementation of the 1992 United Nations Conference on Environment and Development (UNCED) – or the Rio Earth Summit – and to 'reinvigorate' global commitment to sustainable development. The three overarching objectives of the summit were 'eradicating poverty', 'protecting the natural resource base of economic and social development' and 'changing unsustainable patterns of production and consumption'.

In the run-up to the summit, there were calls for the negotiations to focus on just a few multidisciplinary areas. This proved difficult to achieve in practice; but, informally, some focus was achieved through the 'WEHAB agenda', proposed by the UN Secretary-General. This stands for '*water and sanitation, energy, health, agriculture and biodiversity*' and formed the basis for thematic sessions in Johannesburg.

One negotiated outcome of the summit was a 54-page plan of implementation that builds on the achievements in sustainable development made since 1992. WSSD also adopted a political statement, the Johannesburg Declaration on Sustainable Development, in which world leaders committed themselves '*to expedite the achievement of the time-bound, socio-economic and environmental targets*' contained in the Johannesburg Plan of Implementation (JPOI). The summit also provided a unique forum where new multi-stakeholder partnerships or initiatives could be announced. These partnerships aimed to strengthen the implementation of Agenda 21 (the 40-chapter blueprint for action that was adopted at UNCED).

By the final preparatory session in Bali (in May 2002), 70 to 80 per cent of the draft JPOI had been agreed. Negotiators convened two days in advance of the summit to start work on the outstanding issues. These included application of the Rio principles (such as the 'precautionary approach' and the 'common but differentiated responsibility' of states), as well as deliberations over good governance and the establishment of a World Solidarity Fund to address poverty. Other difficult issues included targets on sanitation, energy and climate change, along with proposals on establishing ten-year programmes on sustainable consumption and production patterns, health and human rights, globalization and natural resource issues, including targets on reversing trends in the loss of natural resources and biodiversity, the negotiation of a mechanism on benefit-sharing from the use of biological resources, and issues related to the sustainable use and conservation of fish and ocean resources. Lying at the heart of some of the toughest talks were the financial and technical resources needed to support sustainable development actions and concerns related to trade, especially issues addressed in the World Trade

Organization's (WTO's) Doha 'Development Round' work programme and improved market access for developing countries' agricultural products.

The Johannesburg Declaration and the JPOI represent an important international commitment to continued and increased efforts at bringing about sustainable development. The summit also provided an impetus for the launch of new multi-stakeholder partnerships to address sustainable development problems. Together with the UN Millennium Summit and the Monterrey Summit on Finance for Development, WSSD sets the framework for sustainable development over the first decades of the 21st century.

The Johannesburg Plan of Implementation (JPOI)

The Johannesburg Plan of Implementation is grounded in the outcomes of the 1992 UNCED. It includes well over 20 new targets and draws together significant outcomes from recent international meetings into a sustainable development framework. These include the Millennium Development Goals (MDGs); the Monterrey Consensus on Financing for Development; the WTO Doha Agenda; the Dakar Framework for Action on Education for All; the World Summit on Social Development; the Third United Nations Conference on the Least Developed Countries; and numerous multilateral environmental agreements and regional sustainable development initiatives and strategies.

The Rio Summit focused on environment and development and helped to elaborate both the concept of, and practical approaches to, sustainable development through the integration of the three components of sustainable development (economic development; social development and environmental protection). WSSD recognized that much more had to be done to bring about this integration, strengthening the focus on poverty, social concerns and implementation of Agenda 21.

The JPOI is arranged in 11 chapters, which address the following:

I *Introduction*. Principles for sustainable development, including Rio principles; implementation of Agenda 21 and internationally agreed development goals; good governance within each country and at the international level; peace, security, stability and respect for human rights and fundamental freedoms, including the right to development; the importance of ethics.

II *Poverty eradication*. National programmes and strategies; women's participation in decision-making; indigenous people and their communities; agriculture; rural infrastructure; desertification; sanitation; energy and industrial development for the poor; slum dwellers; child labour.

III *Changing unsustainable patterns of consumption and production*. Policies, programmes, strategies, planning and decision-making; measures and tools to promote sustainable patterns of consumption and production; investment in cleaner production; corporate environmental and social accountability; energy; transport; waste; management of chemicals and hazardous waste; heavy metals.

IV *Protecting and managing the natural resource base of economic and social development*. Water and sanitation; oceans and marine resources; vulnerability; disaster management; climate change; agriculture; desertification; biodiversity; mountains; tourism; forests; mining.

V *Sustainable development in a globalizing world*. Characteristics; opportunities and challenges of globalization.

VI *Health and sustainable development.* HIV/AIDS, tuberculosis (TB), malaria and other epidemics; health services; environmental health.

VII *Sustainable development in small island developing states.* Barbados Programme of Action on the Sustainable Development of Small Island Developing States (BPoA); ocean and coastal resources; freshwater; pollution and waste; tourism; extreme weather events; vulnerability indices; climate change; energy; health; poverty eradication.

VIII *Sustainable development for Africa.* New Partnership for African Development (NEPAD); desertification; health; natural disasters and conflict; water resources; agriculture; management of chemicals; digital divide; tourism; UN-Habitat Agenda.

IX *Other regional initiatives.* Concerns and priorities in the following UN regions: Latin America and the Caribbean; Asia and the Pacific; West Asia; Economic Commission for Europe.

X *Means of implementation.* Trade; finance; debt; technology transfer; role of the scientific community; education; capacity-building; information for decision-making.

XI *Institutional framework for sustainable development.* Role of the United Nations General Assembly (UNGA), the United Nations Economic and Social Council (ECOSOC), the United Nations Commission on Sustainable Development (CSD) and international institutions; strengthening the institutional framework at regional, national and local levels; participation of major groups.

The WSSD's commitments encompassed international targets in the areas of chemicals management, water and sanitation, including:

- a deadline of 2020 to achieve the use and production of chemicals in ways that lead to the minimization of significant adverse effects on human health and the environment;
- a target of 2015 for halving the proportion of people who do not have access to basic sanitation;
- fisheries stocks to be maintained or restored on an urgent basis and, where possible, by 2015; and
- achievement of a significant reduction in the current rate of loss of biological diversity by 2010.

Additionally, governments agreed to negotiate an international instrument, under the auspices of the Convention on Biological Diversity (CBD), on sharing the benefits arising from the use of biological resources. They also established a World Solidarity Fund to help eradicate poverty. Negotiations on trade closely reflected language agreed by trade ministers at the Doha ministerial meeting in 2002; but the agreement promotes 'mutual supportiveness' between the multilateral trading system and multilateral environmental agreements, while recognizing the importance of maintaining the integrity of both sets of instruments. No concrete, time-bound targets could be agreed on renewable energy, though the section on small island developing states (SIDS) has a commitment to the availability of adequate, affordable and environmentally sound energy services by strengthening ongoing, and supporting new, efforts on energy supply and services by 2004. Delegates agreed to take action to phase out energy subsidies that inhibit sustainable development. The way in which partnerships should interact with, or link to, the WSSD process and its follow-up was also debated at length. These partnership initiatives will be free-standing, but the CSD was mandated to act 'as a focal point for the discussion of partnerships that promote sustainable development'.

Origins of the World Summit on Sustainable Development

The first UN environment conference (the United Nations Conference on the Human Environment) took place in Stockholm in June 1972. It was a pioneering event that agreed a declaration and action plan on the human environment and established the United Nations Environment Programme (UNEP), which continues to take forward the environmental agenda set in 1972.

In 1987, the Brundtland Report (*Our Common Future*) was published by Gro Harlem Brundtland, the then prime minister of Norway. It gave the most definitive and well-used explanation of sustainable development as 'development that meets the needs of the present without compromising the ability of future generations to meet their own needs'.[1]

The report was unique in addressing the need for economic development without depleting natural resources or harming the environment, and was central in framing discussions at the United Nations Conference on Environment and Development (UNCED), or the Earth Summit. Convened in June 1992 in Rio de Janeiro, UNCED was attended by over 100 heads of state and government (more than had ever attended an international conference before) and was unique in its size and participation. Though UNCED was seen by some at the time as somewhat disappointing, its outcomes were, nevertheless, significant. They consisted of a political declaration of principles on environment and development (the Rio Declaration), a 40-chapter 'blueprint' for implementing sustainable development (Agenda 21 – so called as it forms an agenda for the 21st century), a declaration of Forest Principles, and two new multilateral environmental conventions on climate change (the United Nations Framework Convention on Climate Change, or UNFCCC) and on biodiversity (the United Nations Convention on Biological Diversity, or CBD). The summit led to new approaches to including different groups of society in policy debate and action and it established a new mechanism within the United Nations (the CSD) to monitor and promote implementation of the outcomes from Rio.

Agenda 21

Agenda 21 is a comprehensive 40-chapter action plan for sustainable development. It addresses both social and economic dimensions of sustainable development, as well as the conservation and management of specific natural resources and ecosystems. Agenda 21 promotes a strongly bottom-up, participatory approach involving a wide range of different civil society groups. Local government has played a particularly constructive role in developing and implementing Agenda 21 at the community level through the Local Agenda 21 process (see 'Major groups' below).

Rio Declaration

The *Rio Declaration on Environment and Development* is a statement of 27 principles to guide action on environment and development. Similar in style to the Stockholm principles of 1972, it was the subject of long and intense negotiations. The Rio Declaration includes the concepts of sustainable development, the precautionary approach and the 'polluter pays' principle and as such has brought these formally to the international arena. It also recognizes that in 'view of the different contributions to global environmental degradation, states have common but differentiated responsibilities'. Here, developed countries acknowledge the responsibility they bear in the international pursuit of sustainable development and the technologies and financial resources they command.

Climate change and biodiversity conventions

Two new conventions were opened for signature at Rio and rapidly came into force. These were the *United Nations Framework Convention on Climate Change* (UNFCCC) and the *Convention on Biological Diversity* (CBD). Both of these conventions have been further elaborated – through the Kyoto Protocol under the UNFCCC and the Cartagena Protocol on Biosafety under the CBD. At the WSSD, the debate on climate concerns remained as vigorous as ever with states that had ratified the Kyoto Protocol urging states that had not yet done so to ratify the protocol in a timely manner. On biodiversity, key issues included the protection of traditional knowledge and agreement to negotiate an international instrument on the fair and equitable sharing of benefits arising out of the utilization of genetic resources.

Forests, desertification and small island developing states

Negotiations at UNCED on forest issues were particularly difficult and could only be concluded through agreement on a non-binding set of *Forest Principles*. Multilateral discussions on forest issues continued after Rio through an Intergovernmental Panel on Forests and subsequently through an Intergovernmental Forum on Forests, and then the United Nations Forum on Forests and Collaborative Partnership on Forests. These processes have deepened the analysis on forest issues; but it has not been possible to secure more concrete or binding international action.

Rio also initiated negotiations on *desertification*, leading to the 1994 United Nations Convention to Combat Desertification (CCD). The CCD has experienced a lack of financing, which was reflected in the discussions at the WSSD on the inclusion of desertification as a focal area for funding by the Global Environment Facility (GEF).

Agenda 21 (Chapter 17) also initiated the 1994 UN Global Conference on the Sustainable Development of Small Island Developing States (SIDS) which adopted the Barbados Programme of Action on the Sustainable Development of *Small Island Developing States* (BPoA), a comprehensive agenda for sustainable development in small island states. These concerns are reflected in Chapter VIII of the Johannesburg Plan of Implementation, which agrees to a review and international meeting, which will take place in Mauritius in January 2005.

Finance

The most difficult and protracted issue for discussion at Rio was the question of *finance* and it remained centre stage at the WSSD, too. Consistently, developing countries have sought new and additional funding for sustainable development actions. However, there is a widespread perception that the continued lack of such funding has been a major constraint in implementing the Rio agreements. Key mechanisms for financing sustainable development include the Global Environment Facility (GEF), established in 1990 to address global environmental problems (ozone depletion, climate change, biodiversity loss and international water pollution). The fund is administered by the World Bank, UNEP and the United Nations Development Programme (UNDP), and finances the incremental costs of those domestic actions which produce global environmental benefits. This stipulation places constraints on the availability of GEF funds to finance actions under Agenda 21. The other important development since Rio was the International Conference on Financing for Development, held in March 2002 at Monterrey in Mexico. Through this, governments committed themselves to a range of actions that would promote a supportive environment for investment, addressing debt concerns and increasing the flow of funding to better support development.

United Nations Commission on Sustainable Development (CSD)

Rio resulted in the creation of a new body in the United Nations, the *Commission on Sustainable Development*, to follow up the outcomes of the Earth Summit. Housed within the UN's Department of Economic and Social Affairs (DESA), CSD's principle role has been to facilitate broad-based policy dialogues on sustainable development, to support the negotiation of texts related to UNCED follow-up and to pioneer stakeholder participation in UN decision-making. While many saw the multidisciplinary dialogues as useful, it was also felt that the CSD was not as effective as it could be. Concerns included the time-consuming nature of the annual negotiations, which it was felt provided little added value to other processes. The low status of the commission within the UN system was another concern, making it difficult for the body to be strategic in its promotion of sustainable development. Reform of the CSD became a focus for negotiation in the run-up to WSSD and after the summit when the CSD considered ways in which to promote the review and implementation of the outcomes (Johannesburg Plan of Implementation, Chapter XI).

Major groups

The 1992 Rio Earth Summit experienced a new level of engagement by civil society in United Nations' negotiations, swept along by a wave of public activism on environment and development issues. Non-governmental organisations (NGOs) had organized a parallel event in Stockholm in 1972, the first of its kind, and their engagement throughout the run-up to Rio – particularly during the work of the Brundtland Commission, which examined issues related to environment and development and the emerging concept of sustainable development – brought a deeper understanding of the need for public engagement in formulating and implementing sustainable development policies and actions. As a result, Agenda 21 calls for new forms of participation at all levels in making sustainable development happen. It devotes individual chapters to the roles and responsibilities of nine 'major groups' of civil society: women; children and youth; indigenous people; NGOs; local authorities; workers and trade unions; business and industry; scientific and technological communities; and farmers. Subsequently, the CSD has engaged the nine major groups through multi-stakeholder dialogues and the key role of major groups in partnerships for sustainable development is well recognized. The 11th session of the CSD (April 2003) highlighted scientists and educators amongst the major groups who should be involved in follow-up work to the WSSD undertaken by the CSD.

 ## Purpose of this book

The aim of this book is to provide a quick way in to the Johannesburg Plan of Implementation to help promote an understanding of the agreement and practical action on the commitments. Throughout the plan there is a call for 'action at all levels' based on the active participation of all groups in society working in fields as diverse as health care; social welfare; education and training; economic planning; natural resources management; environmental protection; trade; investment; and business development. We hope the guide will be particularly useful to those who were not centrally involved in the negotiations, but wish to take forward action on sustainable development in their own areas and in partnership with other groups. This guide does not provide a political analysis of the negotiations or the JPOI: such material is available elsewhere. Rather, it is a resource book for those working in community groups, business, local government, central government departments, regional institutions and the international community.

We recognize that the JPOI is a finely balanced text whose every word has been considered and intensely negotiated. We have tried to be neutral in our summaries of the agreement; but any attempt to simplify the JPOI for the reader runs the risk of upsetting the fine balance of the original. Despite the challenges, we feel this risk is worth taking to bring the JPOI to as wide an audience possible. *However, we urge all readers to refer to the original JPOI text (provided as Annex A in this guide) to consider the precise meaning or intention of the JPOI in any given area.* To help, we have included clear references to the original JPOI paragraph numbers.

 # Resources in this book

Context

Background and context to the decisions taken at the WSSD.

At a glance

Some statistics related to the issues covered in the JPOI chapter.

Key words

A checklist of the key issues addressed in the JPOI chapter.

Chapter in summary

Each chapter of the JPOI is presented in the form of a summary. Bold type has been used by the authors to highlight key words and guide the eye of the reader: these are not intended to give interpretation or emphasis to the text. Actions are almost always signalled in the JPOI as being intended 'at all levels', from local to international.

As far as possible, we have tried to keep the spirit of the original; but a negotiated text can be, by its very nature, ambiguous. *We strongly urge readers to refer to the original text when considering the precise meaning of the JPOI* (see Annex A in this guide). References to each and every paragraph of the JPOI are included within the narrative summaries for each chapter in square brackets – for example, [7m]. A reference to II.8a, indicates paragraph 8a in Chapter II.

Targets and commitments

New and pre-existing targets included in the chapter, drawn from a list prepared by the United Nations CSD.

Themes of the chapter across the JPOI

A narrative review of how key themes within the chapter are dealt with elsewhere in the JPOI. Further cross-referencing is available through the Index.

Key United Nations bodies and Bretton Woods institutions

Key United Nations bodies and Bretton Woods institutions involved in work related to the issues addressed in the chapter and likely to play a role in implementing WSSD outcomes. In Agenda 21, certain UN bodies were identified as the lead agency or 'task manager' for the 40 issues outlined in the agreement. For example, the UN Department of Economic and Social Affairs (DESA) Division for Sustainable Development is the task manager for sustainable consumption and production issues.

Conferences, agreements and processes

International processes and agreements that are related to the themes of the JPOI chapter or directly referred within the text. This is not an exhaustive listing, but provides a rough time-line of key source agreements and events.

Indicators for measuring progress in implementation

Examples of established and accepted indicators, which could be used to assess whether JPOI goals are being met.

Partnership examples

An illustration of the kinds of partnerships that were accepted and announced in connection with the WSSD. All examples given are detailed on the CSD's partnership website and further information is available from the contact points provided.

Other resources

Each chapter has some specific reference material giving short explanations of the processes, institutions, subjects or multilateral agreements that are referred to in the JPOI.

 # Note

1   Brundtland, G (ed) (1987) *Our Common Future: World Commission on Environment and Development*, Oxford University Press, Oxford

Part I

The Johannesburg Plan of Implementation

Introduction

I

 ## Chapter I in summary

The 1992 United Nations Conference on Environment and Development (*UNCED*) in Rio de Janeiro provided the fundamental principles and programme of action for achieving sustainable development. The Johannesburg Plan of Implementation (JPOI) strongly reaffirms:

- The **Rio principles**;
- Full implementation of **Agenda 21**;
- The 1997 Programme for the Further Implementation of Agenda 21; and
- Achievement of **internationally agreed development goals** (for example, the United Nations Millennium Declaration and outcomes of major UN conferences/agreements since 1992) *[1]*.

The JPOI builds on achievements since UNCED and helps to realize the remaining goals. To do this, governments commit themselves to strengthening **international cooperation** and undertaking **concrete actions and measures at all levels**:

- Taking into account the Rio principles, including principle 7 on the **common but differentiated responsibilities** of states in the pursuit of sustainable development; and
- Promoting the **integration of the three pillars** of sustainable development – economic development, social development and environmental protection – as interdependent and mutually reinforcing pillars *[2]*.

AT A GLANCE

Three cross-cutting objectives of, and essential requirements for, sustainable development are:

1. poverty eradication;
2. changing unsustainable patterns of production and consumption; and
3. protecting and managing the natural resource base of economic and social development.

KEY WORDS

- **integrating the three pillars of sustainable development**
- **action at all levels**
- **common but differentiated responsibilities**
- **poverty eradication**
- **consumption and production**
- **natural resource base**
- **implementation to benefit all**
- **partnerships**
- **good governance**
- **peace, security and stability**
- **human rights and fundamental freedoms**
- **right to development**
- **cultural diversity**
- **ethics**

Poverty eradication, changing unsustainable patterns of production and consumption, and protecting and managing the natural resource base of economic and social development are overarching objectives of, and essential requirements for, sustainable development *[2]*. The outcomes of the World Summit on Sustainable Development (WSSD) should be implemented to the benefit of all, and implementation should involve all relevant actors through partnerships *[3]*.

Good governance, within each country and at the international level, is essential for sustainable development. At the national level, the following elements are the basis for sustainable development:

- Sound environmental, social and economic policies;
- Democratic institutions that are responsive to the needs of the people;
- The rule of law;
- Anti-corruption measures;
- Gender equality; and
- An enabling environment for investment.

As a result of globalization, external factors have become critical in determining the success or failure of developing countries in their national efforts. The gap between developed and developing countries shows the continued need for a dynamic and enabling international economic environment, particularly on finance, technology transfer, debt and trade. The importance of the following for sustainable development is recognized:

- Full and effective participation of developing countries in global decision-making *[4]*;
- Peace, security, stability and respect for human rights and fundamental freedoms, including the right to development;
- Respect for cultural diversity *[5]*; and
- Ethics *[6]*.

 ## Rio principles elsewhere in the JPOI

The Rio principles, stated in the 1992 Rio Declaration on Environment and Development, are woven in throughout the JPOI. The principles will be built on in strengthening the institutional framework for sustainable development and taken into account in promoting sustainable consumption and production patterns; cooperation to reduce air pollution; corporate responsibility and accountability; and increased efforts to implement Agenda 21 and internationally agreed development goals. In all but one of these specific areas (corporate responsibility), the principle of common but differentiated responsibilities (principle 7) is referenced, and is quoted in full in Chapter X on the need for increased efforts at implementation. The precautionary approach (principle 15) is evoked with respect to the use and production of chemicals and in science-based decision-making. In its focus on policies and measures to promote sustainable patterns of consumption and production, the application of principle 16 is requested, which states that the polluter should, in principle, bear the cost of pollution caused by their activities. This principle should also be taken into account in promoting the internalization of environmental costs and the use of economic instruments. Industry is encouraged to improve social and environmental performance, bearing in mind principle 11, which addresses the use of environmental legislation and standards, while further efforts should be made to ensure access at the national level to environmental information and public participation in decision-making, in further implementation of principle 10. A number of the Rio principles are addressed in a more general way – for example, principles 5 (poverty eradication) and 8 (production and consumption patterns) are the subject of specific chapters; principle 9 (cooperation to strengthen capacity-building) is addressed all the way through the agreement; or principle 13 (liability and compensation), which has only one related reference addressing the marine transport of radioactive material.

TARGETS AND COMMITMENTS

- Full implementation of Agenda 21 and Millennium Development Goals (MDGs).

- Integration of the three pillars of sustainable development.

- Full involvement of developing countries in decision-making processes.

- Action on poverty, consumption and production patterns, the natural resource base, good governance, peace, security, respect for human rights and fundamental freedoms, the right to development, and cultural diversity.

 # Resources

Agenda 21

www.un.org/esa/sustdev/documents/UNCED_Docs.htm
This 40-chapter action plan, agreed at the United Nations Conference on Environment and Development (UNCED), covers natural resources; the role of different groups; social and economic development; and institutional issues.

Millennium Declaration (2000)

www.un.org/millennium
Adopted by the United Nations General Assembly (UNGA) in September 2000, the

Millennium Declaration contains commitments on human rights, good governance and democracy, as well as measurable goals and targets for combating poverty, hunger, disease, illiteracy, environmental degradation and discrimination against women. It is the basis of the Millennium Development Goals.

Millennium Development Goals (MDGs)

www.un.org/millenniumgoals/index.shtml (UN)
www.undp.org/mdg (UNDP)
www.developmentgoals.org (World Bank)
The United Nations Secretary-General's 'Road Map' (September 2001) set out concrete targets for goals and commitments in the Millennium Declaration. These were further developed into the Millennium Development Goals (MDGs).

Monterrey Consensus

www.un.org/esa/ffd
The Monterrey Consensus was agreed at the International Conference on Financing for Development (March 2002). Its commitments are to increase financial resources for development (domestic and international); promote trade; strengthen cooperation for development; address debt; and improve the international monetary, financial and trading systems.

Programme for the Further Implementation of Agenda 21

www.un.org/esa/earthsummit (on Rio+5)
This programme was adopted by United Nations General Assembly (UNGA) in 1997 following a review of progress on UNCED implementation.

Rio Declaration on Environment and Development

www.un.org/esa/sustdev/documents/UNCED_Docs.htm
The Rio Declaration is a statement of 27 principles on environment and development, adopted at UNCED. They include the following referred to in the background chapter: principle 7 *'In view of the different contributions to global environmental degradation, States have common but differentiated responsibilities'*; principle 15 *'to protect the environment, the precautionary approach shall be widely applied by States according to their capabilities. Where there are threats of serious or irreversible damage, lack of full scientific certainty shall not be used as a reason for postponing cost-effective measures to prevent environmental degradation'*; and principle 16 *'National authorities should endeavour to promote the internalization of environmental costs and the use of economic instruments, taking into account the approach that the polluter should, in principle, bear the cost of pollution'*.

United Nations Commission on Sustainable Development (CSD)

www.un.org/esa/sustdev/csd/about_csd.htm
The CSD reviews UNCED and World Summit on Sustainable Development (WSSD)

implementation. It develops policy recommendations, supports multi-stakeholder dialogues and promotes partnerships.

United Nations Conference on Environment and Development (UNCED)

www.un.org/esa/sustdev/documents/UNCED_Docs.htm

This is the Earth Summit, held in Rio de Janeiro in 1992. Outcomes were the Rio Declaration; Agenda 21; the Forest Principles; the United Nations Framework Convention on Climate Change (UNFCCC) and the Convention on Biological Diversity (CBD), the United Nations CSD.

Key United Nations bodies and Bretton Woods institutions

- United Nations Commission on Sustainable Development (CSD)

- United Nations Department of Economic and Social Affairs (DESA)

- United Nations Development Programme (UNDP)

- United Nations Economic and Social Council (ECOSOC)

- United Nations Environment Programme (UNEP)

- United Nations General Assembly (UNGA)

- United Nations Regional Commissions

- World Bank

CONFERENCES, AGREEMENTS AND PROCESSES

- United Nations Conference on Environment and Development (UNCED), Rio Declaration on Environment and Development, Agenda 21 (1992)

- Programme for the Further Implementation of Agenda 21 (1997)

- Millennium Declaration and Millennium Development Goals (MDGs) (2000)

- United Nations Conference on Financing for Development, Monterrey, Mexico (2002)

Poverty Eradication

2

 ## Context

Poverty eradication was one of three overarching objectives of the World Summit on Sustainable Development (WSSD). Poverty is not simply an issue of income: when asked, the poor highlight a range of other important issues, including health, safety, education, food and basic services. People's experience of poverty can vary widely, but they all speak about their vulnerability and exclusion by the state and society (DFID, 2002). The inter-linkages between poverty and the environment remain an issue of discussion and contention. The livelihoods and well-being of poorer people often depend upon sound environmental management. The poor also suffer disproportionately from the ill effects of environmental decline and poorly planned human activities. Better environmental management is essential to lasting poverty reduction (UNDP, 2002), along with measures promoting social and environmental justice.

KEY WORDS

• **Millennium Development Goals (MDGs)**

• **World Solidarity Fund**

• **gender mainstreaming**

• **indigenous people**

• **health**

• **land and sustainable agriculture**

• **food security**

• **water and sanitation**

• **energy**

• **industrial development**

• **slum dwellers**

• **child labour**

Access to clean water for both urban and rural poor was a priority at the WSSD. In November 2002, the United Nations Committee of Economic, Social and Cultural Rights declared water as a human right, placing an obligation on governments to progressively extend access to sufficient, affordable, accessible and safe water supplies and safe sanitation services to all citizens without discrimination. A right to water will not result in universal access instantly; but the adoption of the right is an encouraging sign that member governments of the UN are placing higher priority on these services (Water Aid, 2003).

Agenda 21 includes chapters on 'combating poverty' and 'promoting human settlement development'. The Johannesburg processes took a further step forward in heightening the profile of links between poverty eradication and sustainable development.

Chapter II in summary

Eradicating poverty

Poverty eradication is the greatest challenge facing the world today and is essential for sustainable development. Each country has responsibility for its own sustainable development and poverty eradication, with national policies

AT A GLANCE

- One in five people on the planet, two-thirds of them women, live in abject poverty (UNDP, 2000).

- Of the world's 6 billion people, 2.8 billion live on less than US$2 a day, and 1.2 billion on less than US$1 a day (International Energy Agency, 2002; UNEP, 2002).

- Water-related diseases such as diarrhoea and cholera kill an estimated 3 million people a year in developing countries, the majority children under the age of five (Water Aid website, 2003).

- 1.2 billion people are without access to clean drinking water (UNEP, 2002).

- 2.4 billion people lack access to adequate sanitation (UNEP, 2002).

- 1.6 billion people – one quarter of the world's population – have no access to electricity (International Energy Agency, 2002).

- 2.4 billion people rely on traditional biomass – wood, agricultural residues, dung – for cooking and heating (International Energy Agency, 2002).

'Improving sanitation and providing clean water are critical if the lives of the urban poor are to be improved. Access to such life saving basic needs is an important first step in the process of slum upgrading' (Anna Tibaijuka, under secretary-general of the UN and executive director of UN-Habitat at the launch of a Water and Sanitation Trust Fund, 7 October 2002).

and development strategies playing an important role. Action is needed at all levels to help developing countries meet **internationally agreed poverty-related goals** *[7]*, including to:

- Halve, by 2015, the proportion of people who have an **income** of less than US$1 a day, suffer from **hunger** and lack access to **safe drinking water** *[7a]*;
- Establish a **World Solidarity Fund** to eradicate poverty and promote social and human development *[7b]*;
- Develop **national programmes for sustainable development and local and community development** to empower poor people and their organizations *[7c]*;
- Promote **women**'s participation in decision-making at all levels; 'mainstream' gender perspectives; eliminate violence and discrimination; and improve women's health and economic status *[7d]*;
- Improve access by **indigenous peoples** and their communities to economic activities and employment *[7e]*;
- Deliver **basic health services** for all and reduce **environmental health threats** *[7f]*;
- Ensure that boys and girls are able to complete a full course of primary schooling and have equal access to all levels of **education** *[7g]*;
- Provide access to **agricultural resources** to people living in poverty, especially women and indigenous communities. This may include land

2

tenure arrangements that support indigenous and common property resource management systems *[7h]*;

- Build **rural infrastructure**: diversify the economy and improve access to markets, market information and credit for the rural poor *[7i]*;
- Transfer **basic sustainable agricultural techniques and knowledge** to small-scale and medium-scale farmers, fishers and the rural poor *[7j]*;
- Increase **food availability and affordability**, through community-based partnerships linking rural and urban people and enterprises *[7k]*; and
- **Combat desertification** and reduce the impacts of drought and floods through better use of weather information and forecasts, early warning systems and conservation practices *[7l]*.

Water and sanitation

The Millennium Development Goal (MDG) of halving the proportion of people who are unable to reach or afford **safe drinking water** by 2015 is complemented by a new target of halving, by the same year, the proportion of people who do not have access to **basic sanitation** *[8]*. Action is required at all levels to strengthen:

'Poverty is pain; it feels like a disease. It attacks a person not only materially but also morally. It eats away one's dignity and drives one into total despair' (a poor woman, Moldova, 1997, cited in Narayan et al, 2000).

- **Household sanitation** systems *[8a]*;
- Sanitation in **public institutions**, especially schools *[8b]*;
- Safe **hygiene practices** *[8c]*; **education/outreach** for children *[8d]*; and affordable and socially and culturally acceptable **technologies** and practices *[8e]*;
- **Innovative financing and partnerships** *[8f]*; and
- Integration of water and sanitation in **national sustainable development and poverty reduction strategies** *[7m]*, and sanitation in **water resources management strategies** *[8g]*.

Energy

To help achieve the MDGs and generate services that alleviate poverty, better collaboration is needed to improve access to reliable and affordable energy services for sustainable development *[9]*. The emphasis is on *'reliable, affordable, economically viable, socially acceptable and environmentally sound energy services and resources'*, with action taken at all levels on:

- Better access, including rural electrification, decentralized energy systems, increased use of renewable energy sources, cleaner liquid and gaseous fuels, and enhanced energy efficiency *[9a]*;
- Modern **biomass** technologies and fuelwood sources; commercialized biomass operations *[9b]*; sustainable use of **biomass** and other renewable energies *[9c]*;
- Cleaner use of **liquid and gaseous fossil fuels**, when these are considered more environmentally sound, socially acceptable or cost effective *[9d]*;

- National energy policies and regulatory frameworks creating energy sector conditions that improve access by the poor to services in rural, peri-urban and urban areas *[9e]*;
- International and regional cooperation on energy services, especially in rural and isolated areas *[9f]*; and
- Accelerated access by the poor to services, facilitated through **financial and technical assistance**, public–private partnerships and national policies on energy for sustainable development *[9g]*.

Industrial development

To strengthen the **contribution of industrial development** to poverty eradication and sustainable natural resource management *[10]*, action at all levels is required to:

- Improve industrial **productivity**, **competitiveness** and **industrial development** in developing countries *[10a]*;
- Increase **income-generating employment**, taking into account the International Labour Organization (ILO) Declaration on Fundamental Principles and Rights at Work *[10b]*;
- Promote **micro-, small-** and **medium-sized enterprises**, especially **agro-industry**, through training *[10c]*;
- Help rural communities in developing countries to benefit from **small-scale mining** *[10d]*;
- Develop safe low-cost **technologies to conserve fuel** for cooking and heating water *[10e]*; and
- Support natural resource management that creates **sustainable livelihoods** for the poor *[10f]*.

'Poverty has so many causes that no one solution will solve all the problems in every country' (Agenda 21, 1992).

Slum dwellers

To secure the MDG of achieving a significant improvement in the lives of at least 100 million **slum dwellers by 2020** *[11]*, actions at all levels addressing the poor is required to:

- Improve access to **land and property, adequate shelter and basic services** especially for female heads of households [11a];
- Use low-cost and **sustainable materials** and appropriate technology for housing *[11b]*;
- Increase decent **employment, credit and income** *[11c]*;
- Remove unnecessary **regulatory** and other obstacles for **micro-enterprises** and the **informal sector** *[11d]*; and
- Support local authorities with **slum upgrade** programmes and facilitate **access to information** on housing legislation *[11e]*.

Child labour

- Immediate measures will be taken to eliminate the worst forms of **child labour** as defined by ILO convention 182 and to put strategies in place to eliminate child labour that is contrary to accepted international standards *[12]*; and
- International cooperation will be offered to developing countries on request to address child labour and its root causes *[13]*.

Poverty eradication elsewhere in the JPOI

'We welcome the Johannesburg Summit focus on the indivisibility of human dignity and are resolved through decisions and targets, timetables and partnerships to speedily increase access to basic requirements such as clean water, sanitation, adequate shelter, energy, healthcare, food security and the protection of biodiversity' (Johannesburg Declaration on Sustainable Development, paragraph 18).

The Johannesburg Plan of Implementation (JPOI) recognizes poverty eradication as one of three overarching objectives of, and essential requirements for, sustainable development. It includes MDGs on poverty, safe drinking water, food security and hunger, and supports frameworks that embody poverty reduction strategies. Action is agreed to integrate health concerns within poverty strategies. The JPOI notes that the risks of climate change mean that poverty and other issues remain central concerns. It also addresses the links between poverty and agriculture, sustainable mountain development, sustainable forest management, and secure equitable access to land tenure. Small island developing states (SIDS) and regional chapters all include poverty eradication objectives. The JPOI acknowledges the benefits of globalization as well as the challenges, including poverty, exclusion and inequality, and the need for resources to achieve internationally agreed goals on poverty. Sound economic policies, solid democratic institutions and improved infrastructure are seen as the basis for sustained economic growth, poverty eradication and employment creation.

TARGETS AND COMMITMENTS

- **Poverty.** Halve, by 2015, proportion of people whose income is less than US$1 a day *[7a]* (MDG).

- **Poverty fund.** Establish World Solidarity Fund to eradicate poverty and promote social and human development *[7b]* (new target).

- **Water and sanitation.** Halve, by 2015, proportion of people unable to reach or afford safe drinking water, and proportion of people without access to basic sanitation *[8]* and *[7a]* (MDG and new target).

- **Hunger.** Halve, by 2015, proportion of people suffering from hunger *[40a]* and *[7a]* (MDG).

- **Slums.** By 2020, achieve significant improvement in the lives of at least 100 million slum dwellers *[11]* (MDG).

EXAMPLES OF INDICATORS FOR MEASURING PROGRESS IN IMPLEMENTATION

- Proportion of population below US$1 per day (Millennium Development Goal, or MDG)

- Poverty gap ration (incidence x depth of poverty) (MDG)

- Proportion of population below minimum level of dietary energy consumption (MDG)

- Literacy rate of 15- to 24-year olds (MDG)

- Proportion of population with sustainable access to an improved water source, urban and rural (MDG)

- Proportion of urban population with access to improved sanitation (MDG)

- Percentage of population living below the poverty line (Commission on Sustainable Development, or CSD)

- Gini Index of income inequality (CSD)

- Unemployment rate (CSD)

Other relevant CSD indicators are found under health, education and housing.

Partnership example

UNDP Capacity 2015

Leading partner: United Nations Development Programme (UNDP)

Dates: January 2003–January 2015

Objective: Building capacity to benefit from globalization and to realize the MDGs while achieving sustainable development.

Capacity 2015 will build on experience gained since the United Nations Conference on Environment and Development (UNCED) to help countries move from strategic planning for sustainable development to effective implementation. The main objectives include helping countries to reap the benefits of globalization; ensuring that sustainable development processes put in place during the 1990s face the challenges of the 21st century; and strengthening capacities to achieve the MDGs.

- Communities, local government and the private sector will have strengthened capacities to sustain vibrant local economies in order to improve livelihoods and to eliminate poverty.

Partnership example (*contd*)

- Legislation will have been reviewed and reformed, governance processes improved and institutional bottlenecks to achieving local sustainable development eliminated.

- There will be increased participation in the global market and increased inward investment.

- National and local development strategies will be under implementation and oriented towards achieving the MDGs.

- National and local development strategies will be in place that support civic engagement and responsible leadership.

- Networks will be in place that engage communities and authorities in monitoring the achievement of the MDGs.

- New national and local strategies, including poverty reduction strategies, will have been developed, reviewed and revised utilizing the principles of sustainable development, ensuring full convergence between Agenda 21 and later developments.

- The principles of the Multilateral Environmental Agreements (MEAs) will have been combined and integrated within activities at the local level and funding will have been mobilized from global sources.

- Programmes will be in place to meet the specific challenges of sustainability and global market access of the small island developing states (SIDS).

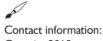

Contact information:
Capacity 2015
United Nations
Development
Programme (UNDP)
304 E 45th street –
FF6
New York, NY, 10017
US
www.undp.org/
capacity2015

 # Resources

Child labour

www.ilo.org/public/english/standards/ipec/index.htm
www.ilo.org/public/english/standards/ipec/ratification/convention/
text.htm (text)
The International Programme on the Elimination of Child Labour (IPEC) is a United Nations/International Labour Organization (ILO) initiative that promotes the ILO Worst Forms of Child Labour Convention, 1999 (No 182).

Cities without Slums Initiative

www.citiesalliance.org/citiesalliancehomepage.nsf
This initiative was developed in 1999 by Cities Alliance, a major alliance of cities and development partners (United Nations, World Bank, regional development banks, NGOs, business leaders, and national and local partners).

International Labour Organization (ILO) Declaration on Fundamental Principles and Rights at Work

www.ilo.org/public/english/standards/decl/index.htm
Agreed on June 1998, this declaration covers freedom of association and the right to collective bargaining; elimination of forced and compulsory labour; abolition of child labour; and elimination of discrimination in the workplace.

Millennium Development Goals (MDGs)

www.un.org/millenniumgoals/index.shtml (UN)
www.undp.org/mdg (UNDP)
www.developmentgoals.org (World Bank)
The United Nations Secretary-General's 'Road Map' (September 2001) set out concrete targets for goals and commitments in the Millennium Declaration. These were further developed into the MDGs.

United Nations Children's Fund (UNICEF)

www.unicef.org
UNICEF champions children's rights, education, HIV/AIDS and child labour, as well as the United Nations Convention on the Rights of the Child.

United Nations Convention to Combat Desertification in Those Countries Experiencing Serious Drought and/or Desertification, Particularly in Africa (CCD)

www.unccd.int/main.php
The Convention to Combat Desertification was completed in 1996. Countries must develop national action programmes in conjunction with local stakeholders; detailed annexes address desertification in specific regions.

United Nations Development Programme (UNDP)

www.undp.org
The UNDP helps to build national capacity for sustainable development, especially the MDGs. It works through country offices and a global network, and publishes the *Human Development Report*.

Universal Declaration of Human Rights (1948)

www.un.org/Overview/rights.html
On 10 December 1998, the UN General Assembly adopted the Universal Declaration of Human Rights. The declaration contains 30 articles which member states have pledged to achieve with the aim of promoting universal respect for and observance of human rights and fundamental freedoms.

United Nations Human Settlements Programme (UN-Habitat)

www.unhabitat.org
This is the lead United Nations agency on human settlements. The Habitat Agenda was adopted at the Habitat II Summit (Istanbul, 1996) and promotes equitable human settlements, poverty eradication and sustainable development.

World Summit for Social Development

www.un.org/esa/socdev/wssd/
Held in Copenhagen in 1995, this summit addressed poverty, unemployment and social integration. It adopted the Copenhagen Declaration on Social Development, as well as a programme of action. Its five-year review was held in Geneva in June 2000.

CONFERENCES, AGREEMENTS AND PROCESSES

- Agenda 21, Chapters 3 and 7 (1992)
- World Conference on Human Rights, Vienna (1993)
- International Conference on Population and Development (ICPD), Cairo (1994)
- World Summit on Social Development (Commitment 2) Copenhagen (1995)
- United Nations Commission on Sustainable Development-3 (CSD-3) Decision 3.6 (1995)
- Fourth World Conference on Women, Beijing (1995)
- Habitat II Conference, Istanbul (1996)
- CSD-4 Decision 4.2 (1996)
- United Nations General Assembly Special Session (UNGASS) Resolution on Eradicating Poverty, paragraph 27 (1997)
- United Nations Decade on Eradication of Poverty (1997–2006)
- CSD-6 (1998)
- United Nations Millennium Declaration (2000)
- Beijing+5 (Women), New York (2000)
- Millennium Development Goals (MDG) on poverty, hunger and drinking water (2000–2015)
- Istanbul+5 (Habitat), New York (2001)
- CSD (2004–2015) to consider poverty eradication as cross-cutting theme

CONFERENCES, AGREEMENTS AND PROCESSES (CONTD)

 World Summit on Sustainable Development (WSSD) target on sanitation (2015)

 MDG target on slum dwellers (2020)

Key United Nations bodies and Bretton Woods institutions

Combating poverty (overall)

International Labour Organization (ILO)

United Nations Children's Fund (UNICEF)

United Nations Conference on Trade and Development (UNCTAD)

United Nations Development Programme (UNDP)

United Nations Food and Agriculture Organization (FAO)

United Nations Human Settlements Programme (UN-Habitat)

World Bank

Millennium Development Goals (MDGs)

United Nations Development Programme (UNDP)

World Bank

Human settlements

United Nations Development Programme (UNDP)

United Nations High Commissioner for Refugees (UNHCR)

United Nations High Commissioner on Human Rights (UNHCHR)

United Nations Human Settlements Programme (UN-Habitat)

World Bank

 # References

DFID (UK Department for International Development) (2002) *Poverty and the Environment*, DFID, London

DFID, EC, UNDP and the World Bank (UK Department for International Development, European Commission, United Nations Development Programme and the World Bank) (2002) *Linking Poverty Reduction and Environmental Management: Policy Challenges and Opportunities*, July 2002, www.undp.org/wssd/docs/LPREM.pdf

International Energy Agency (2002) *World Energy Outlook 2002 – Highlights*, www.worldenergyoutlook.org

Narayan, D, Patel, R, Rademadier, A and Koch-Sholte, S (2000) *Can Anyone Hear Us?* Voices of the Poor Series, World Bank and Oxford University Press, Oxford

2

UN (United Nations) (2002a) *We the Peoples: The Role of the United Nations in the 21st Century*, UN, New York, paragraphs 70, 73, www.un.org/millennium/sg/report/key.htm

UN (2002b) *Johannesburg Plan of Implementation*, Johannesburg Declaration on Sustainable Development and Plan of Implementation of the World Summit on Sustainable Development, www.un.org/esa/sustdev

UNCED (United Nations Conference on Environment and Development) (1992) *Agenda 21*, Chapter 3, 'Combating poverty', www.un.org/esa/sustdev/documents/agenda21/english/agenda21toc.htm

UNDP (United Nations Development Programme) (2000) *Overcoming Human Poverty: Poverty Report 2000*, UNDP, New York

UNDP (2003) *Human Development Report: Millennium Development Goals – A Compact among Nations to End Human Poverty*, UNDP, New York

UNEP (United Nations Environment Programme) (2002) *Global Environmental Outlook 3*, www.unep.org/geo, Earthscan, London

Water Aid (2003) www.wateraid.org.uk

Water Aid and Tear Fund (2000) *Human Waste Report*, www.wateraid.org

World Bank poverty website, www.worldbank.org/poverty/data/trends/index.htm

World Bank (2001) *World Development Report 2000/2001: Attacking Poverty*, Oxford University Press, Oxford

World Bank (2004) *World Development Report: Making Services Work for Poor People*, World Bank, Washington, DC

Changing Unsustainable Patterns of Consumption and Production

3

 ## Context

Twenty per cent of the world's population use an estimated 80 per cent of the world's resources. Such inequality can not continue. Current patterns of resource use *'would push the world beyond what is sustainable; so either the developing world has to be held back or the developed world has to find ways to sustain current standards of living using far fewer resources'* (UK House of Commons Select Committee on Environment, Transport and Regional Affairs, 1998). A working definition of sustainable consumption is *'the use of services and related products which respond to basic needs and bring a better quality of life while minimizing the use of natural resources and toxic materials, as well as the emissions of waste and pollutants over the life cycle so as not to jeopardize the needs of future generations'* (Ministry of the Environment, Norway, 1994).

Environmental pressures are starting to influence the way in which products are designed, manufactured and discarded. Optimizing resource efficiency is the underlying idea behind the *'Factor 4/Factor 10'* concept, initially developed by the Wuppertal Institute in Germany (von Weizacker et al, 1997). This recognizes that developed countries need to reduce the intensity of their material and energy use by at least a factor of four over the next 20 to 30 years and up to a factor of ten in the long term to create 'environmental space' for developing countries to grow. The Johannesburg Plan of Implementation (JPOI) makes several references to the need for clean production centres to act as entrepreneurial drivers for new materials policy and to promote a cyclical, rather than a linear, flow of natural resources. This idea was originally developed by the Organisation for Economic Co-operation and Development (OECD) and has been implemented in several countries, including Germany and Japan (UNEP, www.uneptie.org, 2002).

Moving towards a low pollution, low carbon economy offers a host of opportunities for stakeholders to work collaboratively to address knowledge gaps and numerous technical and economic challenges that include design for low-waste production; product design for longevity, repair, disassembly and reuse; applications for recycled products; and vital changes in consumer awareness and behaviour.

KEY WORDS

- **sustainable consumption and production patterns**
- **ten-year framework of programmes**
- **eco-efficiency**
- **cleaner production**
- **corporate responsibility and accountability**
- **energy for sustainable development**
- **transport**
- **waste**
- **chemicals**

AT A GLANCE

※ Current estimates suggest that we have overshot our global 'carrying capacity' by over 30 per cent (WWF International, 2000).

※ Almost 1 billion people in 70 countries consume less today than 25 years ago, while the richest 20 per cent of the world's population now accounts for 86 per cent of private consumption (UNDP, 1999).

※ The global chemistry industry has grown almost ninefold since 1972, and a 3 per cent annual growth is expected to continue over the next three decades, with a considerable increase in trade (OECD, 2001).

 Chapter III in summary

Global sustainable development depends upon fundamental changes in the way that societies produce and consume. Acknowledging the principle of 'common but differentiated responsibility', the JPOI requests all countries to **promote sustainable consumption and production patterns**, with developing countries taking the lead. Governments, international organizations, the private sector and all major groups have an active role to play *[14]*.

'The Earth has enough for everyone's need, but not for everyone's greed' (Mahatma Gandhi).

Ten-year framework of programmes

A **ten-year framework of programmes** will support regional and national initiatives to accelerate the shift towards sustainable consumption and production. This will promote social and economic development within the **carrying capacity** of ecosystems by addressing the **delinking of economic growth and environmental degradation** and mobilizing resources to help build capacity in developing countries *[15]*. Actions needed at all levels include:

* Identifying specific tools, policies and measures, including **life cycle analysis** and **national indicators** for measuring progress *[15a]*;
* Adopting relevant policies and measures that follow the 'polluter pays' principle (principle 16, Rio Declaration) *[15b]*;
* Developing **policies** to improve products and services while reducing environmental and health impacts *[15c]*;
* **Raising awareness** on the importance of sustainable production and consumption, particularly among young people *[15d]*;
* Employing voluntary, 'effective, transparent, verifiable, non-misleading and non-discriminatory' **consumer information tools** *[15e]*; and
* Developing **financial resources** to increase eco-efficiency through capacity-building, technology transfer and the exchange of technology *[15f]*.

Cleaner production and eco-efficiency

Increasing **investment in cleaner production and eco-efficiency** requires incentives, support schemes and policies that establish necessary regulatory, financial and legal frameworks *[16]*. Actions include:

- Establishing **cleaner production programs and centres**, and particularly assisting small and medium-sized enterprises (SMEs) to improve productivity *[16a]*;
- Creating **incentives** for investment in cleaner production and eco-efficiency *[16b]*;
- Providing **information** on cost-effective examples and best practice *[16c]*; and
- Providing **training** programmes to SMEs about the use of information and communication technologies *[16d]*.

Decision-making processes and corporate responsibility

The issue of production and consumption patterns will be integrated within sustainable development policies and programmes, and poverty eradication strategies *[17]*.

Corporate environmental and social responsibility and accountability will be improved *[18]*, with actions to encourage:

- Industry to improve social and environmental performance through voluntary initiatives, such as environmental management systems, codes of conduct, certification and public reporting *[18a]*;
- Dialogue between enterprises and communities *[18b]*;
- Financial institutions to incorporate sustainability within their decision-making processes *[18c]*; and
- Development of workplace partnerships, including training and education *[18d]*.

Relevant authorities are encouraged to take sustainable development into account in **decision-making processes**, such as planning, infrastructure investment, business development and public procurement *[19]*, with action to:

- Support the development of sustainable development strategies, including decision-making in **investment** *[19a]*;
- Promote the **internalization of environmental costs** and the use of economic instruments *[19b]*;
- Promote **public procurement** policies that encourage environmentally sound goods and services *[19c]*;
- Provide **capacity-building and training** on implementing these measures *[19d]*; and
- Use **environmental impact assessments** *[19e]*.

'Energy is essential for development. Yet 2 billion people currently go without, condemning them to remain in the poverty trap' (UN Secretary-General Kofi Annan, 2002).

Energy

The JPOI calls on governments and stakeholders to implement the recommendations of the ninth session of the United Nations Commission on Sustainable Development (CSD) on energy *[20]*, including actions to:

- Mobilize financial resources, transfer technology, build capacity and help to spread environmentally sound technologies *[20a]*;
- Integrate energy considerations – energy efficiency, affordability and accessibility – within socio-economic programmes, the policies of **major energy-consuming sectors**, and the planning, operation and maintenance of **long-lived energy consuming infrastructures** *[20b]*;
- Develop **alternative energy technologies** to give a greater share of the energy mix to renewable energy, improve energy efficiency and improve reliance on advanced energy technologies, including cleaner fossil-fuel technologies *[20c]*;
- **Combine** the increased use of renewable energy, efficiency and advanced/cleaner fuel technologies with the sustainable use of traditional energy resources to help meet the growing need for energy services in achieving sustainable development *[20d]*;
- **Diversify** energy supply by developing cleaner, more efficient, affordable and cost-effective technologies and their transfer to developing countries. Substantially increase the global share of **renewable energy sources** *[20e]*;
- Reduce **flaring and venting of gas** associated with crude oil production *[20f]*;
- Use **indigenous energy sources** and infrastructures for local uses, promoting participation by rural communities and Agenda 21 groups, and the use of renewable energy to meet daily needs *[20g]*;
- Establish **domestic programmes for energy efficiency** *[20h]*;
- Accelerate development and use of affordable and cleaner **energy efficiency and energy conservation technologies** *[20h]*;
- Transfer technology to developing countries on concessional/favourable terms *[20i]*;
- Recommend that **international financial institutions** and others help to establish policy and regulatory frameworks to create a **level playing field** between renewable energy, energy efficiency, advanced energy technologies and centralized, distributed and decentralized energy systems *[20j]*;
- Promote increased **research and development** (R&D) in energy technology, focusing on strengthening national and regional R&D institutions *[20k]*;
- Network **centres of excellence** on energy for sustainable development *[20l]*;
- Promote **education** about available energy sources and technologies *[20m]*;
- Use **financial instruments and mechanisms**, particularly the Global Environment Facility (GEF), to help developing countries, particularly least

' The public sector, civil society, individuals acting as parents and consumers and voters all have crucial parts to play in the struggle for sustainability. Industry, however, may have the most vital role of all' (Frankel, 1998).

developed countries and small island developing states, meet their needs for training, know-how and institution-building [20n];

- Improve the functioning, transparency and information flows about **energy markets** [20o];
- Use policies to **reduce market distortions** that would promote energy systems compatible with sustainable development [20p];
- Phase out subsidies in this area that hinder sustainable development [20q];
- Improve the **functioning of national energy markets** to support sustainable development, overcome market barriers and improve accessibility [20r];
- Strengthen **national/regional energy institutions/arrangements** for better regional/international cooperation on energy for sustainable development and to assist developing countries in their domestic efforts to provide energy services to all [20s];
- Implement actions within the framework of **CSD-9** relating to access to energy [20t];
- Promote **cooperation** between international and regional institutions dealing with energy for sustainable development [20u];
- Promote **cross-border energy trade**, including interconnection of electricity grids, and oil and natural gas pipelines [20v]; and
- Strengthen dialogue amongst regional, national and international producers and energy consumers [20w].

Transport

The JPOI calls for **integrated approaches to policy-making for transport services and systems**. This includes policies and planning for land use, infrastructure, public transport systems and goods delivery networks to help ensure safe, affordable and energy efficient transportation with less pollution, congestion, negative health impacts and urban sprawl [21]. Actions at all levels will:

- Implement **transport strategies** for sustainable development [21a]; and
- Promote **investment and partnerships** towards sustainable transportation systems [21b].

Waste

Negative environmental effects of **waste** will be minimized, and resource efficiency improved, by preventing and minimizing waste, and by maximizing reuse, recycling and the use of environmentally sound materials [22]. Action is needed to:

- Develop **waste management systems** with a priority on waste prevention, reduction, reuse and recycling. Encourage small-scale waste recycling initiatives that provide opportunities for income generation [22a]; and
- Encourage the production of **reusable consumer goods** and **biodegradable products** [22b].

'Efficiency can safely be called a no-regrets strategy. If it is made a high priority in many countries and by business worldwide, it will buy a lot of time' (von Weizsacker et al, 1997).

23

Chemicals management

The JPOI calls for a renewed commitment towards the **sound management of chemicals** throughout their life cycle and the tackling of hazardous wastes. By 2020, chemicals should be used and produced in ways that minimize significant adverse impacts upon human health and the environment. All processes should be transparent, using science-based risk assessment and management, and based on the precautionary principle. Developing countries will require assistance to strengthen their capacities to meet these objectives *[23]*. Action is needed to:

- Ratify and implement **international instruments on chemicals and hazardous waste**, including the Rotterdam Convention on Prior Informed Consent Procedures for Certain Hazardous Chemicals and Pesticides in International Trade, and the Stockholm Convention on Persistent Organic Pollutants *[23a]*;
- Further develop a **strategic approach to international chemicals management** by 2005, based on the Bahia Declaration and priorities for Action beyond 2000 *[23b]*;
- Implement the globally harmonized system for the **classification and labelling of chemicals** with a view to having the system fully operational by 2008 *[23c]*;
- Encourage **partnerships** to promote environmentally sound management of chemicals and hazardous wastes *[23d]*;
- Prevent **international illegal trafficking** of hazardous chemicals and wastes and damage from **transboundary movement and disposal of wastes** *[23e]*;
- Develop **coherent and integrated information on chemicals** *[23f]*; and
- Reduce risks posed by **heavy metals**, including through a review of relevant studies and assessments *[23g]*.

Consumption and production elsewhere in the JPOI

Changing unsustainable patterns of production and consumption is an overarching goal of the World Summit on Sustainable Development (WSSD). Actions are agreed on increasing access to energy services, increasing the use of renewable energy resources and increasing energy efficiency to assist with poverty alleviation, combat desertification and ensure sustainable development of small island developing states (SIDS), as well as to assist with reaching targets within the New Partnership for African Development (NEPAD). Additionally, effective management and efficient use of resources is fundamental to protecting the natural resource base, and the sound management of chemicals has particular implications for the protection of oceans and coasts. Tools such as corporate accountability are recommended.

TARGETS AND COMMITMENTS

- **Consumption and production**. Ten-year framework of programmes to accelerate the shift towards sustainable consumption and production *[15]* (new target).

- **International agreements**. Ratify and implement relevant international instruments on chemicals and hazardous waste, including the Rotterdam Convention so that it can enter into force by 2003 and the Stockholm Convention so that it can enter into force by 2004 *[23a]*.

- **Chemicals management**. Further develop a strategic approach to international chemicals management, based on the Bahia Declaration and Priorities for Action beyond 2000, by 2005 *[23b]*.

- **Classification**. Implement the new globally harmonized system for the classification and labelling of chemicals as soon as possible, with a view to having it fully operational by 2008 *[23c]*.

- **Health**. By 2020, use and produce chemicals in ways that do not lead to significant adverse effects on human health and the environment *[23]* (new target).

- **Energy supply**. Diversify energy supply and substantially increase the global share of renewable energy in order to increase the renewable contribution to total energy supply *[20e]*.

- **Energy efficiency**. Establish domestic programmes for energy efficiency with the support of the international community. Accelerate the development and dissemination of energy efficiency and energy conservation technologies, including the promotion of research and development *[20b, 20c, 20h, 20i, 20k, 21]*.

EXAMPLES OF INDICATORS FOR MEASURING PROGRESS TO IMPLEMENTATION

- Intensity of material use (United Nations Commission on Sustainable Development, or CSD)

- Intensity of energy use (CSD)

- Annual energy consumption per capita (CSD)

- Generation of industrial and municipal waste (CSD)

- Generation of hazardous waste (CSD)

- Waste recycling and reuse (CSD)

- Distance traveled per capita by mode of transport (CSD)

3

Partnership example

Awareness-raising and training on sustainable consumption and production

Leading partner: United Nations Environment Programme (UNEP) Division of Technology, Industry and Economics (DTIE)

Dates: January 2003–December 2005

This US$2 million capacity-building effort aims to improve decision-makers' ability to implement sustainable consumption and production policies. It relies upon practical training materials, training courses and advisory services. The programme's substantive content is derived from the section on sustainable consumption in the *United Nations Guidelines on Consumer Protection*, and includes segments on how to implement national policy frameworks and how to better market cleaner products and services. The primary target groups are developing and transition countries and small- and medium-sized enterprises (SMEs).

At the project's end, the goal is increased awareness and skills of 300 to 500 staff in governments and heads of SMEs in about 30 countries (in Africa, Asia, Latin America and the Caribbean, and Eastern Europe), as well as increased awareness and improved implementation of the *United Nations Guidelines for Consumer Protection.*

Partners involved include The Netherlands, Sweden and the Czech Republic (as of March 2003); intergovernmental organizations, including inputs from the United Nations Industrial Development Organization (UNIDO) and the United Nations Educational, Scientific and Cultural Organization (UNESCO); and major groups, including Consumers International, in cooperation with partners from the business and industry and scientific community, as well as National Cleaner Production Centres and National Civil Society Groups.

Contact information:
United Nations Environment Programme (UNEP) Division of Technology, Industry and Economics 39–43, quai André Citroën 75739 Paris Cedex 15, France www.uneptie.org/ pc/sustain

Resources

ANPED (Northern Alliance for Sustainability)

www.anped.ord

Bahia Declaration and Priorities for Action beyond 2000, Intergovernmental Forum on Chemical Safety (IFCS)

www.who.int/ifcs
IFCS is an international forum on the environmentally sound management of chemicals, as described in Chapter 19, Agenda 21. The Bahia Declaration (2000) called for global cooperation to tackle priority actions.

Basel Convention on the Control of Transboundary Movements of Hazardous Wastes and their Disposal.

www.basel.int
This convention aims to minimize the generation of hazardous waste in terms of quantity and toxicity; to dispose of it as close to source as possible; and to reduce movement of hazardous materials.

Cleaner Production

www.uneptie.org/pc/home.htm
The United Nations Environment Programme's (UNEP's) Production and Consumption Unit promotes more sustainable forms of industrial development through cleaner production; sustainable consumption; risk reduction; environmental management tools; and waste management.

Global Environment Facility (GEF)

www.gefweb.org
The GEF helps developing countries to fund projects/programmes that protect the global environment. It designated a financial mechanism for conventions on biodiversity, climate change and persistent organic pollutants. It also supports work on desertification, international waters and the ozone layer.

Global Reporting Initiative (GRI)

www.globalreporting.org
The GRI is a multi-stakeholder process and independent institution that is developing and disseminating globally applicable sustainability reporting guidelines for voluntary use by organizations reporting economic, environmental and social dimensions of their activities/products/services. The official UNEP collaborating centre, the GRI works in cooperation with UN Secretary-General Kofi Annan's Global Compact (www.unglobalcompact.org).

International Coalition on Sustainable Consumption and Production (ICSPAC)

www.icspac.net

The ICSPAC is an information exchange and policy advocacy vehicle for non-governmental organizations (NGOs) and citizen organizations in promoting sustainable production and consumption (SPAC) policies and practices.

International Organization for Standardization (ISO)

www.iso.ch

The ISO is a worldwide federation of national standards bodies that promotes standardization to facilitate the international exchange of goods and services. It develops cooperation in all the spheres of intellectual, scientific, technological and economic activity.

Pollutant Release and Transfer Registers (PRTRs)

www.chem.unep.ch/prtr/default.htm

The International Register of Potentially Toxic Chemicals (IRPTC), hosted by UNEP, is an international clearinghouse for PRTRs.

Rotterdam Convention – Agreement on Prior Informed Consents on Hazardous Chemicals (1998)

www.pic.int

This agreement enables countries to monitor and control trade in harmful pesticides and industrial chemicals. It uses a legally binding 'prior informed consent' approach for imports; promotes safe use of chemicals through labelling standards; and provides technical assistance and other support.

Stockholm Convention on Persistent Organic Pollutants (POPs)

www.pops.int

This is a global treaty (2001) to protect human health/environment from POPs by eliminating them or reducing their release in the environment. POPS are chemicals that remain intact for long periods, become widely distributed geographically, persist in the food chain, accumulate in the fatty tissue of living organisms, and are toxic to humans and wildlife.

Sustainable Consumption

www.uneptie.org/pc/sustain

Sustainable consumption is an umbrella term that brings together resource efficiency; renewable energy; waste minimization; life-cycle approaches; meeting needs; quality of life; and equity. It aims to provide the same or better services in a sustainable way to meet basic requirements and aspirations for improvement of current/future generations (UNEP, 1994).

United Nations Environment Programme (UNEP) Global Mercury Assessment

www.chem.unep.ch/mercury/default.htm
This is a process that is developing a global assessment of mercury and its compounds and an outline of options for addressing significant global adverse impacts.

UNEP

Sustainable Consumption, www.uneptie.org/pc/sustain

United Nations Guidelines on Consumer Protection

www.uneptie.org/pc/sustain/guidelines/guidelines.htm
Adopted by the UN in 1999, these guidelines are based on the work of the Commission on Sustainable Development (CSD). It provides a comprehensive framework to promote sustainable consumption and protection. UNEP/Consumers International have surveyed implementation in various countries: recycling and energy and water conservation were the most common activities. The consumer protection approach helps to integrate sustainability issues with safety, quality, functionality and other aspects of product performance (CSD, 2003).

CONFERENCES, AGREEMENTS AND PROCESSES

Consumption and production

- Agenda 21, Chapter 4, 'Changing consumption patterns' (1992)
- United Nations Commission on Sustainable Development (CSD) 2, 3, 4, 7, Decision 2/5, 3/4, 4/13, 7/2, 'Consumption and production patterns' (1994, 1995, 1996, 1999)
- Oslo Symposium on Sustainable Consumption (1994)
- United Nations General Assembly Special Session (UNGASS), Paragraph 28, 'Changing consumption and production patterns' (1997)
- CSD-6 Decision 6/1, 'Consumer protection guidelines for sustainable consumption' (1998)
- United Nations Guidelines for Consumer Protection (1986 and 1999 revision)
- International Expert Meeting on the Ten-Year Framework of Programmes for Sustainable Consumption and Production Patterns, Marrakech (June 2003)
- CSD to address linkages on sustainable consumption and production patterns in each of its annual work cycles (2004–2017)
- CSD to consider progress on the Ten-Year Framework of Programmes on Sustainable Consumption and Production Patterns (2010–2011)

CONFERENCES, AGREEMENTS AND PROCESSES (CONTD)

Chemicals

- Agenda 21, Chapter 19, 'Toxic chemicals' (1992)

- United Nations Commission on Sustainable Development (CSD) 2, 5, Decision 2/1, 5/57, 'Toxic chemicals' (1994, 1997)

- Code of Ethics on the International Trade in Chemicals (1994)

- CSD-3, Decision 3/8/101 (1995)

- International Register of Potentially Toxic Chemicals (IRPTC)

- Prior informed consent (for certain hazardous chemicals) (Rotterdam, 1998)

- Persistent Organic Pollutants Convention (Stockholm, 2001)

- International Register on Biosafety

- CSD to consider chemicals (2010–2011)

Transport

- Agenda 21, Chapter 9, 'Atmosphere', and Chapter 7, 'Human settlements' (1992)

- United Nations Commission on Sustainable Development (CSD) 9, Decision 9/47, 'Transport' (2001)

- CSD to consider transport issues (2010–2011)

Energy

- Agenda 21, Chapter 9, 'Atmosphere', and Chapter 7, 'Human settlements' (1992)

- United Nations General Assembly Special Session (UNGASS), Decision 42, 'Energy' (1997)

- United Nations Commission on Sustainable Development (CSD) 9, Decision 9/1, 'Energy for sustainable development' (2001)

- CSD to consider energy for sustainable development (2006–2007)

Waste

- Agenda 21, Chapter 19, 'Environmentally sound management of hazardous wastes', Chapter 21, 'Environmentally sound management of solid wastes and sewage-related issues' and Chapter 22, 'Safe and environmentally sound management of radioactive wastes' (1992)

CONFERENCES, AGREEMENTS AND PROCESSES (CONTD)

⧗ United Nations General Assembly Special Session (UNGASS) 'Hazardous wastes' and paragraph 59 – 'Radioactive wastes' (1997)

⧗ United Nations Commission on Sustainable Development (CSD) is to include waste management within its work programme for 2010–2011

See the 'Resources' section for other relevant organizations and web links.

Key United Nations bodies and Bretton Woods institutions

Consumption and production

⚙ International Energy Agency (IEA)

⚙ United Nations Conference on Trade and Development (UNCTAD)

⚙ United Nations Department of Economic and Social Affairs (DESA), Division for Sustainable Development (Agenda 21 Task Master)

⚙ United Nations Development Programme's (UNDP's) *Human Development Report*

⚙ United Nations Environment Programme's (UNEP's) Industry and Environment, Sustainable Consumption, Cleaner Production Programme

⚙ United Nations Food and Agriculture Organization (FAO)

⚙ United Nations Industrial Development Organization (UNIDO)

⚙ World Meteorological Organization (WMO)

Chemicals

⚙ United Nations Environment Programme's (UNEP's) International Register of Potentially Toxic Chemicals (IRPTC) (Agenda 21 Task Master)

⚙ World Health Organization (WHO) Global Environmental Epidemiology Network (GEENET)

Transport

⚙ Global Initiative on Transport Emissions

⚙ United Nations Conference on Trade and Development (UNCTAD) transport technical services

> ### Key United Nations bodies and Bretton Woods institutions (*contd*)
>
> **Energy**
>
> - Ad Hoc Inter-Agency Task Force on Energy
> - United Nations Atomic Energy Agency
> - United Nations Development Programme's (UNDP's) Sustainable Energy Programme
> - United Nations Educational, Scientific and Cultural Organization's (UNESCO's) Solar Programme
> - United Nations Environment Programme's (UNEP's) Cleaner Production Programme
> - United Nations Framework Convention on Climate Change (UNFCCC)
> - United Nations Industrial Development Organization (UNIDO)
>
> **Wastes (hazardous, solid, radioactive)**
>
> - International Atomic Energy Agency (IAEA) (Agenda 21 Task Master – radioactive wastes)
> - United Nations Environment Programme (UNEP) (Agenda 21 Task Master – hazardous wastes)
> - United Nations Human Settlements Programme (UN-Habitat) (Agenda 21 Task Master – solid wastes)

 # References

CSD (United Nations Commission on Sustainable Development) (2003) Paper for International Expert Meeting on a Ten-Year Framework of Programmes for Sustainable Consumption and Production, June (Chapter III of the Johannesburg Plan of Implementation), Discussion Paper, prepared for the United Nations Division for Sustainable Development, June 2003

Frankel, C (1998) *In Earth's Company: Business, Environment and the Challenge of Sustainability*, New Society Publishers, Canada, p13

IIED (International Institute for Environment and Development) (1998) *Consumption in a Sustainable World*, Report of the workshop held in Norway, 2–4 June 1998, IIED, London

Internation Symposium on Sustainable Consumption (1994) Ministry for the Environment, Norway

OECD (Organisation for Economic Co-operation and Development) (2001) *Environmental Outlook for the Chemical Industry*, OECD, Paris

Oleson, G B (2002) 'WSSD and Sustainable Energy', *Sustainable Energy News*, INFORSE Europe, no 38, October, pp14–15

UK House of Commons Select Committee on Environment, Transport and Regional Affairs (1998) *Sustainable Waste Management*, HMSO, London

United Nations Secretary-General Kofi Annan (2002) 'cited in Connor, H, Watch the Indicators, Sustainable Energy Watch Global Report for Rio', *Sustainable Energy News*, INFORSE Europe, no 38, October, p12

UNCED (United Nations Conference on Environment and Development) (1992) Rio Declaration on Environment and Development, www.unep.org/ Documents/Default.asp?DocumentID=78&ArticleID=1163

UNDP (United Nations Development Programme) (1999) *Human Development Report 1999*, UNDP, New York

UNEP (United Nations Environment Programme) (1994) *Report of the Oslo Symposium on Sustainable Consumption*, Ministry of Environment, Norway

UNEP (2002a) *Industry as a Partner for Sustainable Development: 10 Years after Rio – The UNEP Assessment*, UNEP, Paris

UNEP (2002b) *Global Environmental Outlook 3*, Earthscan, London.

von Weizacker, E, Lovins, A B and Lovins, L H (1997) *Factor Four: Doubling Wealth, Halving Resource Use – The New Report to the Club of Rome*, Earthscan, London

WWF International (World Wide Fund for Nature) (2000) *Living Planet Report 2000*, WWF, Gland, Switzerland

Protecting and Managing the Natural Resource Base of Economic and Social Development

4

 Context

The well-being of humanity depends upon the wealth of goods and services that natural resources provide. Yet, as the Johannesburg Plan of Implementation (JPOI) acknowledges, 'human activities are having an increasing impact on the integrity of ecosystems' *[24]*. We continue to overuse the natural resource base rather than work in balance with it. The United Nations Environment Programme's (UNEP's) well-respected *Global Environment Outlook 3* (UNEP, 2002), published in the run-up to the World Summit on Sustainable Development (WSSD), noted that '*[p]overty and excessive consumption ... continue to put enormous pressure on the environment. The unfortunate result is that sustainable development remains largely theoretical for the majority of the world's population*' (UNEP, 2002).

Agenda 21 (Chapters 9–18) outlines strategies to conserve and manage natural resources for development, highlighting the impact of human activities on fragile ecosystems such as deserts and mountains, and offers mechanisms to link key environment and development issues. It calls for a collective global responsibility on the part of governments and all sectors of society to take concrete action. Despite the gains made since the Earth Summit in Rio, many areas of Agenda 21 remain a matter for serious concern – in particular, oceans, energy, water resources and sustainable food production. While the WSSD process made commitments to reverse the current trends in natural resource degradation as soon as possible, the question is, how soon is 'soon'? Forestry experts warn that the '*natural forest resource as an asset of the planet is not yet being cared for sustainably*' (Evans, 2002). The Convention on Biological Diversity (CBD) was a major agreement at the 1992 Earth Summit and the WSSD process was seen by non-governmental organizations (NGOs) and many others as a valuable opportunity for this to be taken forward and developed into a more binding agreement (ANPED, 2002). However, the WSSD actually saw a step backwards from Rio's promise to stop the loss of biodiversity by 2010; this time world leaders merely committed to slow it down (Crace, 2003).

Tackling poverty is imperative as degrading natural environments hit the poor hardest of all through greater food insecurity, increased vulnerability to

KEY WORDS

- **water and sanitation**
- **oceans and marine resources**
- **fisheries**
- **maritime safety and pollution**
- **vulnerability and disaster management**
- **climate change**
- **air pollution and atmosphere**
- **sustainable agriculture**
- **poverty eradication**
- **desertification and drought**
- **mountains**
- **sustainable tourism**
- **biodiversity**
- **forests**
- **mining**

AT A GLANCE

- 47 per cent of the main fish stocks or species groups are fully exploited and are producing catches that have reached, or are very close to, their maximum sustainable limits (FAO, 2002).

- 800 million people are chronically malnourished and approximately one third of the world's population lack food security (FAO, 2001a).

- An estimated 97 per cent of natural disaster-related deaths each year occur in developing countries with huge economic impact (ISDR, 2002).

- More than US$1.1 billion has been given to help 114 developing countries phase out ozone depleting substances. By the year 2000, the total consumption of such chemicals had been reduced by 85 per cent. The ozone layer is expected to recover to pre-1980 levels by the middle of the 21st century (UNEP, 2002).

- An estimated 250 million people have been directly affected by desertification, and nearly 1 billion are at risk (FAO, 2001b).

- 75 per cent of the genetic diversity of agricultural crops has been lost since 1900 (FAO, 2001a).

- Ten of the world's 25 top-selling drugs in 1997 were derived from natural sources (UNEP, 2002).

- 13 million people are directly involved in small-scale mining and the livelihoods of a further 80 million to 100 million are affected (IIED and WBCSD, 2002).

'When we try to pick out anything by itself, we find it hitched to everything else in the universe' (John Muir, naturalist, 1869).

natural disasters, inadequate access to the basics of life, poor health and unsuitable settlement location. For sustainable development, poverty alleviation and protection of the natural resource base must go hand in hand.

Chapter IV in summary

Managing the natural resources base in a sustainable and integrated manner is essential for sustainable development. The current trend towards resource degradation must be reversed as soon as possible. To do so will require **strategies** that should include **targets** adopted at the national, and possibly regional, levels to protect ecosystems and achieve integrated management of land, water and living resources. The strengthening of capacity to facilitate this management will be essential at all levels *[24]*.

Water and sanitation

The JPOI includes the Millennium Development Goal (MDG) of halving, by 2015, the proportion of people who are unable to reach or to afford **safe drinking water** and agrees a new target to cut by 2015 the number of people without access to **basic sanitation**. These targets will be achieved through action to *[25]*:

'We express our deep concern that at the beginning of the 21st century 1.2 billion people live a life of poverty without access to safe drinking water, and that almost 2.5 billion have no access to proper sanitation. Safe and sufficient water and sanitation are basic human needs. The worldwide struggle to alleviate poverty must bring safe and decent living conditions to those who are deprived of these basic requirements' (Ministerial Declaration, signed by over 60 ministers who attended the Bonn Conference, 2001).

- Mobilize financial resources, transfer technology, promote best practice and support capacity-building for **water and sanitation infrastructure and services** in a way that meets the **needs of the poor** and is **gender sensitive** *[25a]*;
- Improve access to **public information and participation** (including by women) to support decision-making on water resources management *[25b]*;
- Promote priority action by governments on **water management** and capacity-building. Provide finance and technologies to implement Chapter 18 of Agenda 21 *[25c]*;
- Intensify **water pollution** prevention through affordable sanitation technologies, wastewater treatment, lessening the effects of groundwater contamination, and monitoring systems and legal frameworks *[25d]*; and
- Adopt prevention and protection measures to promote **sustainable water use** and address water shortages *[25e]*.

Integrated water resources management

The JPOI agrees a new target to develop **integrated water resources management and water efficiency plans by 2005**, with support to developing countries *[26]* through actions to:

- Develop national/regional strategies and programmes on **integrated river basin, watershed and groundwater management** and introduce measures to improve **efficiency** in water infrastructure, reducing losses and increasing **water recycling** *[26a]*;
- Employ the **full range of policy instruments**, without cost recovery becoming a barrier to poor people accessing safe water, and adopt an integrated water basin approach *[26b]*;
- Improve the **efficient use** of water resources. Allocate them among **competing uses**, giving priority to basic human needs, and balancing needs to preserve and restore ecosystems with human domestic, industrial and agricultural needs *[26c]*;
- Reduce the effects of **extreme water-related events** *[26d]*;
- Support the spread of technology and capacity-building for **non-conventional water resources** and conservation to developing countries and regions facing water scarcity *[26e]*;

- Support energy-efficient and cost-effective **desalination** of seawater, **water recycling** and **water harvesting from coastal fogs** in developing countries *[26f]*; and
- Use public/private and other forms of partnership that are transparent, accountable and give priority to people living in poverty *[26g]*.

The JPOI supports countries in their efforts to **monitor and assess the quantity and quality of water resources** *[27]* and calls for action to improve:

- Water resources management and scientific understanding of the **water cycle**, through joint observation and research, knowledge-sharing, capacity-building and technology transfer, including **remote sensing and satellite** technologies *[28]*; and
- Coordination among international and intergovernmental bodies/processes working on water issues through the International Year of Freshwater 2003 and beyond *[29]*.

Sustainable development of oceans, seas, islands and coastal areas

Oceans, seas, islands and coastal areas are an essential component of the Earth's ecosystem and are critical for global food security and for sustaining nations' economic development and well-being, particularly in developing countries. To secure the sustainable development of the oceans *[30]*, actions at all levels will:

- Invite states to ratify and implement the **United Nations Convention on the Law of the Sea** *[30a]*;
- Promote implementation of Chapter 17 of Agenda 21, which provides the programme of action for achieving the sustainable development of oceans, coastal areas and seas *[30b]*;
- Establish an **inter-agency coordination mechanism** on ocean and coastal issues within the UN system *[30c]*;
- Apply the **ecosystems approach** by 2010 *[30d]*;
- Promote **integrated coastal and ocean management** at the national level, assisting coastal states to developing ocean policies and measures in this area *[30e]*;
- Strengthen **regional cooperation** between organizations and programmes *[30f]*;
- Assist developing countries in coordinating policies/programmes at regional and sub-regional levels, aimed at **conservation and sustainable management of fishery resources**. Implement **integrated coastal area management plans** *[30g]*; and
- Note the work and review of the UN's open-ended informal consultative process to facilitate an annual review of developments in ocean affairs *[30h]*.

'Sanitation is a dirty word in most societies. Many people, including politicians, seem to prefer other more savoury topics. Often sanitation programmes are tacked on to water projects as an afterthought. This must stop. Sanitation is now a crucial issue in its own right' (cited in Water Aid and Tearfund, 2002).

Sustainable fisheries

To achieve **sustainable fisheries** *[31]*, action will be taken to:

- Maintain or restore fish stocks to levels that can produce the **maximum sustainable yield**, achieving this goal urgently for depleted stocks, if possible by 2015 *[31a]*;
- Ratify/accede to relevant UN and associated regional fisheries agreements and arrangements, including those on **straddling and highly migratory fish stocks**, and conservation and management **measures by fishing vessels on the high seas** *[31b]*;
- Implement the 1995 Code of Conduct for Responsible Fisheries *[31c]*;
- Urgently develop national and regional plans of action to put into effect the **Food and Agriculture Organization (FAO) international action plans** on management of fishing capacity (by 2005) and on illegal, unreported and unregulated fishing (by 2004). Use effective monitoring, reporting and enforcement systems, and **control of fishing vessels**, to achieve the international plan of action to prevent and eliminate **illegal, unreported and unregulated fishing** *[31d]*;
- Encourage fisheries management organizations to give due consideration to the **rights, duties and interests of coastal states**, and the special requirements of developing states, when addressing the issue of the allocations of the share of fishery resources for straddling stocks and highly migratory fish stocks *[31e]*;
- Remove **subsidies** that contribute to illegal, unreported and unregulated fishing, and overcapacity, while completing efforts at the World Trade Organization (WTO) to clarify and improve its disciplines on fisheries subsidies *[31f]*;
- Strengthen **donor coordination and partnerships** between international financial institutions, bilateral agencies and others to help countries to build their capacities in the sustainable management and use of fisheries *[31g]*; and
- Support the sustainable development of **aquaculture**, including small-scale aquaculture *[31h]*.

'More effective prevention strategies would save not only tens of billions of dollars, but save tens of thousands of lives. Funds currently spent on intervention and relief could be devoted to enhancing equitable and sustainable development instead, which would further reduce the risk for war and disaster. Building a culture of prevention is not easy. While the costs of prevention have to be paid in the present, its benefits lie in a distant future. Moreover, the benefits are not tangible; they are the disasters that did NOT happen' (UN Secretary-General Kofi Annan, 1999).

Conservation and management of oceans

The JPOI promotes conservation and management of the oceans *[32]* through actions at all levels to:

- Maintain the productivity and biodiversity of important and vulnerable marine and coastal areas *[32a]*;
- Implement work under the **Jakarta Mandate** of the Convention on Biological Diversity (CBD) on the conservation and sustainable use of marine and coastal biological diversity *[32b]*;

- Adopt diverse approaches, including the ecosystem approach; elimination of destructive fishing practices; **establishment of marine protected areas**, including representative networks by 2012 and **time/area closures** for the protection of nursery grounds/periods; and **integrated planning and management**, including watersheds *[32c]*;
- Develop programmes to halt the loss of **marine biodiversity**, including coral reefs and wetlands *[32d]*; and
- Implement the **Ramsar Convention**, its joint work programme with the CBD and the **International Coral Reef Initiative** to strengthen activities covering wetland ecosystems in coastal zones, such as **coral reefs, mangroves, seaweed beds and tidal mud flats** *[32e]*.

The JPOI also advances implementation of the **Global Programme of Action** (GPA) for the Protection of the Marine Environment from Land-based Activities and the Montreal Declaration on the Protection of the Marine Environment from Land-based Activities, with an emphasis between 2002 and 2006 on **municipal wastewater**, the physical alteration and destruction of **habitats** and **nutrients** *[33]*. Actions will:

- Facilitate partnerships, resources, scientific research, capacity-building and the diffusion of technical knowledge *[33a]*;
- Strengthen capacities to **mainstream the GPA** in national plans *[33b]*;
- Elaborate **regional action** and improve links with strategic plans that cover the sustainable development of coastal and marine resources *[33c]*; and
- Make every effort to achieve **substantial progress** by the GPA conference in 2006 *[33d]*.

Maritime safety and pollution

To improve **maritime safety** and protection of the marine environment from pollution *[34]*, action will be taken to:

- Invite states to ratify/implement relevant instruments of the International Maritime Organization (IMO), including those on **environmental damage caused by ships** and the use of **toxic anti-fouling paints**. Urge the IMO to consider stronger mechanisms to secure implementation *[34a]*; and
- Accelerate measures to address **alien species in ballast water** *[34b]*.

The JPOI calls for efforts to examine/improve measures and internationally agreed regulations related to safety that are relevant to the international maritime transportation and other transboundary movement of **radioactive materials**, radioactive waste and spent fuel, recognizing the importance of having effective **liability mechanisms** in place *[35]*.

To improve the **scientific understanding and assessment of marine and coastal ecosystems** in support of decision-making *[36]*, action will be taken to:

'Hunger, which afflicts one in five of the developing world's people, is a profound impediment to the advancement of individuals and societies. Without proper intervention, undernutrition and the death and disease it causes are repeated with each generation. The hungry suffer in silence and are often invisible: to the casual observer, many of them show no outward sign of the severity of their hunger' (FAO, undated).

4

- Increase **scientific/technical collaboration** including integrated assessments, transfer of marine science, technology and techniques for conservation and management, and expanded ocean-observing capacities *[36a]*;
- Establish,by 2004, a **regular UN process** for global reporting on the state of the marine environment, including the socio-economic aspects *[36b]*;
- Build capacity in **marine science, information and management**, promoting environmental impact assessments and environmental evaluation and reporting techniques for projects/activities that could harm marine/coastal ecosystems *[36c]*; and
- Strengthen the ability of the United Nations Educational, Scientific and Cultural Organization's (UNESCO's) Intergovernmental Oceanographic Commission, the ΓAO and others to build capacity in marine science and the sustainable management of oceans *[36d]*.

Vulnerability, risk assessment and disaster management

'Rapid urban growth, particularly when it is accompanied by a large influx of poor migrants from rural areas, is one of the main factors contributing to increased vulnerability to natural hazards in many parts of the world'
(ISDR, 2002).

An integrated and multi-hazard approach to addressing **vulnerability, risk assessment and disaster management** is an essential element of a safer world. This encompasses all aspects from prevention, mitigation and preparedness, to response and recovery *[37]*. Actions are required to:

- Strengthen the **role of the International Strategy for Disaster Reduction (ISDR)** *[37a]*;
- Establish effective **regional and national strategies** and scientific/technical institutional support for disaster management *[37b]*;
- Strengthen **institutional capacities** and promote joint international **observation/research**, including surface-based monitoring and satellite data *[37c]*;
- Reduce risks of **flooding and drought** in vulnerable countries. Promote **wetland and watershed** protection and restoration and better land-use planning. Widely apply techniques to assess potentially negative effects of climate change on wetlands *[37d]*;
- Improve techniques for assessing effects of climate change. Encourage the Intergovernmental Panel on Climate Change (IPCC) to continue to assess those adverse effects *[37e]*;
- Encourage the use of **traditional and indigenous knowledge** to lessen the impact of disasters. Promote **community-based disaster management planning** by local authorities *[37f]*;
- Support the voluntary contribution of NGOs, the scientific community and others to managing natural disasters *[37g]*;
- Strengthen **early warning systems** and information networks, consistent with the ISDR *[37h]*;

- Develop capacities to collect and disseminate scientific/technical information, including improved early warning systems for extreme weather events such as **El Niño/La Niña** *[37i]*; and
- Cooperate to prevent and address major **technological disasters** and other disasters that affect the environment *[37j]*.

Climate

Changes in the Earth's **climate** and its adverse effects are a common concern of humankind. All countries face increased risks from climate change and, as a result of this, poverty, land degradation, human health, and access to water and food remain at the centre of global attention. The United Nations Framework Convention on Climate Change (UNFCCC) is the key instrument for addressing climate change. In the UN Millennium Declaration, heads of state and government agreed to make every effort to ensure that the **Kyoto Protocol** to the UNFCCC came into force, preferably by the Rio anniversary in 2002, and to embark on the required cuts in greenhouse gas emissions. States that have ratified the Kyoto Protocol strongly urge states that have not done so to ratify the Kyoto Protocol in a timely way *[38]*. Actions are required at all levels to:

- Meet all UNFCCC commitments and obligations *[38a]*;
- Work cooperatively to achieve its objectives *[38b]*;
- Assist developing countries and countries with economies in transition in accordance with the UNFCCC and Marrakech accords *[38c]*;
- Build **scientific and technical capabilities** with continuing support to the IPCC in exchanging data and information *[38d]*;
- Develop and transfer **technological solutions** *[38e]*;
- Develop and transfer **innovative technology** in key sectors of development such as energy *[38f]*;
- Promote systematic **observation and monitoring** of the Earth's atmosphere, land and oceans by improving monitoring stations, increasing satellite use and producing high-quality data for all countries to use *[38g]*;
- Improve implementation of strategies to monitor the Earth's atmosphere, land and oceans, including integrated global observations *[38h]*; and
- Support initiatives, such as the Arctic Council initiative, that assess the consequences of climate change and impacts on **local and indigenous communities** *[38i]*.

Air pollution and atmosphere

In order to effectively reduce **air pollution** (including transboundary pollution, acid deposition and ozone depletion), better cooperation and action at all levels is required, bearing in mind the Rio principles, including the recognition that states have different but common responsibilities in view of their different

'The physical characteristics of mountains have made them important strongholds of biological and cultural diversity. Their remoteness, difficulty of access and rugged terrain have combined to make them among the last places on Earth to be exploited and developed ... the reverence that mountains tend to awaken in cultures around the world provides a powerful source of motivation for preserving biodiversity' (Bernbaum, 1999).

4

contributions to global environmental degradation *[39]*. Action at all levels will help to:

- Strengthen the ability of developing countries and countries with economies in transition to measure, reduce and assess the impacts of air pollution, including **health impacts** *[39a]*;
- Implement the **Montreal Protocol** on Substances that Deplete the Ozone Layer by ensuring an adequate replenishment of its fund by 2003/2005 *[39b]*;
- Support the regime for protection of the ozone layer established in the Vienna Convention and the Montreal Protocol *[39c]*;
- Improve access by developing countries to suitable alternatives to **ozone-depleting substances** by 2010 and help them to comply with the Montreal Protocol's phase-out schedule *[39d]*; and
- Take measures to address illegal traffic in ozone-depleting substances *[39e]*.

'Our planet's essential goods and services depend upon the variety and variability of genes, species, populations and ecosystems. Biological resources feed and clothe us and provide housing, medicines and spiritual nourishment ... the current decline in biodiversity is largely the result of human activity and represents a serious threat to human development' (Agenda 21, 1992, Chapter 15).

Agriculture

Agriculture helps to address the needs of a growing global population and is inextricably linked to poverty eradication. A greater role for **women** is imperative in all aspects of rural development, agriculture, nutrition and food security. **Sustainable agriculture and rural development** are essential to an integrated and environmentally sustainable approach that both increases food production and improves **food security** *[40]*, and require actions to:

- Halve, by the year 2015, the proportion of people who suffer from **hunger** and realize the right to a standard of living, including food, that is adequate for health and well-being. Promote **food security** and fight hunger in combination with anti-poverty measures that are consistent with the World Food Summit outcomes and obligations under the International Covenant on Economic, Social and Cultural Rights *[40a]*;
- Implement **integrated land management and water-use plans**, strengthening the ability of governments, local authorities and communities to monitor and manage those plans *[40b]*;
- Increase understanding of the sustainable use, protection and management of **water resources** *[40c]*;
- Enhance the **sustainable productivity of land and efficient use of water** in agriculture, forestry, wetlands, artisanal fisheries and aquaculture, paying attention to indigenous and local community-based approaches *[40d]*;
- Help developing countries to protect **oases** from silt, land degradation and increasing salinity *[40e]*;
- Improve the participation of **women** in sustainable agriculture and food security *[40f]*;
- Strengthen national research and extension services and farmer organizations to spread **good practice and integrate existing information systems on land-use practices** *[40g]*;

- Protect **indigenous resource management systems** and support the contribution of all stakeholders to rural planning and development *[40h]*;
- Guarantee well-defined and enforceable **land and water rights**, and **security of land tenure**, recognizing that there are different laws and systems of land access and tenure, and providing assistance with land reform *[40i]*;
- Reverse the decline of public-sector **finance** for sustainable agriculture and promote private-sector investment in agricultural research and natural resource management *[40j]*;
- Employ **market-based incentives** to encourage agricultural enterprises and farmers to manage water wisely, using methods such as **small-scale irrigation and wastewater recycling and reuse** *[40k]*;
- Improve access to existing **markets** and develop new markets for value-added agricultural products *[40l]*;
- Increase **brown-field redevelopment** *[40m]*;
- Enhance international cooperation to combat the illicit cultivation of **narcotic plants** *[40n]*;
- Promote environmentally sound, effective and efficient techniques for **soil fertility** and agricultural **pest control** *[40o]*;
- Coordinate existing initiatives on sustainable agriculture and food security *[40p]*;
- Invite countries that have not done so to ratify the **International Treaty on Plant Genetic Resources for Food and Agriculture** *[40q]*; and
- Promote the conservation, sustainable use and management of traditional and **indigenous agricultural systems**. Strengthen indigenous models of agriculture production *[40r]*.

Desertification and drought

To address the causes of **desertification and land degradation**, restore land and address poverty resulting from desertification, the JPOI outlines requirements for **strengthening implementation** of the **United Nations Convention to Combat Desertification** (CCD) *[41]*. They include actions to:

- Mobilize **finance, transfer technologies and building capacity** *[41a]*;
- Formulate **national action programmes**, backed by decentralized local projects *[41b]*;
- Encourage the CCD, the CBD and the UNFCCC to continue to exploring potential **areas of mutual benefit** *[41c]*;
- Integrate measures addressing **desertification** and the effects of **drought** in sectors such as land, water, forests, agriculture, rural development, early warning systems, environment, energy, natural resources, health and education, poverty and sustainable development *[41d]*;
- Provide affordable local access to information to improve monitoring and **early warning** *[41e]*;

'The term 'biodiversity' does not exist in my people's understanding or language. If I were to translate the term in our language, I would say it is everything in this world, down in the sea and things that we can touch. At the same time, it is more than this – more than just things that can be touched or things that are alive. The air, the water and the sun must also be included. If one being or part of biodiversity is disturbed or not kept in the perfect manner, an imbalance is created which will affect all other things' (Segundad, 2001).

- Call on the **Global Environment Facility** (GEF) Assembly to designate land degradation (desertification and deforestation) as a focal area and consider making GEF the financial mechanism of the CCD *[41f]*; and
- Improve the sustainability of **grassland** resources through better management, law enforcement and support *[41g]*.

Mountains

Mountain ecosystems support particular livelihoods, and include significant watershed resources, biological diversity and a unique flora and fauna. Many of these ecosystems are fragile and vulnerable to the effects of climate change *[42]*. Action is needed to:

- Integrate **environmental, economic and social components of sustainable mountain development** at policy and programme levels and strengthen international cooperation to improve **poverty eradication** initiatives *[42a]*;
- Address deforestation, erosion, land degradation, loss of biodiversity, disruption of water flows and the retreat of glaciers *[42b]*;
- Implement **gender-sensitive** policies aimed at eliminating the inequities facing mountain communities *[42c]*;
- **Promote diversification and traditional mountain economies**, sustainable livelihoods and small-scale production systems *[42d]*;
- Promote the full participation and involvement of mountain communities in decisions that affect them and **integrate indigenous** knowledge, heritage and values in all development initiatives *[42e]*; and
- Mobilize support for applied research and capacity-building, provide assistance for the sustainable development of mountain ecosystems, and reduce poverty among people living in mountain areas, taking into account the spirit of the International Year of Mountains in 2002 *[42f]*.

" By degrading forests, engineering rivers, filling in wetlands and destabilizing the climate, we are unravelling the strands of a complex ecological safety net... We have altered so many natural systems so dramatically, their ability to protect us from disturbances is greatly diminished" (Abramovitz, 2001).

Sustainable tourism

The JPOI promotes **sustainable tourism** (including non-consumptive and ecotourism) to increase the benefits flowing from tourism resources to local populations, while maintaining cultural and environmental integrity, protecting ecologically sensitive areas and natural heritages, and strengthening rural and local communities *[43]*. Actions will be taken to:

- Improve international cooperation, foreign direct investment and partnerships *[43a]*;
- Develop programmes, including education/training, that encourage people to participate in ecotourism and enable indigenous local communities to benefit *[43b]*;
- Provide technical assistance to support **sustainable tourism business** development, investment and **tourism awareness** programmes *[43c]*;

- Assist host communities in **managing visits** to maximize the benefits while ensuring the least impact on, or risk to, traditions, culture and the environment *[43d]*; and
- Promote **diversification of economic activities**, including access to markets and commercial information, and participation of emerging local enterprises, especially small- and medium-sized enterprises (SMEs) *[43e]*.

Biodiversity

Biodiversity plays a critical role in sustainable development and poverty eradication. It is essential to the functioning and systems of the planet, human well-being, livelihoods and the cultural integrity of people. However, biodiversity is being lost at an unprecedented rate due to human activities: this trend can only be reversed through enabling local people to benefit from conservation and sustainable use of biological diversity, particularly in countries of origin of genetic resources, as noted in Article 15 of the **Convention on Biological Diversity** (CBD). This convention is the key agreement for the **conservation and sustainable use of biological diversity**, and the **fair and equitable sharing of benefits** arising from the use of genetic resources. Achieving a **significant reduction** in the current rate of loss of biological diversity by 2010, and a more coherent implementation of the three objectives of the CBD, requires new and additional resources for developing countries *[44]* and actions to:

'It is imperative we do more to ensure that mining's [environmental] fallout is mitigated and that local communities – in particular, the millions of artisanal miners – share in the benefits' (UN Secretary-General Kofi Annan, 2002).

- Integrate **CBD objectives** within programmes and policies, especially in economic sectors and international financial institutions *[44a]*;
- Promote ongoing **work under the CBD** on the sustainable use of biological diversity (including sustainable tourism) as a cross-cutting issue *[44b]*;
- Encourage effective links between the CBD and other **multilateral environmental agreements** *[44c]*;
- Implement the CBD through national, regional and global action programmes, particularly **national biodiversity strategies and action plans**. Strengthen their integration into relevant cross-sectoral strategies for sustainable development and poverty eradication, including **community-based use of biological diversity** *[44d]*;
- Promote use of the **ecosystem approach** elaborated through the CBD *[44e]*;
- Promote **international support and partnerships** for the conservation and sustainable use of biodiversity in ecosystems at **World Heritage sites** and to protect **endangered species** *[44f]*;
- Support initiatives for biodiversity **hot spot areas** and the development of national and regional **ecological networks and corridors** *[44g]*;
- Enhance indigenous and community-based biodiversity conservation in developing countries *[44h]*;
- Strengthen control of **invasive alien species** *[44i]*;

- Recognize the rights of local and indigenous communities who are **holders of traditional knowledge**, innovations and practices. With their involvement and approval, develop **benefit-sharing** mechanisms for the use of such knowledge *[44j]*;
- Encourage **all stakeholders** to contribute to CBD implementation, recognizing the role of youth, women and indigenous and local communities in conserving and using biodiversity in a sustainable way *[44k]*;
- Promote effective participation of **indigenous and local communities** in decisions and policy-making concerning the use of their traditional knowledge *[44l]*;
- Support efforts to develop and implement national **sui generis systems** and **traditional systems** *[44m]*;
- Promote implementation of, and work on, the Bonn Guidelines on Access to Genetic Resources and Fair and Equitable Sharing of Benefits Arising out of Their Utilization *[44n]*;
- Negotiate under the CBD an international **regime to promote and safeguard fair and equitable sharing of benefits** arising out of the use of genetic resources *[44o]*;
- Encourage successful conclusion of processes under the World Intellectual Property Organization Intergovernmental Committee on **Intellectual Property and Genetic Resources, Traditional Knowledge and Folklore**, and work on **Article 8(j)** of the CBD *[44p]*;
- Promote measures for access to the results and benefits arising from **biotechnologies** based on genetic resources *[44q]*;
- Promote discussions on relationships between the **CBD** and agreements related to international **trade and intellectual property rights**, as outlined in the Doha Ministerial Declaration, to enhance synergy and mutual supportiveness, but without prejudging the outcomes *[44r]*;
- Promote implementation of the work programme of the **Global Taxonomy Initiative** *[44s]*; and
- Invite all states that have not ratified the **CBD, the Cartagena Protocol on Biosafety** and other biodiversity-related agreements to do so, encouraging signatories to promote effective implementation *[44t]*.

Forests

Sustainable forest management of both natural and planted forests, and for timber and non-timber forest products, is essential to sustainable development. It is a way of eradicating poverty, reducing deforestation, halting the loss of biodiversity, cutting land and resource degradation, improving food security, and providing access to safe drinking water and affordable energy. Achieving sustainable forest management is an essential goal of sustainable development *[45]* and requires actions to:

- Increase political commitment to sustainable forest management, setting it as a priority on the international political agenda *[45a]*;
- Support the United Nations Forum on Forests (with the assistance of the Collaborative Partnership on Forests) to act as the key intergovernmental mechanism for sustainable forest management *[45b]*;
- Take immediate action to enforce **domestic forest law** and tackle **illegal international trade in forest products** (including forest biological resources) *[45c]*;
- Take immediate action to achieve **sustainable timber harvesting** *[45d]*;
- Address the needs of areas currently suffering from **poverty** and the highest rates of deforestation, where international cooperation would be welcomed by affected governments *[45e]*;
- Strengthen **partnerships and international cooperation** to facilitate increased finance, transfer of environmentally sound technologies, trade, capacity-building, forest law and governance, and integrated land and resource management *[45f]*;
- Accelerate implementation of proposals made by the **United Nations Intergovernmental Panel on Forests/Intergovernmental Forum on Forests**, and intensify reporting to the United Nations Forum on Forests to contribute to an assessment of progress in 2005 *[45g]*;
- Recognize/support **indigenous and community-based forest management systems** to ensure their full participation in sustainable forest management *[45h]*; and
- Implement the CBD's work programme on all types of forest biodiversity *[45i]*.

Mining, minerals and metals

Mining, minerals and metals make an important contribution to the economic and social development of many countries *[46]*. Enhancing this contribution to sustainable development requires action at all levels to:

- Address **environmental, economic, health** and **social impacts** and benefits of mining, minerals and metals throughout their life cycle, including work on **workers' health and safety** and partnerships to **promote accountability** for sustainable mining and minerals development *[46a]*;
- Improve the **participation of stakeholders** (including local and indigenous communities and women) to help them play an active role in minerals, metals and mining development, throughout the life cycle of mining operations and taking into account national regulations and significant transboundary impacts *[46b]*; and
- Foster **sustainable mining practices** through support for mining and processing of minerals, including small-scale activities. Where appropriate, this includes better value-added processing, upgrading of scientific and technical information, and efforts to reclaim and rehabilitate degraded sites *[46c]*.

Managing the natural resources base elsewhere in the JPOI

Managing the natural resources base for development is one of the three overarching objectives of, and essential requirements for, sustainable development in the JPOI (Chapter I), and references to natural resources are a continuous thread through all chapters. Many targets, including those on safe drinking water, sanitation, integrated water resource management and chemicals, are closely related to a reversal of trends in environmental degradation, as is the need to maintain the natural resource base to ensure sustainable livelihoods for the poor. Approaches to changing unsustainable patterns of resources use are outlined in Chapter III, while measures to ensure that globalization is managed in a framework that enables rather than inhibits effective natural resources management are addressed in Chapters V and XI.

TARGETS AND COMMITMENTS

- **Drinking water.** Halve, by the year 2015, the proportion of people without access to safe drinking water *[25]* (MDG).

- **Sanitation.** Halve, by the year 2015, the proportion of people who do not have access to basic sanitation *[25]* (new target).

- **Integrated water management.** Develop integrated water resources management and water efficiency plans by 2005 *[26]* (new target).

- **Ecosystem approach for oceans.** Encourage the application, by 2010, of the ecosystem approach for the sustainable development of the oceans *[30d]* (new target).

- **Fish stocks.** On an urgent basis, and where possible by 2015, maintain or restore depleted fish stocks to levels that can produce the maximum sustainable yield *[31a]* (new target).

- **Marine environment.** Use of diverse approaches and tools, including ecosystem approach, elimination of destructive fishing practices and establishment of marine protected areas, including representative networks by 2012 *[32c]* (new target).

- **Global oceans reporting.** Establish, by 2004, a regular process under the UN for global reporting and assessment of the state of the marine environment *[36b]* (new target).

- **FAO action plans.** Put into effect FAO international plans of action by agreed dates: for the management of fishing capacity, by 2005; and to prevent, deter and eliminate illegal, unreported and unregulated fishing, by 2004 *[31d]*.

TARGETS AND COMMITMENTS (CONTD)

- **Fishing.** Eliminate subsidies that contribute to illegal, unreported and unregulated fishing and to overcapacity *[31f]*.

- **Inter-agency coordination on marine issues.** Establish an effective, transparent and regular inter-agency coordination mechanism on ocean and coastal issues within the UN system *[30c]*.

- **Ozone fund.** Ensure adequate replenishment of the Montreal Protocol fund by 2003/2005 *[39b]*.

- **Access to ozone-depleting alternatives.** Improve access by developing countries to alternatives to ozone-depleting substances by 2010; assist them with the Montreal Protocol phase-out schedule *[39d]* (new target).

- **Biodiversity loss.** Achieve, by 2010, a significant reduction in the current rate of loss of biological diversity *[44]*.

- **Forest reporting.** Intensify efforts on reporting to the United Nations Forum on Forests to contribute to an assessment of progress in 2005 *[45g]* (new target).

- **Implementation of Intergovernmental Panel on Forests/Intergovernmental Forum on Forests (IPF/IFF) proposals.** Accelerate implementation of the IPF/IFF proposals for action by countries and by the Collaborative Partnership on Forests *[45g]*.

EXAMPLES OF INDICATORS FOR MEASURING PROGRESS IN IMPLEMENTATION

- Proportion of population with sustainable access to an improved water source, urban and rural (Millennium Development Goal, or MDG)

- Proportion of urban population with access to improved sanitation (MDG)

- Percentage of population with adequate sewage disposal facilities (Commission on Sustainable Development, or CSD)

- Population with access to safe drinking water (CSD)

- Water consumption, price of water (United Nations Human Settlements Programme, or UN-Habitat)

- Concentration of faecal coliform in freshwater (CSD)

- Biological oxygen demand (BOD) in water bodies (CSD)

4

EXAMPLES OF INDICATORS FOR MEASURING PROGRESS IN IMPLEMENTATION (CONTD)

- Percentage of total population living in coastal areas (CSD)
- Algae concentration in coastal waters (CSD)
- Annual catch by major species (CSD)
- Economic and human loss due to natural disasters (CSD)
- Disaster prevention and mitigation instruments (UN-Habitat)
- Carbon dioxide emissions (per capita) and consumption of ozone-depleting chlorofluorocarbons (CFCs) (ozone depleting potential (ODP) tonnes) (MDG)
- Proportion of population using solid fuels (MDG)
- Emissions of greenhouse gases (CSD)
- Consumption of ozone-depleting substances (CSD)
- Ambient concentration of air pollutants in urban areas (CSD)
- Prevalence of underweight children under five years of age (MDG)
- Proportion of population below minimum level of dietary energy consumption (MDG)
- Agricultural support estimate for Organisation for Economic Co-operation and Development (OECD) countries as percentage of their gross domestic product (GDP) (MDG)
- Arable and permanent crop land area (CSD)
- Use of fertilizers (CSD)
- Use of agricultural pesticides (CSD)
- Water availability and quality (UN Food and Agriculture Organization (FAO) Food Security Indicator)
- Soil quality (FAO Food Security Indicator)
- Crop diversity (FAO Food Security Indicator)
- Land tenure, access and control (FAO Food Security Indicator)
- Land affected by desertification (CSD)'
- Ratio of area protected to maintain biological diversity to surface area (MDG)
- Area of selected key ecosystems (CSD)
- Protected area as a percentage of total area (CSD)

EXAMPLES OF INDICATORS FOR MEASURING PROGRESS IN IMPLEMENTATION (CONTD)

- Abundance of selected key species (CSD)
- Proportion of land area covered by forest (MDG)
- Forest area as a percentage of land area (CSD)
- Wood harvesting intensity (CSD)
- Forest resource access (FAO Food Security Indicator)

Partnership example

International Partnership for Sustainable Development in Mountain Regions

Leading partners: United Nations Food and Agriculture Organization (FAO) – International Year of Mountains Coordination Unit and United Nations Environment Programme (UNEP) Mountain Programme.

Dates: 2002–2012

- Improve, strengthen and promote greater cooperation between major groups, all mountain stakeholders, such as donors, implementing agencies, non-governmental organizations (NGOs), the private sector, mountain communities, academia and other field practitioners.

- Focus on the effective implementation of prioritized actions to manage mountain ecosystems through sustainable development and to address chronic poverty in mountain regions through concrete programmes and support from all stakeholders.

- Provide an instrument to implement the Johannesburg Plan of Implementation (JPOI) commitments on mountains (paragraph 42), intended as a way to further implement Chapter 13 of Agenda 21.

- Allow all partners to enter into specific sub-partnerships that could be organized around thematic areas of action – for example, biodiversity conservation, food security and poverty alleviation – or geographic regions or institutional concerns (for example, mountain policy and law).

- Enhance linkages with existing multilateral instruments, such as the United Nations Convention on Biological Diversity (CBD), the United Nations Convention to Combat Desertification (CCD), the United Nations Framework Convention on Climate Change (UNFCCC), the International Strategy for Disaster Reduction (ISDR) and others.

4

> **Partnership example (*contd*)**
>
> Partners involved include governments (Austria, Bhutan, Ghana, Indonesia, Italy, Jordan, Kyrgyz Republic, Lao Republic, Monaco, Peru, Sri Lanka, Switzerland, US, Venezuela – as of August 2002); intergovernmental organizations, including FAO, UNEP, the United Nations Educational, Scientific and Cultural Organization (UNESCO), the United Nations Development Programme (UNDP), the United Nations Population Fund (UNFPA) and CBD; development banks and research centres; and major groups, including the Mountain Forum, the World Conservation Union (IUCN), the Banff Centre for Mountain Coordination, the World Mountain People Association, the World Wide Fund for Nature (WWF-International) and the European Observatory of Mountain Forests.

 # Resources

Water and sanitation

International Year of Freshwater (2003)

www.wateryear2003.org
The International Year of Freshwater focused the attention of individuals, communities, countries and the global family of concerned citizens on protecting and respecting our water resources.

Oceans, seas and marine resources

Agreement on the Conservation and Management of Straddling Fish Stocks and Highly Migratory Fish Stocks (1995)

www.un.org/Depts/los/fish_stocks_conference/fish_stocks_conference.htm
This agreement ensures long-term conservation and sustainable use of straddling fish stocks and highly migratory fish stocks. It covers fish stocks occurring within the exclusive economic zones (EEZs) of two or more coastal states, or both within and beyond the EEZ.

United Nations Food and Agriculture Organization (FAO)

www.fao.org
The FAO is mandated to raise levels of nutrition and standards of living in order to improve agricultural and marine productivity. Fishery concerns include the 1995 Code of Conduct for Responsible Fisheries.

Global Programme of Action for Protection of the Marine Environment from Land-based Activities (GPA), Montreal Declaration

www.gpa.unep.org

The GPA prevents degradation of the marine environment from land-based activities by facilitating the duty of states to preserve and protect the marine environment. It supports an integrated management approach, and mobilizes support for developing countries' activities. Its review in 2001 resulted in the Montreal Declaration.

Intergovernmental Oceanographic Commission (IOC)

www.ioc.unesco.org

The IOC supports oceanic research programmes to increase knowledge about marine resources and their relationship to sustainable development.

International Atomic Energy Agency (IAEA)

www.iaea.org

The IAEA is an intergovernmental forum for scientific and technical cooperation that promotes nuclear safety and non-proliferation.

International Coral Reef Initiative (ICRI)

www.icriforum.org

The ICRI was established in 1994 to stop and reverse the global degradation of coral reefs and ecosystems, including seagrass beds and mangrove forests. The partnership exists to implement Agenda 21 and other agreements related to coral reefs.

International Maritime Organization (IMO)

www.imo.org

The IMO is a UN body concerned with maritime legislation that addresses marine pollution, including through the International Convention for the Prevention of Pollution from Ships, 1973 (MARPOL regime) and related protocols, as well as the movement of hazardous materials, dumping at sea, illegal fishing and invasive species.

International Plan of Action to Prevent, Deter and Eliminate Illegal, Unreported and Unregulated Fishing (2001)

www.fao.org

Addressing the crisis in world fisheries, this non-binding international plan includes activities both on the high seas and within EEZs.

Jakarta Mandate on the Conservation and Sustainable Use of Marine and Coastal Biological Diversity

www.biodiv.org/programmes/areas/marine
Agreed under the United Nations Convention on Biological Diversity (CBD), this mandate focuses on integrated marine and coastal area management, sustainable use of living resources, protected areas, mariculture and alien species.

Ramsar Convention (1971)

www.ramsar.org
The Ramsar Convention is a framework for national action and international cooperation on the conservation and wise use of wetlands (including mangroves/coral reefs) and their resources.

Reykjavik Declaration on Responsible Fisheries (1995)

www.fao.org
This is a voluntary FAO code of conduct that provides principles and standards on the conservation, management and development of fisheries. It also covers the capture, processing and trade of fish and fishery products, fishing operations, aquaculture, research and integrating fisheries within coastal area management.

United Nations Convention on the Law of the Sea (1982)

www.un.org/Depts/los/convention_agreements/convention_overview_convention.htm
This is a globally recognized comprehensive regime that deals with all matters relating to the law of the sea.

United Nations Environment Programme (UNEP) Regional Seas Programme

www.gpa.unep.org/seas/seas.htm
Initiated in 1974, this programme adopts a regional approach to controlling marine pollution and managing marine and coastal resources. It is a means of implementing the GPA.

Vulnerability, risk assessment, disaster management

International Strategy for Disaster Reduction (ISDR)

www.unisdr.org
This is a UN coordinating mechanism on disaster reduction. It supports policy integration, serves as an international information clearinghouse, develops awareness campaigns, and produces articles, journals and other materials related to disaster reduction.

Climate and atmosphere

Arctic Council

www.arctic-council.org
The Arctic Council is a high-level intergovernmental forum that addresses challenges faced by Arctic governments and peoples. Its members are Canada, Denmark, Finland, Iceland, Norway, Russian Federation, Sweden and the US.

Intergovernmental Panel on Climate Change (IPCC)

www.ipcc.ch/index.html
Established by the World Meteorological Organization (WMO) and UNEP, the IPCC assesses published scientific, technical and socio-economic information relevant to understanding the risk of human-induced climate change, its potential impacts and the options for adaptation and mitigation.

Marrakesh Accords

Agreed at the 7th Convention of the Parties to the UNFCCC in 2001, the Marrakesh Accords, among other things, detail the rules, modalities and guidelines for the implementation of the Kyoto Protocol Flexible Mechanism

United Nations Framework Convention on Climate Change (UNFCCC) (1992), Kyoto Protocol

www.unfccc.int
The objective of the UNFCCC is to stabilize greenhouse gas concentrations in the atmosphere at a level that would prevent dangerous anthropogenic interference with the climate system. It should occur within a time frame that is sufficient to allow ecosystems to adapt naturally to climate change, to ensure that food production is not threatened, and to enable economic development to occur in a sustainable manner. The Kyoto Protocol (1997) sets legally binding targets to cut greenhouse gas emissions.

Vienna Convention for the Protection of the Ozone Layer and the Montreal Protocol on Substances that Deplete the Ozone Layer

www.unep.org/ozone
This convention aims to protect human health and the environment from the effects of ozone depletion by controlling the production and consumption of ozone-depleting substances (ODS) and by phasing them out to an agreed schedule. It takes the circumstances of developing countries into account in implementing measures.

Agriculture

International Treaty on Plant Genetic Resources for Food and Agriculture (2001)

www.fao.org/ag/cgrfa/itpgr.htm

This is a legally binding FAO treaty on the conservation and use of plant genetic resources, covering all plant genetic resources relevant for food and agriculture. It balances the rights of different groups and encourages national and international collections of seeds and plants. It will work alongside the Bonn Guidelines on Access to Genetic Resources (2002).

United Nations Food and Agriculture Organization (FAO)

www.fao.org

The FAO is mandated to raise levels of nutrition and standards of living, to improve agricultural productivity, and to improve conditions of rural populations. The FAO helped launch a Sustainable Agriculture and Rural Development (SARD) initiative at the World Summit on Sustainable Development (WSSD) in order to accelerate action to reduce world hunger.

World Food Programme (WFP)

www.wfp.org

The WFP is a frontline UN organization fighting to eradicate world hunger. WFP's vision is a world where every person has access at all times to the food needed for an active and healthy life.

World Food Summit (1996)

www.fao.org

The World Food Summit reaffirmed 'the right of everyone to have access to safe and nutritious food, consistent with the right to adequate food and the fundamental right of everyone to freedom from hunger'. It called for equitable development strategies to reduce poverty, putting an emphasis on social justice and the achievement of better nutrition for all, especially vulnerable and marginalized groups. The 2002 review looked at ways of accelerating progress against a background of persistent food insecurity.

Desertification and drought

Global Environment Facility (GEF)

www.gefweb.org

The GEF helps developing countries fund projects/programmes that protect the global environment. It designates financial mechanisms for conventions on biodiversity, climate change and persistent organic pollutants. It also supports work on desertification, international waters and the ozone layer.

United Nations Convention to Combat Desertification in Those Countries Experiencing Serious Drought and/or Desertification, Particularly in Africa (CCD)

www.unccd.int/main.php
Agreement to negotiate the CCD came out of UNCED in 1996. Detailed annexes address desertification in specific regions; countries must develop national action programmes in conjunction with local stakeholders (UNEP, 2002).

Mountains

International Year of Mountains (2002)

www.mountains2002.org
The International Year of Mountains was coordinated by the FAO to create heightened international awareness of the dangers facing mountain ecosystems/communities; an action plan was developed to tackle the problems and a Global Mountain Summit was held.

Sustainable tourism

World Tourism Organization (WTO)/Global Code of Ethics

www.world-tourism.org
The WTO is an intergovernmental body working with UNEP and the United Nations Educational, Scientific and Cultural Organization (UNESCO) to promote sustainable tourism through guidelines, handbooks, the exchange of good practice and demonstration projects. It adopted a Global Code of Ethics for Tourism.

Biodiversity and biotechnology

Bonn Guidelines on Access to Genetic Resources and Fair and Equitable Sharing of Benefits Arising out of Their Utilization (2002)

www.biodiv.org/programmes/socio-eco/benefit/bonn.asp
These are voluntary guidelines under the Convention on Biological Diversity (CBD) to assist governments to structure national/regional legislation/mechanisms to ensure fair access to genetic resources and the sharing of benefits. It calls for transparency in policy and suggests prior informed consent procedures.

Cartagena Protocol on Biosafety (2002)

www.biodiv.org/biosafety/protocol.asp
This protocol was developed under the CBD to address potential risks to biodiversity posed by living modified organisms (LMOs) resulting from modern biotechnology (also known as genetically modified organisms – GMOs). It seeks the safe transfer, handling and use of LMOs, and takes into account risks to human health.

United Nations Convention on Biological Diversity (CBD)

www.biodiv.org
The CBD was agreed at UNCED (1992) with three main goals: the conservation of biological diversity; the sustainable use of its components; and the fair and equitable sharing of benefits arising from the use of genetic resources. Under the CBD, the Cartagena Biosafety Protocol (2000) focuses on living modified organisms resulting from modern biotechnology and the Jakarta Mandate (1995) addresses marine and coastal biological diversity.

Global Taxonomy Initiative (GTI)

www.biodiv.org/programmes/cross-cutting/taxonomy
The GTI was formed under the CBD to address the lack of taxonomic information and expertise in many parts of the world. Taxonomy is the science of identifying and naming the species of plants, animals and micro-organisms.

World Heritage Sites (UNESCO)

whc.unesco.org/nwhc/pages/home/pages/homepage.htm
Sites designated under the World Heritage Convention are considered to be of outstanding value to humanity. Once listed, their protection becomes a responsibility shared by the international community as a whole.

Forests

Collaborative Partnership on Forests (CPF)

www.un.org/esa/forests
The CPF was formed by 11 international forest-related organizations, within and outside the UN, to support the United Nations Forum on Forests and to enhance coordination/international cooperation.

Forest Principles (1992)

www.un.org/documents/ga/conf151/acon15126-3annex3.htm
This is a non-binding statement of principles on the management, conservation and sustainable development of all types of forests and is an outcome of UNCED.

Intergovernmental Panel on Forests (IPF) (1995–1997)/Intergovernmental Forum on Forests (IFF) (1997–2000)

www.un.org/esa/forests
Following UNCED, the IPF and IFF processes formulated a common vision for the management, conservation and sustainable development of all types of forests. This work is now taken forward by a permanent intergovernmental body: the United Nations Forum on Forests (UNFF).

United Nations Forum on Forests (UNFF)

www.un.org/esa/forests

The UNFF is an intergovernmental policy forum to promote the management, conservation and sustainable development of all types of forests and to strengthen long-term political commitment to this end. It was established in 2000 as part of a new international arrangement on forests to carry on the work of the IPF and IFF. It has expressed concern on the 'continuing high rate of worldwide deforestation, as well as forest and land degradation'.

CONFERENCES, AGREEMENTS AND PROCESSES

Drinking water and sanitation

- Agenda 21, Chapter 18 (1992)
- United Nations General Assembly Special Session (UNGASS) (1997)
- United Nations Commission on Sustainable Development (CSD) 6, Decision 1 (1998)
- International Conference on Freshwater, Bonn (2001)
- Third World Water Forum, Kyoto (March 2003)
- International Year on Freshwater (2003)
- CSD to consider water and sanitation (2003–2005)
- Millennium Development Goal (MDG) on drinking water and World Summit on Sustainable Development (WSSD) sanitation target (2015)

Oceans, seas and coasts

- Agenda 21, Chapter 17 (1992)
- Convention on Biological Diversity (CBD) Convention of the Parties (COP) Decision 5/6
- United Nations Convention on the Law of the Sea (UNCLOS) (1982)
- Global Programme of Action for the Protection of the Marine Environment from Land-based Activities (GPA) and the Washington Declaration (1995)
- Reykjavik Declaration on Responsible Fisheries in the Marine Ecosystem (2001)
- The United Nations Conference on Straddling and Highly Migratory Fish Stocks (1995)
- Food and Agriculture Organization (FAO) Code of Conduct of Responsible Fisheries (1995)
- United Nations Commission on Sustainable Development (CSD) 4 (1996)

CONFERENCES, AGREEMENTS AND PROCESSES (CONTD)

- United Nations General Assembly Special Session (UNGASS), paragraph 36 (1997)

- CSD-7, Decision 1 (1999)

- CSD to consider oceans and seas, and marine resources (2013–2015)

- International Convention for the Prevention of Pollution from Ships (MARPOL) (73/78)

- Antifouling Systems Convention (2002)

- International Maritime Organization (IMO) International Convention for the Control and Management of Ships' Ballast Water and Sediments (2004)

Vulnerability, disaster reduction and management

- United Nations International Decade for Natural Disaster Reduction (1990–1999)

- Yokohama Strategy (1994)

- United Nations General Assembly Special Session (UNGASS) 54/219 (2000)

- United Nations Commission on Sustainable Development (CSD) to consider disaster management and vulnerability (2014–2015)

Climate change

- Vienna Convention for the Protection of the Ozone Layer (1985) and Montreal Protocol (1987)

- Agenda 21, Chapter 9 (incorporates energy and transport) (1992)

- United Nations General Assembly Special Session (UNGASS), paragraphs 42, 47, 48 (1997)

- United Nations Framework Convention on Climate Change (UNFCCC, 1992) and the associated Kyoto Protocol (1998)

- United Nations Commission on Sustainable Development (CSD) 9, Decision 1 (2001)

- CSD to consider climate change, air pollution and atmosphere (2005–2007)

Agriculture

- Agenda 21, Chapter 14 (1992)

- United Nations Commission on Sustainable Development (CSD) 3, Decision 6 (1995)

CONFERENCES, AGREEMENTS AND PROCESSES (CONTD)

- ⧗ United Nations General Assembly Special Session (UNGASS), paragraph 62 (1997)
- ⧗ World Food Summit (1996) CSD-8, Decision 4 (2000)
- ⧗ World Food Summit +5 (2002)
- ⧗ CSD to consider agriculture, rural development and land (2007–2009)
- ⧗ Millennium Development Goal (MDG) on hunger (2015)

Desertification

- ⧗ Agenda 21, Chapter 12 (1992)
- ⧗ United Nations Convention to Combat Desertification (CCD) (1994)
- ⧗ United Nations Commission on Sustainable Development (CSD) 3, Decision 3 (1995)
- ⧗ United Nations General Assembly Special Session (UNGASS), paragraph 64 (1997)
- ⧗ CSD to consider desertification and drought (2007–2009)

Mountains

- ⧗ Agenda 21, Chapter 13 (1992)
- ⧗ United Nations Commission on Sustainable Development (CSD) 3, Decision 4 (1995)
- ⧗ United Nations General Assembly Special Session (UNGASS) Designation of International Year of Mountains (2002)
- ⧗ CSD to consider mountains (2011–2013)

Tourism

- ⧗ United Nations Commission on Sustainable Development (CSD) 7, Decision 3 (1999)
- ⧗ International Year of Ecotourism (2002)
- ⧗ Responsible Tourism Partnership Cape Town Declaration (2002)
- ⧗ World Tourism Eco Summit (Quebec Declaration) (2002)
- ⧗ CSD to consider tourism (2011–2013)

Biodiversity and biotechnology

- ⧗ United Nations Convention on Wetlands of International Importance Especially as Waterfowl Habitat (Ramsar Convention) (1971)

4

CONFERENCES, AGREEMENTS AND PROCESSES (CONTD)

⧗ United Nations Educational, Scientific and Cultural Organization (UNESCO) Convention Concerning the Protection of the World Cultural and Natural Heritage (1972)

⧗ United Nations Convention on International Trade in Endangered Species of Wild Fauna and Flora (CITES) (1973)

⧗ United Nations Convention on the Conservation of Migratory Species of Wild Animals and Further Agreements (1979)

⧗ Agenda 21, Chapters 15, 16 (1992)

⧗ United Nations Convention on Biological Diversity (CBD) (1992)

⧗ United Nations General Assembly Special Session (UNGASS), paragraph 66 (1997)

⧗ United Nations Commission on Sustainable Development (CSD) 3, Decisions 3, 7 (1995) and CSD-6 (1998)

⧗ CSD to consider biodiversity and biotechnology (2011–2013)

Forests

⧗ Forest Principles and Agenda 21, Chapter 11 (1992)

⧗ United Nations Commission on Sustainable Development (CSD) 3 (1995)

⧗ United Nations Economic and Social Council (ECOSOC) Resolution 2000/35

⧗ CSD-8 (2000)

⧗ CSD to consider forests (2011–2013)

Mining

⧗ United Nations Commission on Sustainable Development (CSD) to consider mining (2009–2011)

See the 'Resources' section for other relevant organizations and web links.

Key United Nations bodies and Bretton Woods institutions

Drinking water and sanitation

- Administrative Committee on Coordination Sub-committee on Water Resources (Agenda 21 Task Master)
- United Nations Commission on Sustainable Development (CSD)
- United Nations Department of Economic and Social Affairs (DESA)
- United Nations Development Programme (UNDP)
- United Nations Educational, Scientific and Cultural Organization (UNESCO)
- United Nations Environment Programme (UNEP)
- United Nations Food and Agriculture Organization (FAO)
- United Nations Human Settlements Programme (UN-Habitat)
- Water Supply and Sanitation Collaborative Council (WSSCC)
- World Health Organization (WHO)

Oceans, seas and coasts

- International Atomic Energy Agency (IAEA)
- International Labour Organization (ILO)
- International Maritime Organization (IMO)
- Sub-committee on Oceans and Coastal Areas (SOCA) of the United Nations Administrative Committee on Coordination (ACC)
- UNEP/Global Programme of Action for Protection of the Marine Environment from Land-based Activities (GPA)
- United Nations Convention on Biological Diversity (CBD) (Agenda 21 Task Master)
- United Nations Department of Economic and Social Affairs (DESA)
- United Nations Development Programme (UNDP)
- United Nations Division for Ocean Affairs and the Law of the Sea (DOALOS)
- United Nations Educational, Scientific and Cultural Organization/Intergovernmental Oceanographic Commission (UNESCO/IOC)
- United Nations Environment Programme (UNEP)
- United Nations Food and Agriculture Organization (FAO)

Key United Nations bodies and Bretton Woods institutions (*contd*)

- ☼ United Nations Industrial Development Organization (UNIDO)
- ☼ World Bank

Vulnerability and disaster management

- ☼ United Nations Development Programme (UNDP)
- ☼ United Nations Environment Programme (UNEP)
- ☼ United Nations Human Settlements Programme (UN-Habitat)
- ☼ United Nations Inter-agency Task Force (IATF) on Disaster Reduction
- ☼ United Nations International Strategy for Disaster Reduction (ISDR)
- ☼ World Health Organization (WHO)

Climate change

- ☼ Global Environment Facility (GEF)
- ☼ Intergovernmental Panel on Climate Change (IPCC)
- ☼ International Atomic Energy Agency (IAEA)
- ☼ International Energy Agency (IEA)
- ☼ United Nations Environment Programme and World Meteorological Organization (UNEP/WMO) (Agenda 21 Task Master)
- ☼ United Nations Framework Convention on Climate Change (UNFCCC)

Agriculture

- ☼ International Federation of Agricultural Producers (IFAP)
- ☼ International Fund for Agricultural Development (IFAD)
- ☼ United Nations Food and Agriculture Organization (FAO) (Agenda 21 Task Manager)
- ☼ United Nations Population Fund (UNFPA)
- ☼ World Bank
- ☼ World Food Programme (WFP)

Desertification

- ☼ United Nations Convention on Biological Diversity (CBD)
- ☼ United Nations Development Programme (UNDP)

Key United Nations bodies and Bretton Woods institutions (*contd*)

- ⚙ United Nations Environment Programme (UNEP) (Agenda 21 Task Master)
- ⚙ United Nations Food and Agriculture Organization (FAO)

Mountains

- ⚙ United Nations Educational, Scientific and Cultural Organization (UNESCO)
- ⚙ United Nations Food and Agriculture Organization (FAO) (Agenda 21 Task Master)

Tourism

- ⚙ International Civil Aviation Organization (ICAO)
- ⚙ United Nations Convention on Biological Diversity (CBD)
- ⚙ United Nations Educational, Scientific and Cultural Organization (UNESCO)
- ⚙ United Nations Environment Programme (UNEP) (Agenda 21 Task Master)
- ⚙ World Tourism Organisation (WTO) (Agenda 21 Task Master)
- ⚙ World Travel and Tourism Council (WTTC)

Biodiversity and Biotechnology

- ⚙ UNEP World Conservation Monitoring Centre
- ⚙ United Nations Environment Programme (UNEP) (Agenda 21 Task Master – biodiversity)
- ⚙ United Nations Industrial Development Organization (UNIDO) (Agenda 21 Task Master – biotechnology)
- ⚙ World Bank
- ⚙ World Conservation Union (IUCN)
- ⚙ World Intellectual Property Organization (WIPO)

Forests

- ⚙ United Nations Convention on Biological Diversity (CBD)
- ⚙ United Nations Department of Economic and Social Affairs (DESA)
- ⚙ United Nations Development Programme (UNDP)
- ⚙ United Nations Educational, Scientific and Cultural Organization (UNESCO)

4

Key United Nations bodies and Bretton Woods institutions (*contd*)

◌ United Nations Environment Programme (UNEP)

◌ United Nations Forum on Forests (UNFF)

◌ United Nations Framework Convention on Climate Change (UNFCCC)

◌ World Bank

Mining

◌ International Labour Organization (ILO)

◌ United Nations Conference on Trade and Development (UNCTAD)

◌ United Nations Department of Economic and Social Affairs (DESA)

◌ United Nations Environment Programme (UNEP)

◌ United Nations Industrial Development Organization (UNIDO)

◌ World Bank

See the 'Resources' section for web links.

 # References

Abramowitz, J (2001) 'Human actions worsen natural disasters', Worldwatch Institute press release, Washington, DC, 18 October, www.worldwatch.org/press/news2001/10/18

Annan, K (1999) 'Introduction', in *United Nations Secretary-General's Annual Report on the Work of the Organisation of the United Nations*, UN, New York

Annan, K (2002) 'Executive summary', in *Breaking New Ground: Mining, Minerals and Sustainable Development – the Report of the MMSD Project*, IIED/World Business Council on Sustainable Development, Earthscan, London

ANPED (Northern Alliance for Sustainability) (2000) *World Summit on Sustainable Development*, www.anped.org

Bernbaum, E (1999) Cultural and Spiritual Values of Biodiversity, UNEP, Nairobi

Crace, J (2003) 'Costing the earth', *Guardian*, 10 September 2003, p68

DFID (UK Department for International Development) (2002) *Poverty and the Environment*, DFID, London

DFID, EC, UNDP, World Bank (UK Department for International Development, European Commission, United Nations Development Programme and the World Bank) (2002) *Linking Poverty Reduction and Environmental Management: Policy Challenges and Opportunities*, www.undp.org/wssd/docs/LPREM.pdf, July 2002

Evans, J (2002) 'Sustainable forest management – What has really happened since Rio?' *Sustainable Development International*, spring 2002, pp149–151

FAO (United Nations Food and Agriculture Organization) (undated) 'The spectrum of malnutrition', Briefing sheet, FAO, Italy

FAO (2001a) *The State of Food Insecurity in the World*, www.fao.org

FAO (2001b) *Food Security and the Environment*, Briefing Sheet, www.fao.org

FAO (2002) *The State of World Fisheries and Aquaculture*, FAO, Sofia

IIED and WBCSD (International Institute for Environment and Development and the World Business Council on Sustainable Development) (2002) *Breaking New Ground: Mining, Minerals and Sustainable Development*, Report of the MMSD Project, Earthscan, London

ISDR (International Strategy for Disaster Reduction) (2002) *Natural Disasters and Sustainable Development: Understanding the Links between Development, Environment and Natural Disasters*, Background Paper No 5, ISDR, www.unisdr.org

Price, M (2002) *Ten Years after Rio: The International Year of Mountains*, Sustainable Development International, www.mountains2002.org, pp145–147

Segundad, P (2001) 'Cultural and spiritual values of biodiversity: Excerpted from statements by representatives of indigenous and traditional communities in response to a request from UNEP for information on how they value biodiversity, collected by the Environment Liaison Centre International', in Addison Posey, D (ed) *Cultural and Spiritual Values of Biodiversity*, UNEP and Intermediate Technology Publications, Nairobi, Kenya

UNCHS (United Nations Centre for Human Settlements, UN-Habitat) (2001) *State of the World's Cities 2001*, United Nations Publications, New York

UNDP (United Nations Development Programme) Regional Bureau for Europe and the Commonwealth of Independent States (2003) *Environmental Governance Sourcebook*, UNDP, Bratislava

UNEP (United Nations Environment Programme) (2002) *Global Environment Outlook 3*, Earthscan, London, www.unep.org

United Nations Commission on Sustainable Development (CSD) website, www.un.org/esa/sustdev

United Nations Food and Agriculture Organization (2001a) *The State of Food Insecurity in the World*, www.fao.org

Water Aid and Tearfund (2002) *The Human Waste Report*, Water Aid and Tearfund, London

Worldwatch (2001) 'Human actions worsen natural disasters', Press Release, 18 October 2001

WRI (World Resources Institute) in collaboration with UNEP (United Nations Environment Programme), UNDP (United Nations Development Programme) and the World Bank (2002) *World Resources 2000–2001: People and Ecosystems – The Fraying Web of Life*, WRI, Washington, DC

WRI in collaboration with UNEP, UNDP and the World Bank (2003) *World Resources 2002–2004: Decisions for the Earth – Balance, Voice, and Power*, WRI, Washington, DC

5

Globalization

 Context

Globalization is characterized by a 'growing access to goods and services from all over the world, large flows of capital between countries, and technological advances that can make vast distances a negligible factor in business decisions' (UNDP, UNEP, World Bank and WRI, 2003). It is also a growing interdependence of the world's people through a 'shrinking space, shrinking time and disappearing borders' (UNDP, 1999). While this offers great opportunities for enriching people's lives, the benefits and opportunities have not been shared equitably (UNEP, 2002). Some see globalization as the way forward towards a better standard of living for all or as an inevitable process that requires careful management, if the benefits are to be captured for all. Others are questioning, challenging and even resisting the forces of globalization, and pointing out the manifestation of growing income gaps, increasing environmental damage and increased cultural uniformity. While many international bodies are starting to adjust their policies to include the active participation of civil society and its demands for implementation and enforcement of acceptable trade, labour and environmental standards worldwide (UNEP, 2002), developing countries are also concerned that trade policy measures for labour and environmental purposes should not be a justification for, or a disguised restriction to, international trade. The commitment towards active promotion of corporate responsibility and accountability was welcomed as a step forward, and the pairing of the two concepts – 'responsibility' and 'accountability' – has been seen as an achievement of the World Summit on Sustainable Development (WSSD) in taking forward the Rio agreements.

KEY WORDS

- **opportunities and challenges**
- **policies and measures**
- **trade and finance**
- **Monterrey Consensus**
- **social aspects**
- **corporate responsibility and accountability**
- **information**
- **digital divide**

 Chapter V in summary

Globalization offers both opportunities and challenges for sustainable development. There are new **opportunities** in areas such as trade, investment and capital flows, technology (including information technology), growth in the world economy and improved living standards. The challenges include serious financial crises, insecurity, poverty, exclusion and inequality within and among

AT A GLANCE

- Trade accounts for some 58 per cent of the global economy – up from 27 per cent in 1970 (UNDP, UNEP, World Bank, WRI, 2003).

- One fifth of the world's population living in the highest income countries have 86 per cent of world gross domestic product (GDP), 82 per cent of world export markets, 68 per cent of foreign direct investment and 74 per cent of telephone lines. The one fifth of poorest countries have about 1 per cent in each category (UNDP, 1999).

- In 1991, private finance and official development aid (grants, loans and other assistance) to developing countries were approximately equal at about US$60 billion each. By 2000, private finance had multiplied by a factor of four, to US$226 billion, while development aid had decreased by half to US$35 billion (UNDP, UNEP, World Bank, WRI, 2003).

societies. Developing countries and countries with economies in transition face special difficulties in responding to these challenges. Globalization should be fully **inclusive and equitable**, with **policies and measures** to help these countries respond effectively to the challenges and opportunities *[47]*, including action at all levels on:

- Promoting 'open, equitable, rules-based, predictable and non-discriminatory' **multilateral trading and financial systems** that benefit all countries in pursuit of sustainable development *[47a]*;
- Open and transparent decision-making processes and structures in **international financial and trade institutions** *[47b]*;
- Capacity of developing countries to **benefit from liberalized trade** through national productivity and competitiveness, commodity diversification, and stronger community-based entrepreneurial capacity, transportation and communication infrastructure *[47c]*;
- International Labour Organization (ILO) work on the social dimension of globalization *[47d]*; and
- **Trade-related technical assistance and capacity-building programmes** to, amongst other things, take advantage of market access opportunities and examine the relationship between trade, environment and development *[47e]*.

Further actions relate to:

- **The World Trade Organization's (WTO's) work programme**: implementing the outcomes of the Doha Ministerial Conference; strengthening trade-related capacity-building; and meaningful participation of developing countries in multilateral trade negotiations *[48]*;

'The world is rushing headlong into greater integration, driven mostly by a philosophy of market profitability and economic efficiency. We must bring human development and social protection into the equation... Globalization needs a human face' (Richard Jolly, co-ordinator of the 1999 Human Development Report, cited in UNDP, 1999a).

- Promoting corporate responsibility and accountability through intergovernmental agreements and measures, international initiatives, public–private partnerships and appropriate national regulations *[49]*;
- Building capacities of developing countries to improve ease of access, accuracy, timeliness and coverage of information on countries and financial markets *[50]*;
- Strengthening regional trade and cooperation agreements to help achieve sustainable development *[51]*; and
- Narrowing the digital divide by providing support and transferring technology *[52]*.

 # Globalization elsewhere in the JPOI

' As long as globalization is dominated by economic aspects and by the spread of markets, it will put a squeeze on human development... We need a new approach to governance, one that preserves the advantages offered by global markets and competition while allowing for human, community and environmental resources that will ensure that globalization works for people and not just for profits'
(Sakiko Fakuda-Parr, Director of the Human Development Report Office, 1999).

The Johannesburg Plan of Implementation (JPOI) recognizes the continuing need for a dynamic and enabling international economic environment to support improved opportunities in the areas of finance, technology transfer, debt and trade (JPOI, Chapter X). It calls for the full and effective participation of developing countries in global decision-making and identifies the need for WSSD outcomes to be implemented through partnerships, which were acknowledged in the Monterrey Consensus as being crucial in pursuing sustainable development in a globalizing world. In Africa, poverty remains a major challenge and the majority of African countries have not benefited fully from the opportunities of globalization.

TARGETS AND COMMITMENTS

Actively promote **corporate responsibility and accountability**, including through the full development and effective implementation of intergovernmental agreements and measures, international initiatives and public–private partnerships, and appropriate national regulations *[49]* (new target).

EXAMPLES OF INDICATORS FOR MEASURING PROGRESS IN IMPLEMENTATION

- Percentage of population living below the poverty line (United Nations Commission on Sustainable Development, or CSD)
- Gross domestic product (GDP) per capita (CSD)
- Investment share in GDP (CSD)
- Balance of trade in goods and services (CSD)
- Main telephone lines per 1000 inhabitants (CSD)
- Number of internet subscribers per 1000 inhabitants (CSD)
- Global monitoring of policies for achieving Millennium Development Goals (MDGs) and Monterrey commitments (World Bank)

Partnership example

Capacity-Building Task Force on Trade, Environment and Development, Phase II (CBTF II)

Leading partners: United Nations Environment Programme (UNEP) and United Nations Conference on Trade and Development (UNCTAD)

Dates: 2002–2005 (Phase I initiated in 2000)

The partnership seeks to enhance the human and institutional capacity of developing countries in order to deal with issues arising at the intersection of trade liberalization, environmental protection and economic development. The aims include:

- Assisting beneficiary countries in developing mutually supportive policies that would maximize the net benefits of trade for sustainable development.
- Seeking a close correlation with the Doha Work Programme and the related technical assistance programme administered by the World Trade Organization (WTO) Secretariat.

CBTF II is the main vehicle for capacity-building activities by UNCTAD and UNEP in trade, environment and development in support of the decisions to be taken by the World Summit on Sustainable Development (WSSD). It has a regional emphasis, which accords with the expected outcomes of WSSD with regard to implementation of its work programme. The partnership will undertake thematic research, country projects, training sessions, policy dialogues and networking based on a participatory, 'learning-by-doing' approach and involving national institutions with core competencies in trade and the environment in their design and implementation.

Contact information:
Chief, Economics and Trade Branch
United Nations Environment Programme (UNEP)
15 Chemin des Anémones
1219 Chatelaine
Geneva
www.unep.org

 ## Resources

Capacity-building Task Force on Trade, Environment and Development (CBTF)

www.unep-unctad.org/cbtf/cbtf2/F1.htm
The CBTF is a United Nations Environment Programme (UNEP)/United Nations Conference on Trade and Development (UNCTAD) partnership to strengthen the capacity of developing countries and transition economies in addressing trade, environment and development issues.

5

*'Growing
globalization calls for
mechanisms to
redress
unsustainable
imbalances caused
by unhealthy trade
practices. Not all
countries have the
competitive edge
provided by access
to modern
information and
communication
technologies...
Moreover, countries
and donors will have
to fulfil the promises
they make in
Johannesburg. In the
past, many promises
of financial support
for Agenda 21 have
not been kept... The
same applies to the
slow ratification of
agreements. Many
treaties and
protocols are not yet
operational because
ratification falls short
of what might have
been possible.
Implementation and
action are the key
words for
Johannesburg. Too
much is at stake for
new
disappointments,
which can easily be
avoided if we all
keep our promises'*
(Jan Pronk, Special
Envoy of the UN
Secretary-General for
the WSSD, cited in
UNDP, 2002)

Digital divide

The term 'digital divide' refers to the gap between those who have access to, and effectively use, new information and communication technologies (ICTs), and those who do not have this capacity. See World Summit on the Information Society (WSIS).

Doha Ministerial Declaration

wto.org/english/tratop_e/dda_e/dohaexplained_e.htm
The outcome of the Fourth World Trade Organization (WTO) Ministerial (November 2001) includes a work programme and negotiating agenda for a WTO Development Round. Elements of the declaration include agriculture; services; market access for non-agricultural products; trade-related aspects of intellectual property rights; trade and competition policy; transparency in government procurement; trade facilitation; WTO rules; trade and the environment; electronic commerce; small economies; trade, debt and finance; trade and transfer of technology; technical cooperation and capacity-building; least developed countries; and special and differential treatment.

Global Compact

www.unglobalcompact.org
Proposed by UN Secretary-General Kofi Annan at the World Economic Forum (January 1999), the Global Compact was launched at the UN in July 2000. It is a voluntary international initiative that brings together companies with UN agencies, and labour and civil society, in order to advance responsible corporate citizenship focused on nine principles in the areas of human rights, labour and the environment.

International financial and trade institutions

Principally, these include the Bretton Woods institutions (the World Bank and the International Monetary Fund (IMF) – also referred to as the International Financial Institutions, or IFIs) and the WTO.

Monterrey Consensus

www.un.org/esa/ffd/ffdconf
The Monterrey Consensus is the outcome of the International Conference on Financing for Development (March 2002). Governments committed themselves to increasing resources for development through means to mobilize domestic and international finance; promote trade; strengthen cooperation for development; address debt issues; and improve the international monetary, financial and trading systems.

Multilateral trading and financial systems

This category covers multilateral, plurilateral (between just some members of an institution/agreement), regional and bilateral trade and financial rules, regulations and mechanisms. Principally, it involves those systems developed through the General Agreement on Tariffs and Trade (GATT), which evolved in 2000 into the WTO, and other multilateral arrangements such as the Africa, Caribbean and Pacific group of countries (ACP)/European Union (EU) agreements and regional trade agreements; and multilateral finance mechanisms used by governments that are accessed through the World Bank and the IMF.

International Finance Corporation (IFC)

www.ifc.org
The IFC promotes sustainable private-sector investment in developing countries as a way of reducing poverty and improving people's lives. It is a member of the World Bank Group.

International Telecommunication Union (ITU)

www.itu.int
The ITU is a UN body through which governments and the private sector coordinate global telecom networks and services.

International Trade Centre (ITC)

www.intracen.org/menus/itc.htm
The ITC is a technical cooperation agency of the United Nations Conference on Trade and Development (UNCTAD) and the WTO. It supports developing and transition economies with product and market development; development of trade support services; trade information; human resource development; international purchasing and supply management; and trade promotion.

United Nations Research Institute for Social Development (UNRISD)

www.unrisd.org/
The Business Responsibility for Sustainable Development project (2000–2005) of the UNRISD promotes research and policy dialogue on corporate social and environmental responsibility. It examines whether transnational corporations (TNCs) and others are taking meaningful steps to improve their social and environmental record, particularly in developing countries.

World Summit on the Information Society (WSIS)

www.itu.int/wsis
The WSIS was held in two phases – in Geneva (December 2003) and in Tunis (November 2005) – to develop and foster a clear statement of political will and a concrete plan of action for achieving the goals of the Information Society, while fully reflecting all the different interests at stake.

'We need to build a system, a set of rules, or a framework that will help make globalization a more positive force for improving all people's lives. This new environment must promote equity and involve greater international cooperation, particularly in the areas of finance, capacity-building, technology transfer, debt relief and trade' (Nitin Desai, UN Under Secretary-General for Economic and Social Affairs, cited in United Nations Department of Public Information, October 2001)

CONFERENCES, AGREEMENTS AND PROCESSES

Monterrey Consensus

- International Conference on Financing for Development, Monterrey (March 2002)

Trade

- World Trade Organization (WTO) Doha Ministerial Declaration (November 2001)

- WTO Ministerial Meeting, Cancun (September 2003)

- Africa, Caribbean and Pacific group of countries (ACP)/European Union (EU) Phase II negotiations on Economic Partnership Agreements (from September 2003)

- Regional processes, such as the Free Trade Area of the Americas process and Asian Pacific Economic Cooperation (APEC) (ongoing)

Corporate responsibility

- United Nations Commission on Sustainable Development (CSD) 6: industry and sustainable development (1998)

- Organisation for Economic Co-operation and Development (OECD) Guidelines for Multinational Enterprises: Corporate Governance Principles (1999)

- United Nations Global Compact (July 2000)

- European Community (EC) Green Paper on Corporate Social Responsibility (July 2001)

- EC Communication on Corporate Social Responsibility (2002)

- Guidelines for Good Corporate Governance in the Commonwealth (2002)

- Commonwealth Guidelines for Corporate Citizenship (2003)

- Group of 8 industrialized nations (G8) Declaration on Fostering Growth and Promoting a Responsible Market Economy, Evian (June 2003)

- European Parliament Report on Corporate Social Responsibility (2003)

Digital divide

- Plenipotentiary Conference of the International Telecommunication Union (ITU) (1998)

- World Summit on the Information Society (WSIS): Phase I, Geneva (December 2003); Phase II, Tunis (November 2004)

Key United Nations bodies and Bretton Woods institutions

Monterrey Consensus

- International Monetary Fund (IMF)
- United Nations Development Programme (UNDP)
- United Nations Economic and Social Council (ECOSOC)
- World Bank

Trade

- International Trade Centre (ITC)
- United Nations Conference on Trade and Development (UNCTAD)
- World Trade Organization (WTO)

Corporate Responsibility

- Global Corporate Governance Forum (World Bank, Organisation for Economic Co-operation and Development (OECD) and bilateral partners)
- International Finance Corporation (IFC)
- United Nations Global Compact: Office of the High Commissioner for Human Rights; United Nations Environment Programme (UNEP); International Labour Organization (ILO); United Nations Development Programme (UNDP); United Nations Industrial Development Organization (UNIDO)

Social Dimensions

- International Labour Organization (ILO)
- United Nations Development Programme (UNDP)
- United Nations Research Institute for Sustainable Development

Digital Divide

- International Telecommunication Union (ITU)
- High-Level Summit Organizing Committee (HLSOC) for the World Summit on the Information Society (WSIS): includes Food and Agriculture Organization (FAO); International Atomic Energy Agency (IAEA); International Civil Aviation Organization (ICAO); International Labour Organization (ILO); International Maritime Organization (IMO); ITU; United Nations Conference on Trade and

5

> **Key United Nations bodies and Bretton Woods institutions (*contd*)**
>
> Development (UNCTAD); United Nations Development Programme (UNDP); United Nations Environment Programme (UNEP); United Nations Educational, Scientific and Cultural Organization (UNESCO); United Nations High Commissioner for Refugees (UNHCR); United Nations Industrial Development Organization (UNIDO); United Nations Institute for Training and Research (UNITAR); Universal Postal Union (UPU); United Nations Regional Economic Commissions; World Health Organization (WHO); World Intellectual Property Organization (WIPO); World Meteorological Organization (WMO); World Trade Organization (WTO); and the World Bank.

 References

Annan, K (2003) 'Opening session – ECOSOC', Geneva, July, 2003

UNDP (United Nations Development Programme) (1999) *Human Development Report 1999*, Oxford University Press, New York

UNDP, UNEP (United Nations Environment Programme), the World Bank and WRI (World Resources Institute) (2003) *World Resources 2002–2004: Decisions for the Earth; Balance, Voice and Power*, WRI: Washington, DC

UNEP (United Nations Environment Programme) (2002) *Global Environment Outlook 3*, Earthscan, London, www.unep.org

United Nations Department of Public Information (2001) *Johannesburg Summit 2002. World Summit on Sustainable Development, 2–11 September*, p9

Health and Sustainable Development

6

 ## Context

The Rio principles state that human beings are entitled to a healthy and productive life in harmony with nature. However, the reality for many people is very different. While there is a complex interplay of factors that determine health, the major diseases of poverty and adverse environmental conditions are currently considered an impediment to economic progress, and ill health has the potential to reverse decades of progress, especially in developing countries. Evidence suggests that poor environmental quality is associated with approximately one quarter of all preventable illness in the world, with diarrhoeal diseases and acute respiratory infections the most common. Two-thirds of all preventable ill health due to environmental conditions occurs amongst children (WHO, 2002). A few measures could go a long way towards improving the health of billions of people in the developing world. These include providing greater access to safe drinking water, expanding basic sanitation and waste disposal technologies and improving air quality in urban areas (UNDPI, 2001). Another important measure is the improvement of indoor air quality through increased access to cleaner sources of household energy for cooking and heating. However, problems related to health and the environment cannot be solved if poverty is not addressed. Three diseases – HIV/AIDS, tuberculosis (TB) and malaria – dominate the global burden of disease, causing more than 5.5 million deaths every year. Addressing major causes of ill health and strengthening health services for all, including the most disadvantaged groups such as women and the poor, are major priorities in sustainable development.

 ## Chapter VI in summary

Sustainable development can only be achieved by securing the necessary health gains for the whole population through poverty eradication and by bringing debilitating diseases under control. There is an urgent need to address the root causes of ill health and their impact on development. Particular attention has to be paid to women, children and other vulnerable groups, including the elderly, those with disabilities and indigenous people [53].

KEY WORDS

- **healthcare systems and services**
- **infant and maternal mortality**
- **traditional medicine and knowledge**
- **food**
- **work and health**
- **HIV/AIDS, TB and malaria**
- **public health research**
- **environmental health**
- **water and sanitation**
- **waste and pollution control**
- **respiratory diseases**
- **cleaner fuels**
- **lead in paint and gasoline**

6

AT A GLANCE

- Some 35 people an hour die as a result of armed conflict (WHO, 2002).

- Malaria kills 3000 African children a day (Smith, 2002).

- Every year, environmental hazards kill 3 million children under the age of five (WHO 2002).

- Bathing in polluted seas is estimated to cause 250 million cases of gastroenteritis (GESAMP, 2001).

- In 2001, 3 million people died from AIDS, with the vast majority of these deaths occurring in developing countries (UNAIDS, 2002).

- More than 200 million people live in countries where the average life expectancy is less than 45 years (WHO, 2002).

- Over 250 million work-related incidents per year (WHO, 2002).

- 1.5 million people a year die of tuberculosis (WHO, 2002).

- A woman living in sub-Saharan Africa has a 1 in 16 chance of dying in pregnancy or childbirth. This compares with a 1 in 2800 risk for women in developed regions (WHO, 2003b).

'... an integral approach towards environment, health and sustainable development will only benefit the poor if access to resources necessary for survival and life itself is accepted as a human right for all'
(Jan Pronk, Special Envoy of the UN Secretary-General for the WSSD and chair of IIED, 2003).

Healthcare systems and services

Healthcare systems will be strengthened to deliver basic healthcare services to all in an 'efficient, accessible and affordable manner' and in a way that conforms with human rights and fundamental freedoms, and is consistent with national laws and cultural and religious values [54]. Action is needed at all levels to:

- Integrate health concerns within poverty eradication and sustainable development programmes and strategies [54a];
- Promote equitable and improved access to healthcare services [54b];
- Implement the World Health Organization's (WHO's) Health for All Strategy, including information systems [54c];
- Improve human resources management and development in healthcare services including affordable and safe medicines and vaccines [54d];
- Promote partnerships to increase health literacy by 2010 [54e];
- Reduce by 2015 the mortality rates for infants and children under five years of age by two-thirds and maternal mortality rates by three-quarters, compared to 2000 [54f];
- Target research on priority public health issues [54g];
- Promote and use traditional medicine, knowledge and practices with modern medicine, where appropriate [54h];

- Ensure **equal access of women** to healthcare services, focusing on maternal and emergency obstetric care *[54i]*;
- Promote **healthy lifestyles**, including reproductive and sexual health, in line with recent UN conferences *[54j]*;
- Assess **health and environment linkages** and use the knowledge to develop policy responses *[54k]*;
- Transfer and disseminate **technologies for safe water, sanitation and waste management** *[54l]*;
- Strengthen ILO and WHO programmes to reduce **occupational deaths, injuries and illness** *[54m]*;
- Improve access to, and availability of, **safe, culturally acceptable and nutritionally adequate food** *[54n]*; and
- Address **non-communicable diseases and conditions**, including cardiovascular disease, cancer, diabetes, chronic respiratory conditions, mental health and violence, and associated risk factors, such as alcohol, tobacco, unhealthy diets and lack of exercise *[54o]*.

HIV/AIDS, malaria, tuberculosis

To implement all commitments made at the 2001 United Nations General Assembly Special Session on HIV/AIDS, including the **Millennium Development Goal (MDG) target** to reduce HIV amongst young men and women aged 15 to 24 by 25 per cent in the most affected countries by 2005 and globally by 2010, and to **combat malaria, tuberculosis** and other diseases *[55]*, action is required at all levels to:

- Provide special assistance to **children orphaned by HIV/AIDS** through national strategies, regional cooperation and international initiatives *[55a]*;
- Ensure the **Global Fund to Fight AIDS, Tuberculosis and Malaria** has sufficient resources, and that countries in most need have access to this fund *[55b]*;
- Protect **workers' health** and promote occupational safety, including through the voluntary International Labour Organization (ILO) Code of Practice on HIV/AIDS and the World of Work *[55c]*; and
- Mobilize funding for research and development into diseases of the poor, such as HIV/AIDS, malaria and tuberculosis. This funding will be both public and private and directed at developing **new vaccines and drugs** *[55d]*.

Respiratory disease and air pollution

To address the impact of **respiratory diseases**, particularly on women and children *[56]*, action will be taken to:

- Strengthen regional and national programmes with assistance to developing countries *[56a]*;
- Phase out **lead in gasoline** *[56b]*;

'The most devastating social and economic impacts of AIDS are still to come. Widespread treatment access would substantially mitigate the devastating impact of HIV/AIDS, which affects everything from agriculture to national defence. Effective HIV prevention programmes must be scaled up dramatically if we want a realistic chance at reducing the number of new infections' (Peter Piot, Executive Director of UNAIDS).

- Reduce emissions through use of **cleaner fuels and pollution control techniques** *[56c]*; and
- Provide affordable energy to rural populations, reducing their dependence on **traditional fuel for cooking and heating** *[56d]*.

Lead poisoning

To protect children's health, action will be taken to phase out **lead in lead-based paints** (and other sources of exposure) and step up efforts to monitor and treat lead poisoning *[57]*.

 # Health elsewhere in the JPOI

' It has been estimated that roughly 60 per cent of the global burden of disease from acute respiratory infections, 90 per cent from diarrhoeal disease, 50 per cent from chronic respiratory conditions and 90 per cent from malaria could be avoided by simple environmental interventions ' (Christine K Durbak, 2002).

The Johannesburg Plan of Implementation (JPOI) includes MDGs on access to clean drinking water, food security, mortality rates and action to combat HIV/AIDS, TB and malaria. Health concerns related to poverty are addressed in Chapter II of the JPOI. Detrimental impacts from exposure to chemicals, pesticides, solid waste and other pollution are addressed through commitments on the sound management of chemicals by 2020; the ratification/implementation of relevant international agreements on chemicals; chemical safety and hazardous waste; and the development of sustainable consumption and production programmes and policies that will reduce health impacts (JPOI, Chapter III). A range of health concerns associated with water and sanitation, climate change, air pollution, biosafety and natural disasters are addressed in Chapter IV, while the matter of medicines for all and of the Trade-related Aspects of Intellectual Property Rights (TRIPS) Agreement are addressed in Chapter X. Regional chapters call for action to integrate health concerns within poverty eradication strategies, and to tackle specific health concerns in each region, including HIV/AIDS, TB, malaria, diabetes, dengue fever and the Ebola virus.

TARGETS AND COMMITMENTS

⚙ **HIV/AIDS, malaria, tuberculosis.** Reduce HIV prevalence among young men and women aged 15 to 24 by 25 per cent in the most affected countries by 2005 and globally by 2010, as well as combat malaria, tuberculosis and other diseases [55] (MDG).

⚙ **Health literacy.** Enhance health education to improve health literacy on a global basis by 2010 [54e] (new target).

⚙ **Mortality rates.** Develop programmes and initiatives to reduce, by 2015, mortality rates for infants and children under the age of five by two-thirds, and maternal mortality rates by three-quarters, of the prevailing rate in 2000 [54f] (Millennium Development Goal, or MDG).

EXAMPLES OF INDICATORS FOR MEASURING PROGRESS IN IMPLEMENTATION

- Prevalence of underweight children (under the age of five) (Millennium Development Goal, or MDG)

- Proportion of population below minimum level of dietary energy consumption (MDG)

- Reduction of under five mortality rate by two-thirds between 1990 and 2015 (MDG)

- Infant mortality rate (MDG)

- Proportion of one-year-old children immunized against measles (MDG)

- Maternal mortality ratio (MDG)

- Proportion of births attended by skilled health professional (MDG)

- HIV prevalence among 15- to 24-year-old pregnant women (MDG)

- Number of children orphaned by HIV/AIDS (MDG)

- Prevalence and death rates associated with malaria; proportion of population in malaria risk areas using effective malaria prevention and treatment measures (MDG)

- Prevalence and death rates associated with TB (MDG)

- Life expectancy at birth, by sex (World Health Organization, or WHO)

- Number of hospital beds per 100,000 individuals (WHO)

- Decreased number of people living in areas that fail to meet air quality standards (WHO)

- Decreased number of people whose drinking water fails to meet national safe drinking water standards (WHO)

Other relevant indicators are the WHO Healthy Cities (Health and Sustainability) indicators, and the CSD indicators.

Partnership example

The Healthy Environments for Children Alliance (HECA)

Leading organization: World Health Organization (WHO)

Dates: 2002 – ongoing

The aim of HECA is to build a global alliance to tackle key environment and poverty-related risks to children's health that are responsible for the loss of millions of healthy years of life each year. The alliance will focus on, and catalyse action within, environments where children live, learn, play and sometimes work. Particular attention will be given to improving the home environment – traditionally neglected – but where children spend a major part of their lives, and where the most significant health threats converge. The alliance will focus on health risks associated with lack of access to clean water, to sanitation and to clean indoor and outdoor air. It will act to reduce risks associated with disease vectors, hazardous chemicals and non-intentional injuries. The HECA held its first meeting of stakeholders in December 2002 – attended by over 80 representatives of non-governmental organizations (NGOs), UN and intergovernmental organizations, governments, academia and the private sector.

Contact information:
Agenda 21 and
Manager Healthy
Environments for
Children Alliance
(HECA) Secretariat
World Health
Organization (WHO)
20 Avenue Appia
CH-1211 Geneva 27
Switzerland.
www.who.int/heca

 ## Resources

Millennium Development Goals (MDGs)

www.un.org/millenniumgoals/index.shtml (UN)

www.undp.org/mdg (UNDP)

www.developmentgoals.org (World Bank)

The United Nations Secretary-General's 'Road Map' (September 2001) set out concrete targets for goals and commitments in the Millennium Declaration. These were further developed into the MDGs.

Fourth World Conference on Women, Beijing, (1995)

www.un.org/womenwatch/daw/followup/beijing+5.htm

This conference adopted the Beijing Platform for Action to strengthen women's rights to civic and economic participation, and to education and reproductive health. It was reviewed in 2000.

Global Fund to Fight Aids, Tuberculosis and Malaria

www.theglobalfund.org/en/
This fund was created to finance a dramatic turnaround in the fight against AIDS, tuberculosis and malaria. It will address new and existing programmes to stop the spread of disease.

International Conference on Population and Development (ICPD), Cairo (1994)

www.unfpa.org/icpd/10/index
The ICPD shifted the emphasis from population 'control' towards people-centred development, including human and reproductive rights for women. It called for priority measures to 'improve quality of life and health by ensuring a safe and sanitary living environment' for all, aimed at 'avoiding overcrowded housing conditions, reducing air pollution, ensuring access to clean water and sanitation, improving water management, and increasing the safety of the workplace'. The ICPD set an ambitious 20-year plan of action and was reviewed in 1999.

International Labour Organization (ILO) Code of Practice on HIV/AIDS

www.ilo.org/public/english/protection/trav/aids/code/codemain.htm
The ILO's code of practice comprises fundamental principles that cover prevention; management and mitigation of impacts on the world of work; care and support of workers infected and affected by HIV/AIDS; and elimination of stigma and discrimination.

Joint United Nations Programme on HIV/AIDS (UNAIDS)

www.unaids.org
The goals of UNAIDS are to catalyse, strengthen and support an expanded response to prevent the spread of HIV; provide care and support for those afflicted; reduce vulnerability of individuals and communities; and alleviate socio-economic and human impacts of the epidemic.

Roll Back Malaria Initiative (World Health Organization – WHO)

www.rbm.who.int
This initiative was founded by WHO, the World Bank, the United Nations Children's Fund (UNICEF) and the United Nations Development Programme (UNDP) in 1998. It is a global partnership of governments, the UN, non-governmental organizations (NGOs), researchers, manufacturers and control workers, and is committed to halving the malaria burden by 2010 by building and sustaining partnerships at global and country levels; providing technical and operational support to affected countries; stimulating research and development; and monitoring progress and outcomes.

United Nations General Assembly Special Session (UNGASS) on HIV/AIDS, June 2001

www.unaids.org/en/events/un+special+session+on+hiv_aids.asp
This session agreed a United Nations Declaration of Commitment on HIV/AIDS.

World Health Organization (WHO)

www.who.int
The WHO is a specialized UN agency working on global health strategies to obtain a level of health for all citizens, enabling them to lead socially and economically productive lives.

WHO definition of health (1948)

'[Health] Is a state of complete physical, social and mental well-being and not merely the absence of disease or infirmity. The enjoyment of the highest attainable standard of health is one of the fundamental rights of every human being, without distinction of race, religion, political beliefs, or economic or social conditions.'

WHO Health for All Strategy

www.who.int/archives/hfa
Launched in 1977, this strategy was revised in 1998 to include 21 targets in a framework for action for the 21st century (Health 21). Its underlying principle is to reduce inequalities in health through multi-sectoral strategies involving communities and to find sustainable solutions for health improvement.

WHO Healthy Cities Project

www.healthycities.org
This project puts health and sustainable development on the agenda of decision-makers in cities and builds a lobby for public health at local level. A global initiative, it was developed as part of the WHO European Region's response to the Health for All Strategy. It includes health and sustainability indicators.

World Summit for Children (1990)

www.unicef.org/specialsession
This summit agreed action to improve living conditions for children and their chances for survival by increasing access to healthcare services for women and children; to create more opportunities for education; to provide better sanitation and greater food supply; and to protect children in danger. UNGASS (2001) reviewed progress on implementation and agreed a plan of action to fulfil outstanding commitments.

World Summit for Social Development, Copenhagen (1996) and Five-year Review, 2000

www.un.org/esa/socdev/wssd/index.htm
Key themes of this summit were poverty, meeting basic human needs, reducing economic and social inequalities and providing sustainable livelihoods. Equitable access to primary healthcare was one of ten commitments agreed.

CONFERENCES, AGREEMENTS AND PROCESSES

⧗ World Health Organization (WHO) Health for All Strategy (1977, revised 1998)

⧗ WHO Global Aids Strategy for the Prevention and Control of Aids (1987)

⧗ United Nations General Assembly Special Session (UNGASS) endorses Global HIV/AIDS Strategy (1987)

⧗ Agenda 21, Chapter 6 (1992)

⧗ United Nations Convention on Biological Diversity (CBD) (1992)

⧗ Declaration on the Elimination of Violence against Women (1993)

⧗ United Nations International Conference on Population and Development, Cairo (1994)

⧗ United Nations Commission on Sustainable Development (CSD) 2 (1994) and CSD-3 (1995)

⧗ Fourth World Conference on Women, Beijing (1995)

⧗ United Nations World Summit on Human Settlements, Habitat II, Istanbul (1996)

⧗ United Nations World Summit for Social Development (1996)

⧗ World Food Summit, Rome (1996)

⧗ Renewed Health for All in the 21st Century Strategy adopted at WHO Assembly (1998)

⧗ International Conference on Population and Development (ICPD) +5 review, New York (1999)

⧗ Third Ministerial Conference on Environment and Health (Europe), London (1999)

⧗ United Nations Millennium Declaration, Millennium Development Goals (MDGs) (2000)

⧗ Beijing+5, New York (2000)

⧗ World Food Summit review, Rome (2000)

⧗ Istanbul+5, New York (2001)

⧗ Stockholm Convention on Persistent Organic Pollutants (2001)

⧗ United Nations General Assembly (UNGA) 26th Special Session on HIV/AIDS (2001)

⧗ United Nations Global Fund to fight AIDS, TB and Malaria (2001)

⧗ UNGASS Special Session on Children (2002)

⧗ CSD considers health and sustainable development as a cross-cutting issue each year (2004–2017).

See the 'Resources' section at the end of this chapter for other relevant organizations and web links.

Key United Nations bodies and Bretton Woods Institutions

Health (overall)

- United Nations Children's Fund (UNICEF)
- United Nations Development Programme (UNDP)
- United Nations Environment Programme (UNEP)
- United Nations Food and Agriculture Organization (FAO)
- United Nations Human Settlements Programme (UN-Habitat)
- United Nations Population Fund (UNFPA)
- World Bank
- World Health Organization (WHO) (Agenda 21 Task Manager)

HIV/AIDS, TB and Malaria

- International Labour Organization (ILO)
- Joint United Nations Programme on HIV/AIDS (UNAIDS)
- United Nations Children's Fund (UNICEF)
- United Nations Development Fund for Women (UNIFEM)
- United Nations Development Programme (UNDP)
- United Nations Drug Control Programme
- United Nations Educational, Scientific and Cultural Organization (UNESCO)
- United Nations Environment Programme (UNEP)
- United Nations Population Fund (UNFPA)
- World Bank
- World Health Organization (WHO)

 # References

Durbak, C (2002) 'Childhood antecedents to adult illness', Statement to the World Information Transfer's 11th International Conference on Health and Environment: Global Partners for Global Solutions, New York

GESAMP (2001) *Protecting the Oceans from Land-based Activities: Land-based Sources and Activities Affecting the Quality and Uses of the Marine, Coastal and Associated Freshwater Environment*, GESAMP Reports and Studies No71, Nairobi, United Nations Environment Programme (UNEP), www.gesamp.imo.org./no71/index.htm

Pronk, J (2003) 'Water: Problems and solutions', Speech delivered to World Information Transfer's 12th International Conference on Health and Environment: Global Partners for Global Solutions, New York

Smith, P (2002) 'Roll back malaria – making a sustainable difference', *Sustainable Development International*, spring 2002, pp163–166

UNAIDS (Joint United Nations Programme on HIV/AIDS) (2003) www.unaids.org

UNDPI (United Nations Department of Public Information) (2001) *Johannesburg Summit 2002*, DPI2233, October 2001

UNEP (United Nations Environment Programme) (2002) *Global Environment Outlook 3*, Earthscan, London

UNFPA (United Nations Population Fund) (2002) *State of the World Population Report: People, Poverty and Possibilities*, www.unfpa.org

WHO (World Health Organization) (2002) *Health and Sustainable Development – Key Health Trends*, WHO WSSD Briefing Pack with various WHO publications and summaries prepared by Dr Yasmin von Schindling

WHO (2003a) 'Health provides a model for more effective development aid', Press Release, 20 March 2002, www.who.int/inf/en/pr-2002-20.html

WHO (2003b) 'Maternal deaths disproportunately high in developing countries', WHO Press Release on new findings from WHO, UNICEF and UNFPA, 20 October 2003

Small Island Developing States

7

 Context

Small island developing states (SIDS) are amongst the most vulnerable in the world. Because of their size, SIDS are unable to capture economies of scale in their domestic markets and political, managerial and technical capacities. They are characterized by open economies in which international trade is more significant than it is in larger states, and they tend to rely on just a few external markets and less diverse production. Remoteness brings with it higher costs in energy, transportation and communications, while extreme weather events can also eradicate a country's gross domestic product (GDP) overnight. Ocean and coastal zones are the backbone of well-being and development in SIDS, so the health of these environments is critical. Coastal areas tend to be densely populated areas and may be low lying, making these countries especially vulnerable to the impacts of sea-level rise, climate change and climate variability (Commonwealth Secretariat, 1997; UNGASS, 1999).

Globalization has great potential benefits for SIDS, especially through developments in information and communications technologies; but it can also lead to greater marginalization where least developed SIDS are unable to make the changes needed to take advantage of the new opportunities. The Rio Earth Summit in 1992 recognized SIDS as a special case for sustainable development. This led to the 1994 Global Conference on the Sustainable Development of Small Island Developing States and the Barbados Programme of Action (BPoA), which is the principle international framework for addressing the sustainable development concerns of SIDS.

KEY WORDS

- **Barbados Programme of Action on the Sustainable Development of Small Island Developing States (BPoA)**
- **coastal areas and exclusive economic zones (EEZs)**
- **fisheries**
- **freshwater**
- **pollution and waste**
- **trade**
- **tourism**
- **vulnerability**
- **climate**
- **energy**
- **health**
- **poverty eradication**

 Chapter VII in summary

SIDS are a special case for environment and development [58]. Action is needed at all levels to:

- Accelerate the national and regional implementation of the 1994 **Barbados Programme of Action** (BPoA), with adequate resources [58a];

AT A GLANCE

※ In half of all small island developing states (SIDS), tourism represents 20 to 50 per cent of export earnings (FAO, 1999).

※ Small states' relative importance in global export trade declined by 38 per cent during the last 20 years, suggesting they have not benefited from gains made in world trade (Commonwealth Secretariat, 2002).

※ About 58 per cent of the world's coral reefs and 34 per cent of all fish species are at risk from human activities (World Bank, 2003).

※ Unemployment among young people in the Caribbean ranges from 25 to 50 per cent (UNEP, 1999a).

※ According to the Intergovernmental Panel on Climate Change's (IPCC's) *Third Assessment Report* of 1999, sea levels in SIDS' regions are expected to rise by as much as 5mm per year for the next 100 years as a result of global warming (Nurse, 2002).

- Implement **sustainable fisheries management** and improve financial returns from fisheries by strengthening relevant regional fisheries management organizations *[58b]*;
- Delimit and sustainably manage **coastal areas, exclusive economic zones and continental shelves** *[58c]*;
- Support **SIDS-specific work** relating to marine and coastal biological diversity and freshwater *[58d]*;
- Effectively address **waste and pollution** and health-related impacts by undertaking initiatives by 2004 to implement in SIDS the **Global Programme of Action** for the Protection of the Marine Environment from Land-based Activities (GPA) *[58e]*;
- Ensure that ongoing negotiations and elaboration of the World Trade Organization (WTO) work programme on **trade in small economies** takes due account of SIDS *[58f]*;
- Develop community-based initiatives on **sustainable tourism** by 2004 and capacities to diversify tourism products, while protecting culture and traditions and managing natural resources *[58g]*;
- Assist SIDS in support of local communities and appropriate SIDS' organizations for comprehensive **hazard and risk management**, prevention, mitigation, preparedness and relief related to disasters, extreme weather events and other emergencies *[58h]*;
- Support finalization and early operationalization of economic, social and environmental **vulnerability indices** *[58i]*;
- Assist SIDS in mobilizing resources and partnerships for adapting to the adverse effects of **climate change, sea level rise and climate variability** *[58j]*; and
- Support SIDS' capacity-building efforts to implement **intellectual property regimes** *[58k]*.

'Biodiversity is culture itself' (Kotosata To'o, director of O le Siosiomaga Society Inc, Samoa, cited in Senanayake, 1999).

Energy

Adequate, affordable and environmentally sound **energy services** for the sustainable development of SIDS will be supported through, among other things [59]:

- Efforts on energy supply and services by 2004 [59a];
- Efficient use of different energy sources (including indigenous and renewable sources) [59b]; and
- Building capacity in energy management [59b].

Health

On health issues, action will support SIDS to develop capacity and strengthen [60]:

- Healthcare services for promoting equitable access to healthcare [60a];
- Healthcare systems for making drugs and technology available to fight major diseases, such as HIV/AIDS, tuberculosis, diabetes, malaria and dengue fever [60b];
- Efforts to reduce and manage waste and pollution [60c]; and
- Efforts to implement initiatives aimed at **poverty eradication** [60d].

'The islands of the Caribbean, the Indian and Pacific Oceans face the largest increase in flood risk, with the number of people at risk being some 200 times higher than most other parts of the world'
(Hay, 2000).

Barbados Programme of Action on the Sustainable Development of Small Island Developing States Review

A full and comprehensive review of BPoA implementation will be undertaken in 2004, possibly with an international meeting, to discuss the programme [61].

 # Small island developing states elsewhere in the JPOI

Elements in the Johannesburg Plan of Implementation (JPOI) that are of particular concern to SIDS are those on energy; waste management; sustainable fisheries; oceans, seas, islands and coastal areas; climate change; health; poverty eradication; sustainable tourism; and disaster management. The WTO work programme on small, vulnerable economies is further highlighted in Chapter X of the JPOI, while Chapter IV includes actions to support implementation of the BPoA and Agenda 21's programme of action on the sustainable development of oceans, coastal areas and seas, and efforts to assist coastal states in the area of integrated coastal management. Improved access to, and availability of, safe, reliable and affordable energy supplies are essential for enabling SIDS to capitalize on the potential benefits offered by globalization (JPOI, Chapter II). The commitment of reducing by half the number of people without access to sanitation by 2015 will be critical to the development of SIDS through improved living standards and health of the population (JPOI, Chapter IV).

TARGETS AND COMMITMENTS

⬚ **Barbados Programme of Action.** Undertake a full and comprehensive review of the implementation of the BPoA in 2004 (new target).

⬚ **Global Programme of Action.** Undertake initiatives by 2004 to implement the Global Programme of Action for the Protection of the Marine Environment from Land-based Activities (GPA) (new target).

⬚ **Tourism.** Develop community-based initiatives on sustainable tourism by 2004 (new target).

⬚ **Energy.** Support the availability of adequate, affordable and environmentally sound energy services by strengthening ongoing, and supporting new, efforts on energy supply and services by 2004 (new target).

EXAMPLES OF INDICATORS FOR MEASURING PROGRESS IN IMPLEMENTATION

⬚ Date of ratification/signature of United Nations Framework Convention on Climate Change (UNFCCC) and/or the Kyoto Protocol

⬚ Date of ratification/signature of the United Nations Convention on the Law of the Sea (UNCLOS) (and other related agreements), the Convention on Biological Diversity (CBD) and/or the Cartagena Protocol on Biosafety

⬚ Annual catch by major species (United Nations Commission on Sustainable Development, or CSD)

⬚ Disaster prevention and mitigation instruments (United Nations Human Settlements Programme , or UN-Habitat)

⬚ Abundance of selected key species (CSD)

⬚ Proportion of population using solid fuels (Millennium Development Goal, or MDG)

⬚ Waste recycling and reuse (CSD)

⬚ Annual energy consumption per capita (CSD)

⬚ Life expectancy at birth, by sex (World Health Organization, or WHO)

⬚ *National Assessment Report* for Barbados Plan of Action (BPoA)

'The 1990 UN Disaster Relief Organization's review of the economic impact of disasters over the past 20 years found that of the 25 most disaster prone countries, 13 are SIDS [small island developing states]. With few exceptions, SIDS are prone to extremely damaging cyclones, storm surges, volcanic eruptions, earthquakes, forest fires, extended drought and extensive floods' (FAO 1999).

7

Partnership example

Pacific Island Initiative: Capacity-building through Education and Training for the Sustainable Use and Management of Natural Resources and the Environment in the Pacific

Leading partners: South Pacific Regional Environment Programme (SPREP) and the University of the South Pacific (USP)

Dates: 2002–2012

The initiative was launched by countries of the Pacific sub-region during the World Summit on Sustainable Development (WSSD) and will include, as key players, Pacific Island countries and several South Pacific organizations – the South Pacific Regional Environment Programme (SPREP), the University of the South Pacific (USP) and the Pacific Islands Development Programme (PIDP); the Secretariat of the Pacific Community; the South Pacific Applied Geoscience Commission (SOPAC); the South Pacific Board of Education and Assessment; the Pacific Islands Forum Secretariat; international agencies and non-governmental organizations (NGOs); and national NGOs and civil society. Its aim is to establish a regional training and education framework aimed at developing and strengthening mechanisms, processes and tools to support training and education for environmental management, protection and sustainable development in the region. The overall vision is of achieving 'increased and strengthened capacity for Pacific Islands' governments and people to manage their island environment and achieve sustainable development, poverty reduction and sustainable livelihoods'.

 ## Resources

Barbados Programme of Action on the Sustainable Development of Small Island Developing States (BPoA)

www.unep.ch/islands/dsidspoa.htm
Adopted in 1994 by the UN, the BPoA addresses climate change/sea-level rise; disasters; wastes; coastal/marine resources; freshwater; land; energy; tourism; biodiversity; institutions; technical cooperation; transport/communications; science/technology; human resources; implementation; and monitoring and review.

Global Environment Facility (GEF)

www.gefweb.org/
The GEF was established 1991 and helps developing countries to fund projects that protect the global environment. It is a financial mechanism for conventions on biodiversity,

climate change, persistent organic pollutants, desertification, protecting international waters and the ozone layer.

United Nations Convention on the Law of the Sea (UNCLOS)

www.un.org/Depts/los/index.htm
Adopted in 1982, UNCLOS covers all aspects of sea/ocean use and resources, such as agreed limits (between national and international waters and zonal delimitation); navigation; exclusive economic zones (EEZs); continental shelves; high seas; the seabed; protection of the marine environment; marine scientific research; and settlement of disputes.

Caribbean Regional Fisheries Mechanism

www.caricom-fisheries.com/
This mechanism promotes the sustainable use of fisheries/aquaculture resources. A network of stakeholders, it is comprised of a ministerial body, the Caribbean Fisheries Forum for Technical/Scientific Decisions and the Caribbean Fisheries Technical Unit.

Convention on the Conservation and Management of Highly Migratory Fish Stocks in the Western and Central Pacific Ocean

www.ocean-affairs.com/convention.html
Agreed in 2000, this seeks to ensure long-term conservation and sustainable use of highly migratory fish stocks in the western and central Pacific Ocean.

Global Programme of Action for the Protection of the Marine Environment from Land-based Activities (GPA)

www.gpa.unep.org/
Adopted in 1995, the GPA is a source of guidance on sustained action to prevent, reduce, control and/or eliminate marine degradation from land-based activities. Its secretariat is the United Nations Environment Programme (UNEP).

Agreement on the Conservation and Management of Straddling Fish Stocks and Highly Migratory Fish Stocks

*www.un.org/Depts/los/convention_agreements/convention_overview_fish_*
  stock.htm
www.unep.ch/seas/main/legal/lstrad.html
Opened for signature in 1995, this agreement seeks to ensure long-term conservation/sustainable use of straddling fish stocks and highly migratory fish stocks through effective implementation of UNCLOS (see above). It covers stocks in EEZs of two or more coastal states, or both within and beyond the EEZ.

Vulnerability indices

- www.un.org/esa/sustdev/sids/sidsvind.htm: UN review of vulnerability indices in 1999;
- www.cobalt.sopac.org.fj/Projects/Evi/Index.htm: South Pacific Applied Geoscience Commission (SOPAC) environmental vulnerability index;
- www.commonwealthsmallstates.org: Commonwealth vulnerability index;
- www.home.um.edu.mt/islands/research.html: work since 1990 by Professor Lino Briguglio, Islands and Small States Institute, University of Malta, on an economic vulnerability index (Briguglio, 1995, 2003);
- United Nations Conference on Trade and Development (UNCTAD) statistical profiles of least developed countries and use of an economic vulnerability index; and
- United Nations Economic Commission for Latin America and the Caribbean (UNECLAC): Sub-regional Headquarters for the Caribbean work on a social vulnerability index.

Small Island Developing States (SIDS)

The UN identifies 53 small islands and coastal states as SIDS: they are members and observers of the Alliance of Small Island States (AOSIS) and members/associate members of the UN Regional Economic Commissions.

Alliance of Small Island States (AOSIS)

www.sidsnet.org/aosis/
AOSIS is a coalition of small island and low-lying coastal countries that share similar development challenges and vulnerability. It is the principle lobby and negotiating voice for small states in the UN system.

United Nations Office of the High Representative for the Least Developed Countries, Landlocked Developing Countries and Small Island Developing States (OHRLLS)

www.un.org/special-rep/ohrlls/ohrlls/default.htm
Established in 2001, OHRLLS provides support and advocacy on focus countries.

Regional Organizations of Small Island Developing States (SIDS)

In addition to the institutions listed, some key regional institutions supporting implementation of the Barbados Programme of Action (BPoA) are the following:

Pacific

The Council of Regional Organizations in the Pacific (CROP) brings together ten main regional organizations in the Pacific: the Pacific Islands Forum Secretariat (PIFS); the South Pacific Applied Geoscience Commission (SOPAC); the Secretariat for the Pacific Community (SPC); the South Pacific Regional Environment Programme (SPREP); the University of the South Pacific (USP); the Pacific Islands Development Programme (PIDP); the South Pacific

Forum Fisheries Agency (FFA); the South Pacific Board for Educational Assessment (SPBEA); the South Pacific Tourism Organization (SPTO); and the Fiji School of Medicine (FSM).

Caribbean

Key institutions in the Caribbean include the Caribbean Community Secretariat (Caricom); the Organization of Eastern Caribbean States (OECS); the Caribbean Environmental Health Institute (CEHI); the Caribbean Disaster Emergency Response Agency (CDERA); the Caribbean Centre for Development Administration (Caricad); the Caribbean Community Climate Change Centre (CCCCC); the Caribbean Development Bank (CDB); the University of the West Indies (UWI); and the Eastern Caribbean Central Bank (ECCB).

AIMS Region (Atlantic, Indian Ocean, Mediterranean, South China Seas)

Key institutions include the Indian Ocean Commission Secretariat (IOC) and the Singapore Environment Institute (SEI).

CONFERENCES, AGREEMENTS AND PROCESSES

- Agenda 21, Chapter 17 (1992)

- Barbados Programme of Action on the Sustainable Development of Small Island Developing States (BPoA) (1994)

- United Nations General Assembly (UNGA) Resolution 50/116 of 20 December beginning work on a vulnerability index (1995)

- United Nations Commission on Sustainable Development (CSD) 7 on the five-year review of implementing the BPoA (1999)

- United Nations General Assembly Special Session (UNGASS) on implementing the BPoA (1999)

- Fourth World Trade Organization (WTO) Ministerial Conference, Doha, Qatar, Doha Ministerial Declaration, paragraph 35 on small economies (2001)

- International meeting on implementation of BPoA (Mauritius, 2004/5)

7

Key United Nations bodies and Bretton Woods institutions

- Alliance of Small Island States (AOSIS)

- United Nations Conference on Trade and Development (UNCTAD)

- United Nations Department of Economic and Social Affairs (DESA)

- United Nations Development Programme (UNDP)

- United Nations Educational, Scientific and Cultural Organization (UNESCO)

- United Nations Environment Programme (UNEP)

- United Nations International Strategy for Disaster Reduction (ISDR)

- United Nations Office of the High Representative for the Least Developed Countries, Landlocked Developing Countries and Small Island Developing States (OHRLLS)

- United Nations Regional Commissions

 # References

Briguglio, L (1995) 'The economic vulnerability of small island developing states', *World Development*, vol 23, pp1615–1632

Briguglio, L (2003) 'The economic vulnerability index – some conceptual and methodological issues', *Occasional Papers on Islands and Small States,* no 5, Islands and Small States Institute, Malta

Commonwealth Secretariat (1997) *A Future for Small States: Overcoming Vulnerability*, Report by a Commonwealth Advisory Group, Commonwealth Secretariat, London

Commonwealth Secretariat (2002) 'Small States: Economic Review and Basic Statistics', Annual Series, vol 7, autumn 2002, Commonwealth Secretariat, London

FAO (United Nations Food and Agriculture Organization) (1999) *State of the World's Forests*, FAO, Rome

Hay, J E (2000) 'Climate change and small island states: A popular summary of science-based findings and perspectives and their links with policy', Paper presented at the Second Alliance of Small Island States, Workshop on Climate Change Negotiations, Management and Strategy, 26 July–4 August 2000, Samoa

Hughes, A and Brewster, H (2002) *Lowering the Threshold*, Commonwealth Secretariat, London

Nurse, L (2002) 'Climate change and coastal vulnerability in small island states', Presentation at the Alliance of Small Island States' Inter-regional Preparatory Meeting for the World Summit on Sustainable Development, Singapore, 7–11 January 2002, www.sidsnet.org/workshop/singapore_agenda.html

Senanayake, R (1999) *Voices of the Earth, Cultural and Spiritual Values of Biodiversity: A Complementary Contribution to the Global Biodiversity Assessment*, Intermediate Technology Publications, on behalf of UNEP, Kenya, p165

Turner, R K, Subak, S and Adger, N (1996) 'Pressures, trends and impacts in coastal zones: Interactions between socioeconomic and natural systems', *Environmental Management*, vol 20, no 2, pp159–173

UNEP (United Nations Environment Programme) (1999a) *Caribbean Environment Outlook*, UNEP, Regional Office for Latin America and the Caribbean, Mexico

UNEP (1999b) *Western Indian Ocean Environment Outlook*, UNEP, Regional Office for Latin America and the Caribbean, Mexico

UNGASS (United Nations General Assembly Special Session) (1999) *Report of the Ad Hoc Committee of the Whole of the Twenty-second Special Session of the General Assembly*, United Nations, New York, UN General Assembly Official Records, Twenty-second Special Session, Supplement No 3 (A/S-22/9/Rev.1)

World Bank (2001) *Atlas 2001*, World Bank, Washington, DC

World Bank (2003) *World Bank Development Report 2003: Sustaining Development in a Dynamic World, Transforming Institutions, Growth and Quality of Life*, World Bank/Oxford University Press, Washington, DC, New York

WTO (World Trade Organization) (2001) *Doha WTO Ministerial Declaration*, WTO, Geneva, 20 November 2001, WT/Min(01)/Dec/1

Sustainable Development for Africa

8

Context

Africa's wealth of resources offers myriad opportunities for sustainable development; yet the region has not been able to realize the full potential of these opportunities and entered the 21st century with enormous challenges. The demand for energy in Africa is set to grow exponentially; but the continuing lack of access to affordable and appropriate technologies is seriously constraining Africa's sustainable development options. Increasing numbers of African countries face water stress and scarcity, as well as critical levels of land degradation (UNEP, 2002), and the region is likely to be hit hardest by climate change (UNEP, 2001). The rising costs of water treatment, food imports, medical treatment and soil conservation measures are increasing human vulnerability and health insecurity and draining African countries of their economic resources (UNEP, 2002). The HIV/AIDS pandemic is affecting all aspects of human, social and economic development and weakening 'the ability of today's generation to pass on its skills and knowledge to the next' (Devarajan, 2003). In the face of these challenges, Africa's commitment to implementing multilateral environmental agreements is impressive (UNEP, 2002), and there are many regional and local sustainable development initiatives underway that address the concerns of the poor. The New Partnership for African Development (NEPAD) is key amongst these and was identified at the World Summit on Sustainable Development (WSSD) for special attention and support to direct international efforts towards Africa's development needs.

KEY WORDS

- **New Partnership for African Development (NEPAD)**
- **technology transfer**
- **education**
- **HIV/AIDS**
- **energy**
- **land degradation**
- **desertification**
- **disasters and conflicts**
- **water and sanitation**
- **land**
- **agriculture and food security**
- **chemicals**
- **digital divide**
- **tourism**
- **human settlements**

Chapter VIII in summary

Sustainable development remains elusive for many African countries. Poverty is a major challenge and most African countries have not benefited fully from the opportunities of globalization, exacerbating the continent's marginalization. Efforts to achieve sustainable development have been hindered by conflicts, insufficient investment, limited market access opportunities and supply-side constraints, unsustainable debt burdens, declining levels of official

AT A GLANCE

* In 2000, there were 3.6 million refugees in Africa, 56 per cent of whom were under 18 years of age (UNHCR, 2001).

* In Africa, 340 million people or half the population live on less than US$1 per day (UNEP, 2002).

* The mortality rate of children under five years of age is 140 per 1000 (UNEP, 2002).

* Life expectancy at birth is only 54 years of age (UNEP, 2002).

* Only 58 per cent of the population have access to safe water (UNEP, 2002).

* The rate of illiteracy for people over 15 is 41 per cent (UNEP, 2002).

* Two-thirds of Africa's mountain area has been affected by 'high intensity conflict' (UNEP, 2002).

* There are only 18 mainline telephones per 1000 people in Africa, compared with 146 for the world as a whole and 567 for high-income countries (UNEP, 2002).

development assistance, and the impact of HIV/AIDS. The international community welcomes the **New Partnership for Africa's Development** (NEPAD) and pledges support towards the implementation of this vision and other development frameworks that are owned and driven by African countries and which embody poverty reduction strategies *[62]*. Action is required at all levels to:

* Create an **enabling environment** to achieve economic growth and sustainable development, and support African efforts for peace, stability and security, conflict resolution and prevention, democracy, good governance, and respect for human rights and fundamental freedoms, including the right to development and gender equality *[62a]*;
* Implement the vision of NEPAD and other efforts, including through **financing, technical and institutional cooperation** and **capacity-building** *[62b]*;
* Promote **technology** development, transfer and diffusion to Africa, and develop African centres of excellence *[62c]*;
* Develop **effective science and technology institutions** and research activities capable of developing and adapting world class technologies *[62d]*;
* Support national programmes and strategies on **education**, helping to ensure all children are able to complete a full course of primary schooling by 2015, with boys and girls having equal access to all levels of education *[62e]*;

- Enhance **industrial productivity, diversity and competitiveness** [62f] and the contribution of industry to Africa's sustainable development, especially **mining, minerals and metals** [62g];
- Strengthen capacities in **environmental impact assessment, environmental legislative and institutional reform** for sustainable development, and in negotiating and implementing **multilateral environmental agreements** [62h];
- Implement the **African Process for the Protection and Development of the Marine and Coastal Environment** [62i];
- Deal with **energy** problems in Africa, including through support for NEPAD, which seeks to secure access for at least 35 per cent of the African population, especially people in rural areas, within 20 years [62j(i)];
- Promote cleaner, more efficient use of natural gas, increased use of renewable energy, improved energy efficiency and access to advanced energy technologies [62j(ii)];
- Mobilize resources for adaptation to the negative effects of **climate change, extreme weather events, sea level rise and climate variability**, and assist national climate change strategies and mitigation programmes [62k];
- Develop affordable **transport systems and infrastructure** [62l];
- Address the poverty affecting **mountain communities** [63m]; and
- Support afforestation, reforestation and **sustainable forest management**, including by combating deforestation, providing finance and technical support, and improving the policy and legal framework of the forest sector [62n].

'Johannesburg must deliver a concrete programme of action if it is to have real impact on the lives of the millions of people around the world who still live in poverty'
(Mohammed Valli Moosa, Minister of Environmental Affairs and Tourism, Republic of South Africa, 2002).

The Johannesburg Plan of Implementation (JPOI) calls for financial and technical support for national implementation of the **Convention to Combat Desertification** (CCD) and to **integrate indigenous knowledge systems** within land and natural resources management practices. Measures are needed to improve **extension services** to rural communities, and to promote better **land, watershed management and agricultural practices** to overcome land degradation [63].

Health

To strengthen healthcare systems in Africa [64], finance and other support will be mobilized to:

- Promote **equitable access to healthcare** [64a];
- Make available drugs and technology to fight and control **communicable diseases**, including HIV/AIDS, malaria, tuberculosis, and trypanosomiasis and **non-communicable diseases**, including those caused by poverty [64b];
- Build the capacity of **medical and paramedical personnel** [64c];
- Promote **indigenous knowledge**, including traditional medicine [64d]; and
- Research and control **Ebola** disease [64e].

Disasters and vulnerability

The JPOI calls for action to deal effectively with **natural disasters and conflicts**, recognizing that conflicts in Africa have hindered, and in many cases obliterated, the gains and efforts made towards sustainable development. The most vulnerable members of society, including women and children, have borne the brunt of the impact *[65]*. Efforts at all levels will include support for:

- **Disaster management** capacities, including early warning and observation systems, assessments, prevention, preparedness, response and recovery *[65a]*;
- **Rapid response mechanisms** to enable Africa to deal more effectively with displaced people *[65b]*;
- Prevention, resolution, management and mitigation of **conflicts** and an early response to help avert tragic humanitarian consequences *[65c]*; and
- **Refugee host countries** in rehabilitating infrastructure and environments damaged in the process of receiving and settling refugees *[65d]*.

Water and sanitation

To promote **integrated water resources development**, measures will be taken to develop and effectively manage water resources while protecting water quality and aquatic ecosystems *[66]*. This includes action at all levels to:

- Provide access to **drinkable domestic water**, **hygiene education** and **improved household sanitation** and **waste management** through encouraging investment prioritizing the poor *[66a]*;
- Develop **integrated river basin and watershed management** strategies and plans for all major water bodies *[66b]*;
- Strengthen capacities for **data collection and processing** for planning, monitoring and enforcement purposes and water resource management arrangements *[66c]*; and
- Protect water resources and combat **water pollution**, and develop non-conventional water resources, including **desalination, rainwater harvesting** and **water recycling** *[66d]*.

Agriculture and food security

To achieve significantly **improved agricultural productivity and food security** and to achieve the Millennium Development Goals (MDGs), including halving by 2015 the proportion of people who suffer from hunger *[67]*, initiatives will be taken at all levels to:

- Support **national programmes and investment** in infrastructure, technology and extension services to regenerate the African agricultural sector and develop sustainable fisheries. African countries should be in the process of developing and implementing **food security strategies** by 2005 *[67a]*;

8

- Secure **equitable access to land tenure** and clarify **resource rights and responsibilities** through reform processes that respect the law, provide access to credit, enable poverty eradication and promote efficient and ecologically sound use of land. Enable women producers to become decision-makers and landowners, including the right to inherit land *[67b]*;
- Improve **market access for goods** particularly from least developed countries *[67c]*;
- Invest in **regional trade, market infrastructure and economic integration** *[67d]*; and
- Support **livestock development programmes** aimed at controlling animal diseases *[67e]*.

Management of chemicals

Measures will be taken to achieve the sound management of chemicals, focusing on hazardous chemicals and wastes, through assistance with:

- National chemical profiles;
- Regional and national frameworks for chemicals management; and
- Establishing chemical focal points *[68]*.

Digital divide

To bridge the digital divide and create digital opportunities, action will help to:

- Create an enabling environment for investment;
- Accelerate programmes to connect essential institutions; and
- Stimulate the adoption of information and communication technologies in government, commerce and elsewhere *[69]*.

Tourism and biodiversity

Sustainable tourism that contributes to Africa's social, economic and infrastructure development will be supported *[70]* through action at all levels on:

- Implementing local, national and sub-regional projects, with an emphasis on **marketing African products** such as adventure tourism, ecotourism and cultural tourism *[70a]*;
- National and cross-border conservation areas to promote ecosystem conservation and sustainable tourism *[70b]*;
- Promoting the use of indigenous knowledge in natural resource management and ecotourism *[70c]*;
- Assisting host communities to manage tourism projects to maximize benefits while limiting negative impacts on their traditions, culture and environment *[70d]*; and

'Every one of us can make a contribution. And quite often we are looking for the big things and forget that, wherever we are, we can make a contribution... Sometimes I tell myself, I may only be planting a tree here; but just imagine what's happening if there are billions of people out there doing something. Just imagine the power of what we can do' (Wangari Maathai, founder of Kenya's Green Belt Movement; now Deputy Prime Minister of Environment, Natural Resources and Wildlife, Kenya, 1977).

- Conservation of Africa's **biological diversity**, sustainable use of its components and the fair and equitable sharing of benefits arising from the use of genetic resources *[70e]*.

Habitat agenda

African countries will be supported in their efforts to implement the Habitat Agenda and the Istanbul Declaration by initiatives to:

- Strengthen capacities on sustainable urbanization and human settlements;
- Provide support for adequate shelter and basic services, and development of effective governance systems in cities and settlements; and
- Strengthen the United Nations Human Settlements Programme (UN-Habitat)/United Nations Environment Programme (UNEP) on managing water for African cities *[71]*.

 # Africa elsewhere in the JPOI

Commitments throughout the Johannesburg Plan of Implementation (JPOI) are pertinent to Africa. They include those on poverty eradication, water, sanitation and energy. The JPOI supports integrated land and water management, based upon the ecosystem approach, to help manage limited resources more effectively and to help combat the growing impact of climate change. Commitments to strengthen implementation of the United Nations Convention to Combat Desertification (CCD) are highlighted, along with actions to improve sustainable agricultural productivity and food security in line with the MDGs. Land reform issues identified in Chapter IV are critical to Africa's progress and efforts towards stemming the HIV/AIDS epidemic, including a new WSSD target on health literacy, are highly relevant to the NEPAD vision and all African countries. Other relevant commitments include those on access to energy and the use of financial instruments and mechanisms to increase capacity-building, training and strengthened technical knowledge.

TARGETS AND COMMITMENTS

- **Food security.** Support African countries in developing and implementing food security strategies by 2005 *[67a]* (new target).

- **Agriculture.** Improve sustainable agricultural productivity and food security in accordance with the Millennium Development Goals (MDGs), in particular to halve, by 2015, the proportion of people who suffer from hunger *[67]* (new target).

- **Energy.** Support Africa's efforts to implement New Partnership for African Development (NEPAD) objectives on energy, which seek to secure access for at least 35 per cent of the African population within 20 years, especially in rural areas *[62j(i)]* (new target).

EXAMPLES OF INDICATORS FOR MEASURING PROGRESS IN IMPLEMENTATION

- Proportion of the population living on below US$1 per day (Millennium Development Goal, or MDG)

- Prevalence of underweight children under five years of age (MDG)

- Proportion of the population below minimum level of dietary energy consumption (MDG)

- Net enrolment ratio in primary education (MDG)

- Literacy rate of 15- to 24-year olds (MDG)

- Under five mortality rate (MDG)

- Number of children orphaned by HIV/AIDS (MDG)

- Prevalence and death rates associated with malaria (MDG)

- Prevalence and death rates associated with tuberculosis (MDG)

- Proportion of population with sustainable access to an improved water source, urban and rural (MDG)

- Proportion of households with access to secure tenure (MDG)

- Economic and human loss due to natural disasters (United Nations Commission on Sustainable Development, or CSD)

- Proportion of urban population with access to improved sanitation (MDG)

- Proportion of population with sustainable access to an improved water source, urban and rural (MDG)

- Proportion of population with access to affordable essential drugs on a sustainable basis (MDG)

- Telephone lines and cellular subscribers per 100 population (MDG)

- Personal computers in use per 100 population and internet users per 100 population (MDG)

 # Resources

United Nations Environment Programme (UNEP)

www.unep.org

UNEP was the outcome of the 1972 Stockholm Conference on the Human Environment. It provides leadership and encourages partnership in caring for the environment by inspiring, informing and enabling nations/peoples to improve their quality of life without compromising that of future generations.

Partnership example

Global Network on Energy for Sustainable Development (GNESD)

Leading partner: United Nations Environment Programme (UNEP)

Dates: January 2003–December 2006

The objective of the Global Network on Energy for Sustainable Development (GNESD) is to make it easier for partners to contribute to the provision of environmentally sound energy services that underpin sustainable development. It will do so by supporting (amongst its partners) information exchange, learning, analysis and study, policy support, and capacity-building. It will work with a number of 'centres of excellence' in, amongst other places, Dakar, Nairobi, Cape Town, New Delhi, Beijing, Bangkok and Rio de Janeiro, as well as with partnerships established by governments, industry, international institutions and non-governmental organizations (NGOs). This North–South network of energy, development and environment institutions will allow members to cooperate on a range of energy for sustainable development topics; improve their ability to acquire and apply knowledge and experience; access quality advisory services; and improve their understanding of the links between sustainable energy and other environment/development priorities, as well as technology and policy options. It will ideally result in changes in government policies and programmes to favour energy for sustainable development approaches.

Contact information:
Interim Secretariat
Global Network on
Energy for Sustainable
Development
(GNESD)
Risoe National
Laboratory, Bldg 142
Frederiksborgvej 399
PO Box 49
DK 4000 Roskilde
Denmark
www.gnesd.org

United Nations Human Settlements Programme (UN-Habitat)

www.unhabitat.org
UN-Habitat is the lead UN agency for human settlements, including the Habitat Agenda (a practical road map to an urbanizing world, adopted by 171 governments at Habitat II, Istanbul, 1996).

United Nations Convention to Combat Desertification in Those Countries Experiencing Serious Drought and/or Desertification, Particularly in Africa (CCD)

www.unccd.ch
The CCD came into force in 1996 following the United Nations Conference on Environment and Development (UNCED) mandate to negotiate. In March 2003, 186 countries were parties. Activities to control/alleviate desertification are closely linked to needs/participation of local land users. UNEP has adopted a regional focus and requires national action programmes developed with local stakeholders (UNEP, 2002).

United Nations Convention on Biological Diversity (CBD)

www.biodiv.org

The CBD was also an outcome of UNCED. Three main goals of the CBD are the conservation of biological diversity; the sustainable use of its components; and the fair/equitable sharing of benefits arising from the use of genetic resources. The CBD includes the Cartagena Biosafety Protocol (living/genetically modified organisms) and the Jakarta Mandate (marine and coastal biodiversity).

Convention on International Trade in Endangered Species of Wild Fauna and Flora (CITES)

www.cites.org

CITES came into force in 1975 and ensures that the international trade in species of wild animals and plants does not threaten their survival.

New Partnership for African Development (NEPAD)

www.nepad.org

Adopted in July 2001 at the Summit of Organization of African Unity, NEPAD is a commitment by leaders to the people of Africa, addressing current challenges (Moosa, 2002). Objectives include to eradicate poverty; place African countries on the path of sustainable growth and development; halt marginalization of Africa in globalization; and accelerate empowerment of women. NEPAD recognizes the value of partnerships between African countries and with the international community.

Tokyo International Conference on African Development (TICAD)

Launched in 1993 by governments, the private sector and other stakeholders, the TICAD promotes high-level dialogue between African leaders and their partners, and mobilizes support for Africa's own development efforts.

 # References

Devarajan, S (2003) 'Economic cost of AIDS', World Bank Press Release, 23 July 2003, www.worldbank.org

Moosa, M V (2002) 'African Renaissance', *Our Planet*, UNEP, vol 13, no 2, pp13–14

UNCHS (United Nations Centre for Human Settlements) (2000) *Habitat*, vol 6, no 1, p36

UNEP (United Nations Environment Programme) (2001) *Annual Report, 2001*, UNEP, Nairobi

UNEP (2002) *Global Environment Outlook 3*, Earthscan, London, www.unep.org/geo

UNHCR (United Nations High Commissioner for Refugees) (2001) *Refugee Children in Africa. Trends and Patterns in the Refugee Population in Africa Below the Age of 18 Years, 2000*, UNHCR, Geneva

World Bank (2000) *World Development Report, 2000/2001*, World Bank and Oxford University Press, Oxford, www.worldbank.org/wdr

CONFERENCES, AGREEMENTS AND PROCESSES

⧗ African Convention on the Conservation of Nature and Natural Resources (1968)

⧗ United Nations Convention to Combat Desertification (CCD) (1994)

⧗ World Summit on Social Development (Commitment 7) Copenhagen (1995)

⧗ South African Development Community (SADC) Policy and Strategy for Environment and Sustainable Development (1996)

⧗ United Nations Millennium Declaration (2000)

⧗ United Nations Decade to Roll Back Malaria, Particularly in Africa (2001–2010)

⧗ African Union launched; New Partnership for African Development (NEPAD) adopted (June 2001)

⧗ Pan-African Conference on Water in Africa (2003)

See the 'Resources' section at the end of this chapter for other relevant processes, organizations and web links.

Key United Nations bodies and Bretton Woods institutions

⚙ International Fund for Agricultural Development (IFAD)

⚙ International Monetary Fund (IMF)

⚙ Joint United Nations Programme on HIV/AIDS (UNAIDS)

⚙ United Nations Children's Fund (UNICEF)

⚙ United Nations Conference on Trade and Development (UNCTAD)

⚙ United Nations Development Programme (UNDP)

⚙ United Nations Economic Commission for Africa

⚙ United Nations Environment Programme (UNEP)

⚙ United Nations Food and Agriculture Organization (FAO)

⚙ United Nations High Commissioner for Refugees (UNHCR)

⚙ United Nations Human Settlements Programme (UN-Habitat)

⚙ World Health Organization (WHO)

⚙ World Bank

Other Regions

9

 Context

With Small Island Developing States (SIDS) and African countries given their own chapters within the Johannesburg Plan of Implementation (JPOI), Chapter IX addresses the priorities of the following UN regions: Latin America and the Caribbean; Asia and the Pacific; West Asia; and the Economic Commission for Europe, which includes North America. Of course, these regions exhibit startling differences in all three pillars of sustainable development. Chapters VII to IX are a recognition of this diversity and reflect a growing concern to strengthen regional and sub-regional responses to sustainable development. The JPOI reflects a number of regionally agreed strategies and priorities. Experience gained through the World Summit on Sustainable Development (WSSD) preparatory process, and the preparation of participatory national strategies for sustainable development, should further support the policy cohesion and coordination that is called for in the JPOI.

 Chapter IX in summary

Important sustainable development initiatives have been developed within the UN regions. The Johannesburg Plan of Implementation (JPOI) recognizes the value of these efforts and calls for further action, and coordination at all levels, to take these initiatives further *[72]*.

Latin America and the Caribbean

Initiative of Latin America and the Caribbean on Sustainable Development:

- Recognizes the importance of **regional action** towards sustainable development;
- Builds on the **Platform for Action on the Road to Johannesburg 2002**; and
- Seeks **concrete actions** in areas such as biodiversity; water resources; vulnerabilities and sustainable cities; social aspects; and economic aspects

AT A GLANCE

◻ Latin America and the Caribbean is the most urbanized region in the developing world. 75 per cent of the population live in urban areas, with 40 to 60 per cent of urban residents living in informal settlements (UNEP, 2002; UN Population Division, 2001).

◻ The Asia and Pacific region contains 12 megacities – Beijing, Calcutta, Delhi, Dhaka, Jakarta, Karachi, Metro Manila, Mumbai, Osaka, Seoul, Shanghai and Tokyo – with 12 per cent of the world's urban population (UN Population Division, 2001).

◻ In many countries of West Asia, water rationing is used to limit domestic demand. Jordan restricts water supplies in Amman to only three days a week. In Damascus, water can be used for less than 12 hours a day (UNEP, 2002).

◻ The pollution of surface and groundwater by excess nutrients from agricultural sources is a major cause for concern in Europe (EEA, 2002).

'... the significance of the Aarhus Convention is global. It is by far the most impressive elaboration of principle 10 of the Rio Declaration, which stresses the need for citizen's participation in environmental issues and for access to information on the environment held by public authorities ... it is the most ambitious venture in the area of 'environmental democracy' so far undertaken under the auspices of the United Nations' (UN Secretary-General Kofi Annan, 2002).

and institutional arrangements, taking into account ethics for sustainable development [73].

The initiative envisages **actions among countries** in the region, fostering South–South cooperation and **attracting support** from groups of countries and multilateral and regional organizations. It is a framework for cooperation open to **partnerships** [74].

Asia and the Pacific

The **Phnom Penh Regional Platform on Sustainable Development for Asia and the Pacific**:

- Recognizes that the region contains over half of the world's population and the largest number of people living in poverty; sustainable development in Asia and the Pacific is critical to achieving sustainable development globally [75];
- Identifies **seven initiatives for action**: capacity-building for sustainable development; poverty reduction; cleaner production and sustainable energy; land management and biodiversity conservation; protection and management of freshwater resources; oceans, coastal and marine resources and sustainable development in small island developing states (SIDs); and action on atmosphere and climate change; and
- Identifies follow-up action of these initiatives through national strategies and relevant regional and sub-regional initiatives, including the **Regional**

Action Programme for Environmentally Sound and Sustainable Development and the Kitakyushu Initiative for a Clean Environment *[76]*.

West Asia

The West Asia Region is known for **scarce water** and **limited fertile land**. Progress has been made towards a more knowledge-based production of higher value-added commodities *[77]*. **Priorities** include: poverty alleviation; relief of debt burden and sustainable management of natural resources; integrated management of water resources and coastal zones; control of land and water pollution; and programmes to combat desertification *[78]*.

Economic Commission for Europe region

The Economic Commission for Europe (ECE) Regional Ministerial Meeting for the WSSD recognized the major role and responsibilities of the region in global efforts to achieve sustainable development. Priority actions, identified in the Ministerial Statement to the WSSD and **different approaches and mechanisms** to implement Agenda 21, may be needed in each country *[79]*:

'*We learned with the elders that we are a tiny part of this immense universe with all the animals, the plants and the waters. Together we have to take care of the vessel in which we are all journeying*' (Ailton Krenak, indigenous leader, Brazil, 2002).

- **Ongoing efforts** include: the **Environment for Europe process**; the fifth ECE Ministerial Conference (Kiev, May 2003); development of an environmental strategy for the 12 countries of Eastern Europe; the Caucasus and Central Asia; the Central Asian Agenda 21; Organisation for Economic Co-operation and Development (OECD) work on sustainable development; and the European Union (EU) sustainable development strategy.
- Relevant **conventions and processes** include: the Convention on Access to Information, Public Participation in Decision-Making and Access to Justice in Environmental Matters (Aarhus Convention); the Alpine Convention; the North American Commission for Environmental Cooperation; the International Boundary Waters Treaty Act; the Iqaluit Declaration of the Arctic Council; and processes to implement Agenda 21 in the Baltic and Mediterranean *[80]*.

Other regional initiatives elsewhere in the JPOI

Regional frameworks and structures figure prominently throughout the Johannesburg Plan of Implementation (JPOI). Specific issues highlighted as requiring inter- and intra-regional cooperation and coordination include: oceans; coastal and marine resources; desertification; biodiversity; human settlements (JPOI, Chapter IV); and poverty reduction programmes (JPOI, Chapter II). Chapter X of the JPOI makes reference to the need for regional coordination in sharing information, making the best use of existing resources and for all forms of capacity-building. Concerns of Latin America/Caribbean and Asia/Pacific regions with respect to their small island developing states are discussed in Chapter VII. Recognizing that environmental impacts transcend state boundaries, Chapter XI urges the strengthening of institutional arrangements for protecting ecosystems and their individual components. It is noted that people's vulnerability to natural disasters can be lessened through effective regional strategies, including monitoring and early warning systems. Regional cooperation is called for to provide assistance to children orphaned by HIV/AIDS, and for more effective regional responses to environmental threats to health (JPOI, Chapter VI).

The UN's Regional Commissions are tasked with assisting in mobilizing technical and financial assistance from regional development banks for the implementation of regionally and sub-regionally agreed sustainable development programmes for education, technology transfer and capacity-building (JPOI, Chapter X). In its refocused remit, the United Nations Commission on Sustainable Development (CSD) is urged to make more effective use of existing regional structures and, in particular, to use regional reports more fully in planning and decision-making. Multi-stakeholder participation and partnerships are promoted in this context. Overall, it is recognized that strengthened regional capacities are essential for sustainable development (JPOI, Chapter XI).

TARGETS AND COMMITMENTS

Commitments in Chapter IX of the JPOI relate to the implementation of previously agreed regional initiatives and priorities, including the:

- Initiative of Latin America and the Caribbean on Sustainable Development;

- Phnom Penh Regional Platform on Sustainable Development for Asia and the Pacific;

- Regional Action Programme for Environmentally Sound and Sustainable Development (Asia and the Pacific Region);

- Kitakyushu Initiative for a Clean Environment;

- Arab Declaration to the World Summit on Sustainable Development (WSSD);

- Ministerial Statement to the WSSD adopted by the Economic Commission for Europe (ECE) Regional Ministerial Meeting for the WSSD;

- Environment for Europe Process.

EXAMPLES OF INDICATORS FOR MEASURING PROGRESS IN IMPLEMENTATION

- Proportion of population below US$1 a day (Millennium Development Goal, or MDG)

- Proportion of urban population with access to improved sanitation (MDG)

- Proportion of population with sustainable access to an improved water source, urban and rural (MDG)

- Proportion of population below minimum level of dietary energy consumption (MDG)

- Literacy rate of 15- to 24-year olds (MDG)

- Under five mortality rate (MDG)

- Proportion of births attended by skilled health professional (MDG)

- Prevalence and death rates associated with malaria (MDG)

- HIV Prevalence among 15- to 24-year-old pregnant women (MDG)

- Proportion of population with access to affordable essential drugs on a sustainable basis (MDG)

Partnership example

HIV/AIDS in the World of Work: A Tripartite Response in the Caribbean

Leading partner: International Labour Organization (ILO)

Dates: 2004–2007 (expected time frame)

This project aims to prevent HIV/AIDS among workers, enhancing workplace protection and reducing the adverse consequences of the epidemic on Caribbean development. More specifically, it will focus on:

- reducing the spread of HIV;

- a comprehensive strategic response to HIV/AIDS on work;

- implications of HIV/AIDS on work;

- capacity of governments, organizations of employers and workers, and people living with HIV/AIDS in education, awareness-raising and implementation;

- reducing stigma and discrimination; and

- improving capacity to determine financial costs of the epidemic and its impact on the social security system.

Contact information:
Technical Cooperation and Advisory Services
International Labour Organization (ILO)
International Labour Office
4, Route des Morillons
CH-1211 Geneva 22
Switzerland
www.mirror/public/english/protection/trav/aids/

Resources

Other regional initiatives

www.un.org/jsummit/html/documents/prep2reg_outcomes.html
See this website for outcomes of regional preparatory processes for the World Summit on Sustainable Development (WSSD).

Initiative of Latin America and the Caribbean on Sustainable Development

This initiative was endorsed at the First Special Meeting of the Forum of Ministers of the Environment of Latin America and the Caribbean in Johannesburg on 31 August 2002.

Platform for Action on the Road to Johannesburg 2002

This platform was adopted by the governments of Latin America and the Caribbean in Rio de Janeiro (23–24 October 2001), meeting as the regional preparatory conference for the WSSD.

Phnom Penh Regional Platform on Sustainable Development for Asia and the Pacific

The Phnom Penh platform was adopted by members of the United Nations Economic and Social Commission for Asia and the Pacific (ESCAP) at the high-level regional meeting for the WSSD (Phnom Penh, 27–29 November 2001).

Fourth Ministerial Conference on Environment and Development in Asia and the Pacific

www.unescap.org/mced2000/outcom.htm
Occurring in Kitakyushu, Japan (31 August–5 September 2000), this conference adopted the *Regional Action Programme for Environmentally Sound and Sustainable Development 2001–2005*, as well as the Kitakyushu Initiative for a Clean Environment.

West Asia Regional Preparatory Committee Meeting for the WSSD

Attended by 10 North African and 12 Middle Eastern countries (Cairo, 24 October 2001), this meeting adopted the Arab Declaration to the WSSD.

Economic Commission for Europe (ECE) Regional Ministerial Meeting for the WSSD

Attended by members of the United Nations Economic Commission for Europe (ECE) region (includes Europe, North America, Nordic countries and Israel) (Geneva, 24–25 September 2001), this meeting adopted the Ministerial Statement to the WSSD.

Environment for Europe Process

www.unece.org/env/europe/welcome.html
United Nations ECE ministers have met since 1991. The Third Ministerial (1995) adopted an Environmental Programme for Europe. The Fourth Ministerial (1998) adopted the Aarhus Convention (see below).

Fifth ECE Ministerial Conference (Kiev, 21–23 May 2003)

www.kyiv-2003.info/main/index.php
The Fifth ECE Conference considered 'Environment for Europe: Progress and priorities for future years'. A number of regional environmental agreements were also signed.

Organisation for Economic Co-operation and Development (OECD)

www.oecd.org/home/
The OECD is based in Paris with a membership of 30 industrialized nations. It fosters good governance in the public sphere and private sector, and develops internationally agreed instruments, decisions and recommendations to promote rules where multilateral agreement is necessary for individual countries to make progress in a globalized economy. Work covers macro-economics, trade, education, development and science and innovation.

European Union (EU) Sustainable Development Strategy

www.europa.eu.int/comm/sustainable/pages/strategy_en.htm
Proposed by the European Commission (EC) and discussed by the EU (Göteborg, June 2001), this strategy outlines measures to address important threats to well-being, including climate change, poverty and emerging health risks.

Aarhus Convention

www.unece.org/env/pp/treatytext.htm
The Aarhus Convention on Access to Information, Public Participation in Decision-Making and Access to Justice in Environmental Matters was adopted in 1998 at the Fourth ECE Ministerial Conference. It entered into force on 30 October 2001.

Convention on the Protection of the Alps (Alpine Convention)

www.convenzionedellealpi.org/
The Alpine Convention was adopted in Salzburg on 7 November 1991. Parties pursue a comprehensive policy for the preservation/protection of the Alps by applying the principles of prevention, payment by the polluter and cooperation. Measures cover population and culture; regional planning; prevention of air pollution; soil conservation; water management; conservation of nature and the countryside; mountain farming; mountain forests; tourism and recreation; transport; energy; and waste management.

North American Commission on Environmental Cooperation

www.cec.org/home/index.cfm?varlan=english
Created by Canada, Mexico and the US under the North American Agreement on Environmental Cooperation (NAAEC) to address regional environment concerns, this commission helps to prevent potential trade and environment conflicts and promotes effective enforcement of environmental law.

Boundary Waters Treaty

www.ijc.org/rel/agree/water.html
Adopted on 1 November 1909, the Boundary Waters Treaty entered into force on 5 May 1910 to prevent uses, obstructions or diversions that materially affect the level or flow of boundary waters between the US and Canada (unless permitted by special agreement or approved by the International Joint Commission established under the treaty). The two parties also agree not to cause cross-border pollution of boundary waters.

Iqaluit Declaration of the Arctic Council

www.eppr.arctic-council.org/reports/980917.html
The Iqualuit Declaration was adopted at the First Ministerial Meeting of the Arctic Council (Iqaluit, Canada, 17–18 September, 1998) to promote cooperation/consultation among Arctic states with involvement of Arctic indigenous communities and other inhabitants, especially on sustainable development and environmental protection.

Baltic Agenda 21

www.ee/baltic21/
The Baltic Agenda was adopted at the Seventh Ministerial Session of the Council of the Baltic Sea States (Nyborg, Denmark, 22–23 June 1998). It was a joint, long-term effort by 11 countries of the Council of the Baltic Sea States to attain sustainable development in the region.

CONFERENCES, AGREEMENTS AND PROCESSES

Latin America and the Caribbean

- Global Conference on the Sustainable Development of Small Island Developing States (SIDS) adopts the Barbados Programme of Action (BPoA) (1994)

- Platform for Action on the Road to Johannesburg, Rio de Janeiro (E/CN.17/2002/PC.2/5/Add.2) (October 2001)

- Initiative of Latin America and the Caribbean on Sustainable Development (2002)

- International Meeting on the Barbados Programme of Action (BPoA) (2004)

CONFERENCES, AGREEMENTS AND PROCESSES (CONTD)

Asia and Pacific

- Global Conference on the Sustainable Development of Small Island Developing States (SIDS) adopts the Barbados Programme of Action (BPoA) (1994)

- Fourth Ministerial Conference on Environment and Development in Asia and the Pacific adopted the Kitayushu Initiative for a Clean Environment; and the Regional Action Programme for Environmentally Sound and Sustainable Development (2001–2005) (2000)

- Regional Platform on Sustainable Development for Asia and the Pacific, Phnom Penh (2001)

- Regional Action Programme for Environmentally Sound and Sustainable Development (2002)

- International Meeting on the Barbados Programme of Action (BPoA) (2004)

- Likely review of the Regional Action Programme for Environmentally Sound and Sustainable Development (2001–2005) by the Fifth Ministerial Conference on Environment and Development in Asia and the Pacific (2005)

West Asia

- Fourth Ministerial Conference on Environment and Development in Asia and the Pacific (Economic and Social Commission for Asia and the Pacific (2000)

- Jeddah Declaration on the Islamic Perspective on the Environment (2000)

- Tehran Declaration on Religions, Cultures and the Environment (2000)

- Abu Dhabi Declaration on the Future of the Arab Environment Programme (2001)

- West Asia Regional Preparatory Committee meeting for World Summit on Sustainable Development (WSSD) adopts the Arab Declaration to WSSD (2001)

Europe

- International Boundary Waters Treaty Act (1909)

- Environment for Europe process (initiated 1991 – ongoing)

- Towards Sustainability: European Community (EC) programme of policy and action in relation to the environment and sustainable development (better known as the Fifth EC Environmental Action Programme) (1993)

CONFERENCES, AGREEMENTS AND PROCESSES (CONTD)

⧖ Mediterranean Agenda 21 (1994)

⧖ Alpine Convention (1995)

⧖ Nordic Strategy on Sustainable Development (1998)

⧖ The Iqaluit Declaration of the Arctic Council (1998)

⧖ The Baltic Agenda 21 (1998)

⧖ Convention on Access to Information, Public Participation in Decision-Making and Access to Justice in Environmental Matters (Aarhus Convention) (1998)

⧖ European Union (EU) Sixth Environmental Action Plan 'Environment 2010: Our Future, Our Choice' (2001)

⧖ Ministerial statement to World Summit on Sustainable Development (WSSD) adopted by the United Nations Economic Commission for Europe (ECE) Regional Ministerial Meeting for WSSD (2001)

⧖ Central Asian Agenda 21 – type II partnership (2003–2012)

⧖ Fifth ECE Ministerial Conference – Environment for Europe, Kiev (May 2003)

⧖ Review of progress in the implementation of priority actions for the ECE region as set out in the 2001 Ministerial Statement (2011)

Key United Nations bodies and Bretton Woods institutions

Latin America and the Caribbean

⚙ United Nations Children's Fund (UNICEF) Americas and the Caribbean

⚙ United Nations Development Programme (UNDP) country offices

⚙ United Nations Economic Commission for Latin America and the Caribbean (ECLAC) – Santiago, Chile and Port-of-Spain, Trinidad

⚙ United Nations Environment Programme (UNEP) Regional Office – Mexico City, Mexico

⚙ United Nations Human Settlements Programme (UN-Habitat) Regional Office for Latin America and the Caribbean, Rio de Janeiro, Brazil

Key United Nations bodies and Bretton Woods institutions (*contd*)

Asia and the Pacific

- United Nations Children's Fund (UNICEF) East Asia and Pacific
- United Nations Development Programme (UNDP) country offices
- United Nations Economic and Social Commission for Asia and the Pacific (ESCAP) – Bangkok, Thailand
- United Nations Environment Programme (UNEP) Regional Office – Bangkok, Thailand
- United Nations Human Settlements Programme (UN-Habitat) Regional Office for Asia and the Pacific, Fukuoka, Japan

West Asia

- United Nations Development Programme (UNDP) country offices
- United Nations Economic and Social Commission for Western Asia (ESCWA) – Beirut, Lebanon
- United Nations Environment Programme (UNEP) Regional Office for West Asia (ROWA) – Manama, State of Bahrain

Economic Commission for Europe Region

- North American Commission for Environmental Cooperation
- Organisation for Economic Co-operation and Development (OECD)
- UNEP Regional Office for North America (RONA) – Washington, DC, US
- United Nations Children's Fund (UNICEF) Central and Eastern Europe and Baltic States
- United Nations Development Programme (UNDP) Regional Bureau for Europe and the Commonwealth of Independent States (CIS)
- United Nations Economic Commission for Europe (UNECE) – Geneva, Switzerland
- United Nations Environment Programme (UNEP) Regional Office – Geneva, Switzerland

References

Annan, K, Secretary-General of the UN (2002) In: Stakeholder Forum Network 2015 Bulletin Issue No 1, 2003

Arab Declaration to the World Summit on Sustainable Development (WSSD) (2001) United Nations Economic and Social Council, Commission on Sustainable Development acting as the Preparatory Committee for the WSSD, second preparatory session (28 January–8 February 2002), 1 December 2001, New York (E/CN.17/2002/PC.2/)

Commission of the European Communities (2001) *A Sustainable Europe for a Better World: A European Union Strategy for Sustainable Development*, Commission of the European Communities, Brussels, 15 May 2001, Communication from the Commission, COM(2001)264 final

CSD (United Nations Commission on Sustainable Development) (2001) *Rio de Janeiro Platform for Action on the Road to Johannesburg 2002*, United Nations Economic and Social Council, Commission on Sustainable Development acting as the Preparatory Committee for the WSSD, second preparatory session (28 January–8 February 2002), 1 December 2001, Brussels (E/CN.17/2002/PC.2/5/Add.2)

ECOSOC (United Nations Economic and Social Council) (2002) Ministerial Statement to the World Summit on Sustainable Development (WSSD) (adopted by the Economic Commission for Europe Regional Ministerial Meeting for the Summit on 25 September 2001), United Nations Economic and Social Council, Commission on Sustainable Development acting as the Preparatory Committee for the WSSD, second preparatory session (28 January–8 February 2002), 7 December 2001, New York (E/CN.17/2002/PC.2/5/Add.1)

EEA (European Environment Agency) (2002) *European Environment Agency, Europe's Environment: The Third Assessment*, EEA, Environmental Assessment Report No 10, 2003

ESCAP (United Nations Economic and Social Commission for Asia and the Pacific) (2000a) *Kitakyushu Initiative for a Clean Environment*, ESCAP, Bangkok

ESCAP (2000b) *Regional Action Programme for Environmentally Sound and Sustainable Development, 2001–2005*, ESCAP, Bangkok, 2000

ESCAP (2001) *Phnom Penh Regional Platform on Sustainable Development for Asia and the Pacific*, Task Force for the Preparation of WSSD in Asia and the Pacific (ESCAP, Asian Development Bank, UNDP, UNEP), Bangkok, 29 November 2001 (ENR/HRM/WWS/1/Rev.1) (also available as: E/CN.17/2002/PC.2/8)

Groombridge, B and Jenkins, M D (2000) *Global Biodiversity: Earth's Living Resources in the 21st Century*, The World Conservation Press, Cambridge

Krenak, A (2002) cited in Liz Hosken, 'Earth Democracy', *Resurgence Magazine*, no 214, September/October, p12

UNDP (United Nations Development Programme) (2003) *Human Development Report 2003, Millennium Development Goals: A Compact among Nations to End Human Poverty*, hdr.undp.org/reports/global/2003

UNEP (United Nations Environment Programme) (2002) *Global Environment Outlook – 2 (GEO-2)*, Earthprint, www.unep.org/geo/geo2000

UNEP–ROLAC (Regional Office for Latin America and Caribbean) (2002) *Latin America and Caribbean Initiative for Sustainable Development*, UNEP, Regional Office for Latin America and the Caribbean, Mexico, 30 August 2002, UNEP/LAC-SMIG.I/2

UN-Habitat (United Nations Human Settlements Programme) (2001) General Assembly, Special Session for an Overall Review and Appraisal of the Implementation of the Habitat Agenda, New York, 6–8 June 2001

UNPD (United Nations Population Division) (2001) *World Urbanisation Prospects Revision 2001*, UNPD, Istanbul

10 Means of Implementation

 ## Context

Agenda 21 agreed that official development assistance (ODA) would be a main source of financing for implementation in developing countries and that substantial new and additional funding was required for funding sustainable development. At the World Summit on Sustainable Development (WSSD), the perception that developed countries had fallen short of their 1992 commitments on financing formed the backdrop of what became some of the toughest negotiations of the summit. In the end, the WSSD reiterated existing commitments on financing, and placed a stronger emphasis on mobilizing resources and creating an enabling environment for investment, private international financial flows, public–private partnerships and the effective use of ODA. The other means of implementation outlined in Agenda 21 (transfer of environmentally sound technologies; science for sustainable development; promoting education; public awareness and training; capacity-building; and information for decision-making) all remain within the Johannesburg Plan of Implementation (JPOI) under Chapter X. National mechanisms and international institutional arrangements are addressed in Chapter XI.

Implementation was a central theme at WSSD and remains the litmus test of commitment to the JPOI. Klaus Töpfer of the United Nations Environment Programme (UNEP) called for the summit to be one of:

> '... implementation of existing declarations. We have very important and very good declarations, first and foremost the Earth Summit's Agenda 21. Now it is high time to implement them, with a targeted, benchmarked timetable-orientated action programme... It must be a summit of concrete actions, reliable and accountable, with the aim of overcoming poverty ... and changing unsustainable consumption patterns in the developed countries' (UNEP, 2002).

KEY WORDS

- **enabling environment**
- **foreign direct investment (FDI)**
- **official development assistance (ODA)**
- **debt**
- **trade**
- **human rights**
- **right to self-determination**
- **environmentally sound technologies**
- **science and technology**
- **issues of global public interest**
- **terrorism**
- **education**
- **capacity-building (human, institutional, infrastructure)**
- **information**

AT A GLANCE

⚙ In 2001, net private flows of external financing to emerging market economies was US$133.2 billion compared to US$11.1 billion in official flows (IIF, 2003).

⚙ Monterrey commitments would raise the official development assistance (ODA) gross national income (GNI) ratio to 0.26 per cent by 2006, still well below the ratio of 0.33 per cent consistently achieved until 1992. The amount promised also falls considerably short of the US$50 billion annual additional resources that have been projected as needed to meet the Millennium Development Goals (MDGs) (Commonwealth Secretariat, 2003).

⚙ The banks involved in the Equator Initiative (a partnership which addresses poverty through the conservation and sustainable use of biodiversity in the equatorial belt by fostering community partnerships) provided over US$9 billion in loans for infrastructure projects in 2002 (WRI, 2003).

⚙ In 2002, net transfers on foreign investment (after taking account of profit remittances), though positive for all regions except the Middle East and North Africa, were insufficient to offset the net transfer on debt for all developing countries (Commonwealth Secretariat, 2003).

Chapter X in summary

Implementation of Agenda 21, the JPOI and internationally agreed development goals requires:

'A lot of people believe that there must be a global deal, with contributions from both developed and developing countries. Economic cooperation is not a matter of charity, but of investment, and investment with a very high return' (Klaus Töpfer, executive director of UNEP, 2002).

- A **substantially increased effort** by countries and the international community, based on the recognition that each country has primary responsibility for its own development and that the role of national policies and development strategies cannot be overemphasized;
- Rio principles to be taken into account, including the **common but differentiated responsibility** of states;
- A significant increase in financial resources, as set out in the Monterrey Consensus, including **new and additional financial resources**, particularly for developing countries;
- Implementation of the commitments of relevant **major UN conferences**, such as the Third United Nations Conference on the Least Developed Countries and the Global Conference on the Sustainable Development of Small Island Developing States; and
- Implementation of relevant **international agreements** made since 1992, particularly the International Conference on Financing for Development and

the Fourth World Trade Organization (WTO) Ministerial Conference that was held in Doha in 2001, including building on them as part of a process of achieving sustainable development *[81]*.

Enabling financial environment

Governments' first step towards ensuring that the 21st century becomes the century of sustainable development for all will be action to **mobilize and increase the effectiveness of financial resources** and to achieve the national and international economic conditions needed to fulfil the internationally agreed development goals *[82]*. In the common pursuit of growth, poverty eradication and sustainable development, critical challenges are:

* Ensuring necessary **internal conditions**;
* Improved efficacy, coherence and consistency of **macro-economic policies**; and
* An **enabling domestic environment** for mobilizing domestic resources, increasing productivity, reducing capital flight, encouraging the private sector and attracting and making effective use of international investment and assistance.

The international community should support efforts to create such an environment *[83]*.

Foreign direct investment

Greater flows of **foreign direct investment** (FDI) will be facilitated to support sustainable development activities in developing countries, including infrastructure development *[84]*, including through:

* Domestic and international conditions that will increase the flow of FDI to developing countries *[84a]*; and
* Use of **export credits** to encourage sustainable development and FDI *[84b]*.

Official development assistance

Substantial increases in **official development assistance** (ODA) and other resources are needed if developing countries are to achieve the internationally agreed development goals. To build support for ODA and **improve aid effectiveness**, governments will cooperate to improve policies and development strategies at both the national and international levels *[85]*. Actions include:

* Making available increased ODA commitments announced at the International Conference on Financing for Development in Monterrey. Developed countries that have not done so are urged to make concrete

efforts to fulfil the **target of 0.7 per cent of gross national product (GNP) as ODA**, and to implement their commitments on ODA in the Programme of Action for the Least Developed Countries for the Decade 2001–2010. Developing countries are encouraged to build on the progress achieved in ensuring that ODA is used effectively *[85a]*; and

* Targeting ODA more effectively towards poverty eradication, sustained economic growth and sustainable development. Institutions should intensify efforts to **harmonize operational procedures** *[85b]*.

Financial mechanisms and institutions

Full and effective use will be made of **existing financial mechanisms and institutions** *[86]* by actions to:

* Strengthen ongoing efforts to reform the existing **international financial architecture** to foster a transparent, equitable and inclusive system *[86a]*;
* Improve **transparency and information about financial flows** to contribute to stability in the international financial environment. Measures that lessen the impact of **excessive volatility** in short-term capital flows must be considered *[86b]*;
* Ensure that funds are **made available on a timely and predictable basis to international organizations** and agencies for their sustainable development activities *[86c]*;
* Encourage the **private sector, private foundations and civil society** to provide financial and technical assistance to developing countries *[86d]*; and
* Support new and existing **public–private financing mechanisms** to improve infrastructure and benefit small entrepreneurs, small- and medium-sized enterprises (SMEs) and community-based enterprises *[86e]*.

Governments welcomed the third replenishment of the **Global Environment Facility (GEF)**, which was encouraged to leverage additional funds from public and private organizations and to streamline procedures and its project cycle *[87]*. Governments will also explore new public and private **innovative sources of finance** for development, noting the possibility of using **special drawing rights** allocations *[88]*.

Debt

Debt relief and, where appropriate, debt cancellation will be used to reduce unsustainable **debt burdens** and address the debt problems of developing countries, especially the poorest and most heavily indebted ones. There should be an increase in the use of **grants** for the poorest debt-vulnerable countries. Countries are encouraged to develop **national comprehensive strategies** to monitor and manage external liabilities *[89]*. Action is required to:

- Implement the enhanced **heavily indebted poor countries (HIPC) initiative** *[89a]*;
- Encourage the participation of all creditors in the HIPC initiative *[89b]*;
- Bring together international **debtors and creditors** in relevant international forums to restructure unsustainable debt *[89c]*;
- Acknowledge the problems of debt sustainability in some **non-HIPC low-income countries** *[89d]*;
- Encourage exploration of **innovative mechanisms** to address debt problems, including **'debt for sustainable development' swaps** *[89e]*; and
- Ensure that resources provided for debt relief do not detract from ODA *[89f]*.

Doha development round

Trade plays a major role in achieving sustainable development and eradicating poverty. The JPOI encourages WTO members to pursue the work programme agreed at the **Fourth WTO Ministerial Conference in Doha** in 2001 *[90]*, and urges them to:

- Facilitate the accession of developing countries that apply for **WTO membership** *[90a]*;
- Support the **Doha work programme** as a commitment by countries to mainstream appropriate trade policies in their development programmes and policies *[90b]*;
- Implement substantial **trade-related technical assistance and capacity-building**, supporting the Doha Development Agenda Global Trust Fund *[90c]* and implementing the New Strategy for World Trade Organization Technical Cooperation for Capacity-building, Growth and Integration *[90d]*; and
- Support implementation of the Integrated Framework for Trade-related Technical Assistance to Least Developed Countries *[90e]*.

Exports of developing countries

In accordance with the **Doha Ministerial Declaration** (DMD), governments are determined to take concrete action to address the concerns raised by developing countries on implementing WTO agreements and decisions *[91]*. They call on WTO members to:

- Fulfil the commitments of the DMD on **market access**, particularly for products of export interest to developing countries *[92]*;
- Review all **special and differential treatment** provisions with a view to strengthening them and making them more precise *[92a]*;
- Reduce or eliminate **tariffs on non-agricultural products**, especially on products of export interest to developing countries *[92b]*;

- Fulfil, without prejudging the outcome of negotiations, the commitment for comprehensive negotiations initiated under article 20 of the **Agreement on Agriculture**, take note of the **non-trade concerns** reflected in negotiating proposals submitted by WTO members and confirm that these will be taken into account in the negotiations *[92c]*; and
- Work towards the objective of **duty-free and quota-free access for all least developed countries' exports** *[93]*.

Small and vulnerable economies and commodity-dependent countries

Actions include to:

- Actively pursue the WTO work programme related to **small, vulnerable economies** in a way that supports their efforts towards sustainable development *[94]*; and
- Build the capacity of **commodity-dependent countries** to diversify their exports and address the instability of commodity prices and declining terms of trade. Strengthen activities covered by the Second Account of the Common Fund for Commodities to support sustainable development *[95]*.

To enhance the benefits for developing countries and economies in transition from trade liberalization *[96]*, action will be taken to:

- Improve **trade infrastructure and institutions** *[96a]*;
- Increase the capacity of developing countries to **diversify and increase exports** to cope with commodity price instability *[96b]*; and
- Increase the **value added** of developing country exports *[96c]*.

Mutual supportiveness of trade, environment and development

To continue to enhance the **mutual supportiveness of trade, environment and development** *[97]*, action at all levels will:

- Encourage the **WTO committees** on trade and environment and on trade and development to act as a forum for identifying and debating developmental and environmental aspects of the negotiations *[97a]*;
- Support the completion of the Doha Declaration's work programme on subsidies in order to promote sustainable development and encourage the **reform of subsidies that have considerable negative effects on the environment** *[97b]*;
- Encourage cooperation on trade, environment and development between the secretariats of the WTO, the United Nations Committee on Trade and Development (UNCTAD), the United Nations Development Programme

'A strategy for sustainable development involves people who understand what is needed, have the necessary information at their fingertips, are part of an integrated national drive towards a sustainable future, and have participated in the vital decisions that affect them' (Philip Dobie of UNDP, undated).

(UNDP) and the United Nations Environment Programme (UNEP), and other relevant international and regional organizations *[97c]*; and

- Encourage the voluntary use of **environmental impact assessments** as a national-level tool to help identify trade, environment and development linkages *[97d]*.

Mutual supportiveness between the multilateral trading system and multilateral environmental agreements will be promoted in a way that is consistent with sustainable development goals, supportive of the WTO's work programme, and recognizes the importance of maintaining the integrity of both sets of instruments *[98]*.

To complement and support the Doha Declaration and Monterrey Consensus, further action is agreed to **enhance the benefits of trade liberalization**, especially for developing countries and countries with economies in transition *[99]*, by:

- Establishing and strengthening existing **trade and cooperation agreements** aimed achieving sustainable development *[99a]*;
- Supporting voluntary WTO compatible, market-based initiatives to create and expand markets for **environmentally friendly goods and services**, including **organic products** *[99b]*; and
- Introducing measures to simplify, and make more transparent, **domestic regulations and procedures** that affect trade *[99c]*.

'The ability of a country to follow a path of sustainable development is determined by the capabilities of its peoples and institutions. Capacity-building is the sum of efforts needed to nurture, enhance and utilize the skills of people and institutions to progress towards sustainable development' (Capacity 21, UNDP, www.undp.org).

Health and the Agreement on Trade-Related Aspects of Intellectual Property Rights

To address the **public health problems** that affect many developing countries, especially in relation to HIV/AIDS, tuberculosis, malaria and other epidemics, the JPOI reiterates its commitment to the Doha Declaration on the **Trade-Related Aspects of Intellectual Property Rights (TRIPS) Agreement and public health**, and reaffirms that the agreement can and should be interpreted in a manner that is supportive of WTO members' right to protect health and to promote access to **medicines for all** *[100]*.

Trade policy for environmental purposes/ environmental measures

States should cooperate in promoting a **supportive and open international economic system** that leads to economic growth and sustainable development in all countries in order to better address the problems of environmental degradation:

- **Trade policy measures for environmental** purposes should not constitute a means of arbitrary or unjustifiable trade discrimination or a disguised restriction on international trade.

- Unilateral actions to deal with environmental challenges outside the importing country should be avoided.
- As far as possible, environmental measures to address **transboundary or global environmental problems** should be based on international consensus *[101]*.

Human rights

Steps will be taken to avoid **unilateral measures** that are not in accordance with international law and the Charter of the United Nations, and which impede the full achievement of economic and social development by the population of affected countries, particularly women and children, and that creates obstacles that hinder their well-being or full enjoyment of their human rights. This includes the right of everyone to have a standard of living that is adequate for their heath as well as their right to food, medical care and necessary social services. Governments will ensure that food and medicine are not used as tools for political pressure *[102]*.

Right to self-determination

Effective measures will be taken to remove obstacles to the realization of the right of peoples to **self-determination**, particularly peoples living under colonial and foreign occupation *[103]*. This will not be construed as supporting any action that would dismember or impair the territorial integrity or political unity of sovereign and independent states that conduct themselves in compliance with the principle of equal rights and self-determination of peoples, and therefore have a government that represents the whole people of the territory *[104]*.

Environmentally sound technologies/technology transfer

With respect to **environmentally sound technologies** (ESTs), the JPOI focuses on addressing the needs of developing countries and countries with economies in transition, including through the use of **favourable trade terms** such as concessional and preferential terms on a mutually agreed basis *[105]*. Commitments are made to:

- Provide **information** more effectively *[105a]*;
- Improve existing **national institutional capacities** in developing countries on ESTs *[105b]*;
- Facilitate country-driven **technology needs assessments** *[105c]*;
- Establish **legal and regulatory frameworks** in supplier and recipient countries to assist EST transfer *[105d]*; and
- Promote access to, and transfer of, technology related to **early warning systems** and programmes to help reduce the impacts of natural disasters to developing countries *[105e]*.

In order to improve the transfer of technologies to developing countries, especially from country to country and at a regional level *[106]*, urgent action at all levels will:

- Improve the **collaboration among universities, research institutions, government agencies and the private sector** *[106a]*;
- Develop networks of technology and productivity centres, research, training and development institutions and **centres for cleaner production** *[106b]*;
- Create **partnerships** that bring about investment and technology transfer, development and diffusion, sharing of best practices, and collaboration between corporations and research institutes to improve industrial efficiency, agricultural productivity, environmental management and competitiveness *[106c]*;
- Assist with accessing knowledge and ESTs that are publicly owned or in the public domain *[106d]*; and
- Support mechanisms for the **development, transfer and diffusion of ESTs** *[106e]*.

Science and technology

Assistance will be provided to developing countries in building **centres for sustainable development**, enabling them to access a larger share of multilateral and global research and development programmes *[107]*. Their capacity will also be built in **science and technology for sustainable development** through collaboration, partnerships and networking between **centres of scientific excellence** *[108]*.

To improve policy and decision-making at all levels based on better **collaboration between natural and social scientists, and between scientists and policy-makers** *[109]*, urgent action will be taken to:

- Increase the use of scientific knowledge and technology, and the beneficial use of local and indigenous knowledge *[109a]*;
- Make greater use of **integrated scientific assessments, risk assessments and interdisciplinary and inter-sectoral approaches** *[109b]*;
- Support international scientific assessments that help inform decision-making (such as the Intergovernmental Panel on Climate Change – IPCC) with the broad participation of developing country experts *[109c]*;
- Assist developing countries in **implementing science and technology policies** *[109d]*;
- Establish **partnerships** between scientific, public and private institutions, and integrate **scientists' advice** within decision-making bodies *[109e]*; and
- Improve **science-based decision-making**, reaffirming the **precautionary approach** as set out in principle 15 of the Rio Declaration on Environment and Development *[109f]*.

Developing countries' capacities in **environmental protection and management** will be increased *[110]* through urgent actions to:

* Improve the use of science and technology for environmental monitoring and modelling *[110a]*;
* Promote the use of satellite technologies for data collections and better aerial and ground-based observations *[110b]*; and
* Set up or develop **national statistical services** to provide sound data on science education and research and development activities *[110c]*.

Regular channels will be established between policy-makers and the scientific community to deliver science and technology advice in implementing Agenda 21. **Networks on science and education** for sustainable development will help countries to share their knowledge and experiences *[111]*, while **information and communication technologies (ICTs)** will be used to increase the frequency of communication and knowledge-sharing and access to ICTs. This work will build on the efforts of the United Nations Information and Communication Technology Task Force, amongst others *[112]*.

The JPOI calls for support of publicly funded research and development entities in building strategic alliances to create **cleaner production and product technologies** *[113]*, and for the better integration of publicly funded research and development with development programmes *[119]*.

Issues of global public interest

Commitments include to examine **issues of global interest** through open, transparent and inclusive workshops *[114]* and to take concerted action against **international terrorism** *[115]*.

Education

Education is critical for promoting sustainable development and, as such, it is essential to mobilize resources at all levels to complement the efforts of national governments *[116]* towards the following goals and actions:

* The **Millennium Development Goal (MDG)** of ensuring that, by 2015, children everywhere, boys and girls alike, will be able to complete a full course of primary schooling *[116a]*; and
* Providing all children, particularly those living in rural areas and those living in poverty, and especially girls, with the chance to complete a full course of primary education *[116b]*.

Support will be provided to **education, research, public awareness programmes and development institutions** in developing countries and countries with economies in transition *[117]* to:

10

- Sustain educational infrastructures and programmes *[117a]*; and
- Avoid the frequent and serious financial constraints faced by many institutions of higher learning *[117b]*.

The JPOI calls for the **impact of HIV/AIDS on the educational system** to be addressed *[118]* and for resources to be used to improve the integration of sustainable development in education development programmes. Resources need to be allocated for **basic education** *[119]* and **gender disparity** must be eliminated in primary and secondary education by 2005, as well as at all levels of education no later than 2015 to meet the MDGs. These objectives will be achieved with '**gender mainstreaming**' and by creating a gender-sensitive education system *[120]*.

Sustainable development will be integrated within education systems at all levels to promote education as a key agent for change *[121]*. Education for sustainable development will be part of **education action plans** that are relevant to local conditions and lead to community development *[122]*. The JPOI calls for community members to be provided with a wide range of **continuing education** opportunities to end illiteracy and promote life-long learning and sustainable development *[123]*. To support the use of education to promote sustainable development *[124]*, urgent actions will:

- Integrate information and communication technologies (**ICTs**) within school curriculum development, ensuring access by communities and establishing an enabling environment for ICTs *[124a]*;
- Promote greater access by students, researchers and engineers from developing countries to the **universities** and research institutions of developed countries *[124b]*;
- Further implement **United Nations Commission on Sustainable Development (CSD)** work on education for sustainable development [124c]; and
- Recommend that the United Nations General Assembly (UNGA) adopts a **decade of education for sustainable development starting in 2005** *[124d]*.

Capacity-building

Capacity-building initiatives and partnerships will be stepped up, with the focus on human, institutional and infrastructure capacity *[125]*. The JPOI supports initiatives from local to regional levels within **centres of excellence** for education, research and training *[126]*. It also supports stronger capacity-building for developing countries, including the **UNDP's Capacity 21 programme** *[127]* to:

- Assess their own capacity development needs and opportunities at different levels *[127a]*;

- Design capacity-building programmes that will focus on meeting the challenges of globalization and attaining internationally agreed development goals *[127b]*;
- Develop the capacity of civil society and youth to participate in the design and implementation of sustainable development policies and strategies *[127c]*; and
- Build national capacities for effective implementation of Agenda 21 *[127d]*.

Information

Governments will ensure access at the national level to **environmental information, judicial and administrative proceedings and public participation in decision-making**. This relates to principle 10 of the Rio Declaration on Environment and Development (on access to environmental information and public participation): principles 5 (poverty eradication), 7 (common but differentiated responsibilities) and 11 (on the use of environmental legislation and standards) will also be taken into account *[128]*. Actions include:

- Strengthening national and regional **information and statistical services** that are relevant to sustainable development, using disaggregated data *[129]*;
- Working at the national level on **indicators for sustainable development**, including its gender aspects *[130]*; and
- Working in accordance with paragraph 3 of Decision 9/4 of the CSD (on information for decision-making and participation) *[131]*.

The JPOI promotes the development and wider use of **Earth observation technologies**, including satellite remote sensing, global mapping and geographic information systems (GIS). These will help to provide data on environmental impacts, land use and land-use changes *[132]*. Urgent actions will:

- Coordinate **global observing systems** and research programmes, and build capacity to provide integrated global observations *[132a]*;
- Develop information systems that make possible the sharing of valuable data such as **Earth observation data** *[132b]; and*
- Encourage initiatives and partnerships for **global mapping** *[132c]*.

Developing countries, in particular, will be supported in their efforts to *[133]*:

- Collect data that are accurate, long term, consistent and reliable *[133a]*;
- Use **satellite and remote sensing** technologies to improve ground-based observations *[133b]*; and
- Access, explore and use geographic information by using satellite remote sensing, satellite global positioning, mapping and GIS *[133c]*.

Efforts to prevent and lessen the impacts of natural disasters will be supported *[134]* by the provision of affordable **disaster-related information for early-warning** purposes *[134a]* and the translation of data from global meteorological observation systems into timely and useful products *[134b]*.

With respect to **support for decision-making**, the JPOI calls for wider application of **environmental impact assessments** *[135]* and the promotion of methodologies to be used in policies, strategies and projects in sustainable development decision-making at the local and national levels. The choice of methodology should be adequate to country-specific conditions and voluntary *[136]*.

Means of implementation elsewhere in the JPOI

Elements that make up the means of implementation are deeply cross-cutting in nature and occur throughout the Johannesburg Plan of Implementation (JPOI). There are links, in particular, with issues in Chapter V (on globalization) and Chapter XI (on the institutional framework for sustainable development). These relate to the need to create internal national conditions conducive to investment and efforts to promote an open, equitable, rules-based, predictable and non-discriminatory multilateral trading and financial system. Actions that support commitments on finance, capacity-building and information are addressed at different levels (international, regional and national) in Chapter XI. Trade issues are addressed in Chapter V, but also with respect to energy, chemicals, fisheries, biodiversity and forests in Chapter IV. The JPOI includes commitments to provide 'financial and technical assistance' in a wide range of areas. It acknowledges the need to maximize the use of existing resources, including ODA, and to find new and innovative sources of finance. Funding issues related to multilateral agreements and mechanisms occur throughout the JPOI, focusing on areas such as desertification, disaster management, climate change, capacity-building and the sustainable development of small island developing states (SIDS).

TARGETS AND COMMITMENTS

- **Education.** By 2015 ensure that children everywhere, boys and girls alike, will be able to complete a full course of primary schooling (Millennium Development Goal, or MDG).

- **Education.** Eliminate gender disparity in primary and secondary education by 2005 (Dakar Framework for Action on Education for All) and at all levels of education no later than 2015 (MDG).

- **Education.** Recommend a United Nations Decade of Education for Sustainable Development, starting in 2005 (new target).

TARGETS AND COMMITMENTS (CONTD)

Further commitments in Chapter X of the JPOI relate to the MDG on developing a global partnership for development. Broadly, they include efforts to:

- **Finance.** Mobilize and increase the effectiveness of financial resources and achieve the national and international conditions to fulfil internationally agreed development goals; create the necessary conditions to increase foreign direct investment (FDI) in developing countries; build support for official development assistance (ODA); make full and effective use of existing financial mechanisms and institutions; foster a transparent, equitable and inclusive (financial) system; and ensure timely provision of funds to international organizations for their sustainable development activities.

- **Debt.** Reduce unsustainable debt burdens and address the debt problems of developing countries.

- **Trade.** Support the Doha work programme (including its aspects on market access and small, vulnerable economies); enhance the mutual supportiveness of trade, environment and development; address public health problems that affect many developing countries; develop the capacity of commodity-dependent countries; and enhance the benefits of trade liberalization for developing countries and countries with economies in transition.

- **Environmentally sound technologies** (ESTs). Support existing, or establish new, mechanisms for development, transfer and diffusion of ESTs.

- **Science and technology.** Strengthen centres for sustainable development and networking of centres of excellence in developing countries; make greater use of scientific advice and integrated scientific assessments, risk assessments and interdisciplinary and inter-sectoral approaches; and improve use of environmental monitoring and modelling.

- **Education.** Integrate sustainable development within education systems; use education to promote sustainable development; and address the impact of HIV/AIDS on the education system.

- **Capacity-building.** Enhance capacity-building and partnerships with the focus on human, institutional and infrastructure capacity, and on meeting the challenges of globalization and attaining internationally agreed development goals.

TARGETS AND COMMITMENTS (CONTD)

🔅 **Information.** Ensure access at the national level to environmental information and public participation in decision-making (Rio principle 10); undertake further work at the national level on indicators for sustainable development, including gender aspects; strengthen national statistical services; promote wider use of Earth observation technologies and coordination of global observing systems for integrated global observations; make available affordable disaster-related information for early warning; and apply environmental impact assessments and other tools for sustainable development decision-making and policy-making more widely.

EXAMPLES OF INDICATORS FOR MEASURING PROGRESS IN IMPLEMENTATION

🔅 Total official development assistance (ODA) given or received as a percentage of gross national product (GNP) (United Nations Commission on Sustainable Development , or CSD)

🔅 Donor countries reaching their UN target of 0.7 per cent of GNP as ODA (Monterrey Consensus)

🔅 Global monitoring of policies for achieving Millennium Development Goals (MDGs) and Monterrey commitments (World Bank)

🔅 Debt to GNP ratio (CSD)

🔅 Progress reports on implementation of the heavily indebted poor countries (HIPC) initiative (International Monetary Fund, or IMF)

🔅 Number of countries that have eliminated tariffs on goods originating from least developed countries (World Trade Organization, or WTO)

🔅 Expenditure on research and development as a percent of GDP (CSD)

Partnership example

Capacity-building on the applications of information and communication technology (ICT) for the establishment of environmental information systems for sustainable development in Africa – SISEI

Leading partner: United Nations Institute for Training and Research (I INITAR)

Dates: September 2002–December 2005

Significant efforts are underway in Africa to manage natural resources and the environment, involving scientific and technical research, implementation of appropriate programmes, projects in the field and the harnessing of local know-how. The results (products, information, data) represent a unique scientific, technical and cultural heritage for sustainable development and the fight against poverty in Africa. An identified problem is the uneven dispersal of this information through inadequate systems and compartmentalization. This loss of 'institutional memory' is recognized as a major obstacle to sustainable development in Africa.

The SISEI (Système de Circulation d'Information et de Suivi de l'Environnement sur Internet en Afrique) initiative responds to calls in Agenda 21 and other international instruments (the United Nations Framework Convention on Climate Change – UNFCCC – and the Convention on Biological Diversity – CBD) to strengthen the collection and exchange of information. It builds upon several International Telecommunication Union (ITU) conferences where the role of telecommunication and information technologies for environmental protection and sustainable development has been highlighted. SISEI will provide countries and regional organizations with systems for the validation, circulation and harnessing of relevant environmental information with a view to strengthening the participative approach at the different decision-making and operational levels, thereby promoting more informed decision-making. It also encourages the environmental community to share experiences and information. This approach aims to create synergy between human and financial resources, establishing environmental information systems within national programmes, such as development plans, national environmental action plans and poverty eradication plans.

Contact information: United Nations Institute for Training and Research (UNITAR) UNITAR Palais des Nations CH-1211 Genève 10 Suisse www.sisei.net

Resources

Programme of Action for the Least Developed Countries for the Decade 2001–2010

www.un.org/special-rep/ohrlls/ldc/reports.htm
This programme was adopted at the Third United Nations Conference on the Least Developed Countries (LDCs) (Brussels, May 2001) to accelerate development in LDCs. Paragraph 83 relates to implementation of donor commitments on official development assistance (ODA) and support to LDCs with information systems and indicators on aid effectiveness (UN, 2001).

Global Environment Facility (GEF)

www.gefweb.org/
Established 1991, the GEF helps developing countries fund projects that protect the global environment. It is a financial mechanism for international agreements on biodiversity, climate change, persistent organic pollutants, desertification, international waters and the ozone layer. The third replenishment of the GEF Trust Fund (Washington, DC, 6–7 August 2002) completed with about US$2.92 billion.

Heavily Indebted Poor Countries (HIPC) Initiative

www.worldbank.org/hipc/
The HIPC initiative was established in 1996 to reduce the external debt of the poorest countries facing an unsustainable debt situation that can not be resolved through traditional mechanisms. Creditors provide assistance beyond current mechanisms and a trust fund supports activities under HIPC.

Monterrey Consensus

www.un.org/esa/ffd/ffdconf
The Monterrey Consensus was the outcome of the International Conference on Financing for Development (March 2002). Governments committed to increase resources for development. Elements of the consensus include domestic and international finance; trade; debt; development assistance; and reform of international financial and trading systems.

Paris and London Clubs for Debt Restructuring

www.clubdeparis.org/
The Paris Club is an informal body where debt restructuring is negotiated with bilateral official creditors. Its secretariat is the French Ministry of Finance. The London Club is a process for restructuring sovereign debt owed to commercial banks. Each club is formed by the debtor country and has an advisory committee chaired by a leading financial firm. Clubs are dissolved when restructuring is completed.

Doha Ministerial Declaration

wto.org/english/tratop_e/dda_e/dohaexplained_e.htm

The outcome of the Fourth World Trade Organization (WTO) Ministerial (November 2001), the Doha Declaration includes a work programme and negotiating agenda for a WTO Development Round. Elements of the declaration include agriculture; services; market access for non-agricultural products; trade-related aspects of intellectual property rights (TRIPS); trade and competition policy; transparency in government procurement; trade facilitation; WTO rules; trade and environment; electronic commerce; small economics, trade, debt and finance, trade and transfer of technology, technical cooperation and capacity-building; least developed countries (LDCs); and special and differential treatment.

Article 20 of the Agreement on Agriculture

Process adopted under the Agreement on Agriculture (negotiated as part of the Uruguay Round of trade negotiations) to bring agricultural trade issues into the General Agreement on Tariffs and Trade (GATT), now the WTO. Article 20 provides that negotiations for further liberalization of trade, and improvements in rules and preferential treatment for developing countries, would be launched before the end of 1999.

Agreement on Trade-Related Aspects of Intellectual Property Rights (TRIPS)

www.wto.org/

The TRIPS Agreement was negotiated in the Uruguay Round of trade negotiations and sets out minimum standards for the protection of intellectual property rights and procedures for their enforcement. Provisions relate to patents, copyright, trademarks, industrial designs, layout designs for integrated circuits, undisclosed information and geographical indications.

Declaration on the TRIPS Agreement and Public Health

www.wto.org/

Agreed at the Doha Ministerial Meeting on 14 November 2001 (WTO, 2001b), this declaration agrees that the Trade-Related Aspects of Intellectual Property Rights (TRIPS) Agreement should be implemented in a manner supportive of WTO members' right to protect public health and to promote access to medicines for all.

Doha Development Agenda Global Trust Fund (DDAGTF)

www.wto.org/

The DDAGTF was created following the Doha WTO Ministerial Conference in November 2001 to support technical assistance and help developing countries build capacity and participate fully in the Doha Development Agenda. A pledging meeting in March 2002 raised 30 million Swiss francs for the fund.

New Strategy for WTO Technical Cooperation for Capacity-building, Growth and Integration

www.wto.org/
Prepared through the WTO Committee on Trade and Development, this strategy endorses paragraph 38 of the Doha Declaration on technical cooperation and capacity-building, and provides definition, objectives and core elements of a WTO technical assistance comprehensive strategy (WTO, 2001c).

Integrated Framework for Trade-related Technical Assistance to Least Developed Countries

www.wto.org/
This framework was undertaken by six core agencies (International Trade Centre – ITC; International Monetary Fund – IMF; United Nations Conference on Trade and Development – UNCTAD; United Nations Development Programme – UNDP; the World Bank; and WTO) to support developing and least-developed countries in the new round of trade negotiations and the negotiations of the Doha Development Agenda on the basis of complementary expertise of the agencies.

Common Fund for Commodities

www.common-fund.org/
This is an intergovernmental UN financial institution to improve socio-economic development of commodity producers, concentrating on commodity development projects. It is financed through voluntary contributions; capital subscriptions that are transferred to the 'Second Account'; and interest. Voluntary funds are used for either grants or loans. Capital of the Second Account is used for loan-financing of projects. Capital of the First Account is an endowment fund and cannot be used directly.

Dakar Framework for Action on Education for All

www.unesco.org/education/efa/ed_for_all/framework.shtml
Adopted at the World Education Forum in April 2000, the Dakar framework reaffirms the goals set at the World Conference on Education for All agreed at Jomtien, Thailand, in 1990 (UNESCO, 2000).

Decision 9/4 of the United Nations Commission on Sustainable Development (CSD) on Information for Decision-making and Participation, New York, April 2001

www.un.org/esa/sustdev/csd/ecn172001-19e.htm#Decision%209/4
Decision 9/4 offers recommendations for action at different levels to enhance information for decision-making in support of sustainable development.

United Nations Charter

www.un.org/aboutun/charter/
This is a founding UN document, agreed and signed on 26 June 1945, in San Francisco at the United Nations Conference on International Organization. When the charter came into force on 24 October 1945, the UN officially came into being.

Intergovernmental Panel on Climate Change (IPCC)

www.ipcc.ch/
The IPCC assesses the scientific, technical and socio-economic information relevant to understanding the scientific basis of the risk of human-induced climate change, its potential impacts and options for adaptation and mitigation. Reports are based on published and peer-reviewed research. It supports the United Nations Framework Convention on Climate Change (UNFCCC) on methodologies for national greenhouse gas inventories.

United Nations Information and Communication Technology Task Force

www.unicttaskforce.org/
Established 2001, this task force provides overall leadership in the UN on strategies for developing information and communication technologies to bridge the digital divide.

United Nations Development Programme's (UNDP's) Capacity 21

www.undp.org/capacity21/
The UNDP's Capacity 21 Trust Fund has its origins in the 1992 United Nations Conference on Environment and Development (UNCED) and works with countries to build national capacities for implementing Agenda 21.

CONFERENCES, AGREEMENTS AND PROCESSES

General

⧖ United Nations Commission on Sustainable Development (CSD) discussions on 'means of implementation' elements as cross-cutting themes (1993–1999)

⧖ Barbados Programme of Action on the Sustainable Development of Small Island Developing States (BPoA) (1994)

⧖ Programme of Action for the Least Developed Countries for the Decade (2001–2010)

⧖ Third United Nations Conference on the Least Developed Countries, Brussels (2001)

⧖ World Trade Organization (WTO) Ministerial Meeting, Doha (2001)

CONFERENCES, AGREEMENTS AND PROCESSES (CONTD)

⏳ WTO Ministerial Meeting, Cancun (2003)

⏳ International Meeting on the Barbados Programme of Action, Mauritius (2004)

⏳ WTO Ministerial Meeting (2005)

Finance

⏳ Heavily indebted poor countries (HIPC) initiative established (1996)

⏳ Adoption of the Monterrey Consensus at the International Conference on Financing for Development, Monterrey (2002)

⏳ Third replenishment of the Global Environment Facility (GEF) Trust Fund completed (2002)

⏳ International conference to review implementation of the Monterrey Consensus (details to be decided not later than 2005)

Trade

⏳ World Trade Organization (WTO) Ministerial Meeting, Doha (2001)

⏳ Pledging conference held for the Doha Development Agenda Global Trust Fund (DDAGTF) (2002)

⏳ WTO Ministerial Meeting, Cancun (2003)

⏳ Africa, Caribbean and Pacific group of countries (ACP)/European Union (EU) Phase II negotiations on economic partnership agreements commence (2003)

⏳ WTO Ministerial Meeting (2005)

Education

⏳ Dakar Framework for Action on Education for All adopted by the World Education Forum in Thailand (2000)

⏳ Decade of Education for Sustainable Development commences (2005)

Information

⏳ Plenipotentiary Conference of the International Telecommunication Union (ITU) (1998)

⏳ Decision 9/4 of the United Nations Commission on Sustainable Development (CSD) on information for decision-making and participation (2001)

⏳ World Summit on the Information Society (WSIS): Phase I, Geneva (December 2003); Phase II, Tunis (November 2005)

Key United Nations bodies and Bretton Woods institutions

Finance

- Global Environment Facility (GEF)
- International Monetary Fund (IMF)
- United Nations Development Programme (UNDP)
- United Nations Economic and Social Council (ECOSOC)
- World Bank

Trade

- United Nations Conference on Trade and Development (UNCTAD)
- United Nations Development Programme (UNDP)
- United Nations Environment Programme (UNEP) Economics and Trade Unit
- World Trade Organization (WTO)

Education

- Joint United Nations Programme on HIV/AIDS (UNAIDS)
- United Nations Educational, Scientific and Cultural Organization (UNESCO)

Capacity-building

- United Nations Commission on Sustainable Development (CSD)
- United Nations Conference on Trade and Development (UNCTAD)
- United Nations Development Programme (UNDP) Capacity 21 (and successor initiative, Capacity 2015)
- United Nations Environment Programme (UNEP)
- United Nations Human Settlements Programme (UN-Habitat)

Information

- High-level Summit Organizing Committee (HLSOC) coordinating efforts in the UN system for the World Summit on the Information Society (WSIS) (includes FAO, IAEA, ICAO, ILO, IMO, ITU, UNCTAD, UNDP, UNEP, UNESCO, UNHCR, UNIDO, UPU, WHO, WIPO, WMO, WTO, UNITAR, UN Regional Economic Commissions, World Bank)
- International Strategy for Disaster Reduction (ISDR)
- International Telecommunication Union (ITU)
- United Nations Educational, Scientific and Cultural Organization (UNESCO)
- United Nations Environment Programme (UNEP)

References

Commonwealth Secretariat (2001) 'Rio+10 – Key issues and concerns related to implementation of the Rio Agreements: Technology transfer, finance, capacity-building and global governance for sustainable development', Paper for the Commonwealth Consultative Group on Environment, London, CCGE(01)1, www.thecommonwealth.org/

Commonwealth Secretariat (2003) *World Economic Situation and Prospects (with particular reference to the Commonwealth)*, London, Commonwealth Finance Ministers Meeting, FMM(03)3, p2

Dobie, P (undated) 'Models for national strategies: Building capacity for sustainable development', *Capacity 21 (UNDP) Series, Approaches to Sustainability*, UNDP, New York

IIF (Institute of International Finance, Inc) (2003). *Capital Flows to Emerging Market Economies*, 21 September 2003, www.iif.com

Töpfer, K (2002) 'Towards Johannesburg', *Our Planet*, UNEP, vol 13, no 1, p20

UN (United Nations) (2001) *Programme of Action for the Least Developed Countries for the Decade 2001–2010*, Adopted by the Third United Nations Conference on the Least Developed Countries in Brussels on 20 May 2001, UN, New York, 8 June 2001, p51 (A/CONF.191/11)

UN (2002) *Report of the International Conference on Financing for Development, Monterrey, Mexico, 18–22 March 2002*, UN, New York (A/CONF.198/11)

UNEP (2002) *Global Environment Outlook 3*, Earthscan, London

UNESCO (United Nations Educational, Scientific and Cultural Organization) (2000) *The Dakar Framework for Action, Education for All: Meeting our Collective Commitments*, Adopted by the World Education Forum, Dakar, Senegal, 26–28 April 2000, UNESCO, Paris (ED-2000/WS/27)

WRI, in collaboration with UNEP, World Bank and UNDP (2003) *World Resources 2002–2004: Decisions for the Earth – Balance, Voice and Power*, WRI, Washington, DC, p165

WTO (World Trade Organization) (1999) *The Legal Texts: The Results of the Uruguay Round of Multilateral Trade Negotiations*, Cambridge University Press, Cambridge

WTO (2001a) *Ministerial Declaration*, Adopted 14 November 2001, WTO Ministerial Conference Fourth Session, Doha, 9–14 November 2001, WTO, Geneva, 20 November 2001 (WT/MIN(01)/DEC/1)

WTO (2001b) *Declaration on the TRIPS Agreement and Public Health*, Adopted on 14 November 2001, Ministerial Conference Fourth Session, Doha, 9–14 November 2001, WTO, Geneva. (WT/MIN(01)/DEC/2)

WTO (2001c) *A New Strategy for WTO Technical Cooperation: Technical Cooperation for Capacity-building, Growth and Integration*, WTO, Geneva, Committee on Trade and Development, 21 September 2001 (WT/COMTD/W/90)

Institutional Framework for Sustainable Development

11

 ## Context

A reform and strengthening of institutions, and the wider framework within which they work, is needed to support sustainable development. The integration of economic, social and environmental policies continues to challenge institutions at all levels (UNEP, 2002). Wider participation by all stakeholders and good governance are also needed, and these are based on greater accountability, transparency, access to information, equity and social justice. Such issues have been well recognized. In 2002, the **Human Development Report** called for more democratic principles in global institutions and reiterated not only the need for new frameworks to be efficient and effective, but also to be just, equitable and conducive to human development (UNDP, 2002). Similarly, the 2002–2004 World Resources Institute (WRI) report **Decisions for the Earth: Balance, Voice and Power** makes it clear that 'poor environmental governance – decisions taken without transparency, participation of all stakeholders, and full accountability – is a failure we can no longer live with in an era when human decisions, not natural processes, dominate the global environment' (WRI, 2003). Others have noted that voluntary processes and non-governmental organizations (NGOs) could also benefit from improved governance and processes.

Discussions on institutional reform in the run-up to the World Summit on Sustainable Development (WSSD) looked for greater consistency within and between different sectors and at all levels of policy and decision-making. Strengthening the institutional framework for sustainable development at the regional level was a major focus of discussions. With respect to the UN, the emphasis was on coordination mechanisms and closer integration of the three pillars of sustainable development, as well as reform of the United Nations Commission on Sustainable Development (CSD) to maximize its effectiveness. There were inputs to the process from the United Nations Environment Programme (UNEP), which undertook an extensive process to examine 'international environmental governance', including the structure, role and financing of UNEP; coordination of multilateral environmental agreements; capacity-building and technology transfer; and UN coordination. The

KEY WORDS

* **United Nations General Assembly (UNGA)**

* **United Nations Economic and Social Council (ECOSOC)**

* **United Nations Commission on Sustainable Development (CSD)**

* **international institutions**

* **United Nations Regional Economic Commissions**

* **regional development strategies**

* **national institutional frameworks**

* **national strategies for sustainable development**

* **sustainable development councils**

* **public participation**

* **local authorities**

* **participation of major groups**

* **environment and human rights**

AT A GLANCE

▣ Good governance at all levels is essential for sustainable development.

▣ It requires a stronger institutional framework at every level: international, regional, national and local.

▣ There should be full participation of all stakeholders through transparent and accountable processes.

Johannesburg Plan of Implementation (JPOI) recognizes these processes and provides recommendations to strengthen and reform governance at every level.

 Chapter XI in summary

An **effective institutional framework** for sustainable development is essential to full implementation of Agenda 21 and the WSSD, and to meet emerging challenges. Measures to strengthen the framework must build on Agenda 21, the Programme for the Further Implementation of Agenda 21 (1997) and the Rio Declaration. Actions should promote **internationally agreed development goals**, including the Millennium Development Goals (MDGs), taking into account the Monterrey Consensus and outcomes of major UN conferences/international agreements since 1992. The framework should respond to the needs of all countries, especially developing countries, and include the means for implementation. It should lead to stronger international, regional, national and local institutions and organizations *[137]*.

'We are made wise not by the recollections of our past, but by the responsibility for our future'
(George Bernard Shaw, from A Treatise on Parents and Children).

Good governance is essential for sustainable development. Sustained economic growth, poverty eradication and employment opportunities depend upon sound economic policies, democratic institutions and improved infrastructure. Other essential elements are **freedom**; **peace** and **security**; **domestic stability**; respect for **human rights**, including the **right to development**; the **rule of law**; **gender equality**; **market-orientated policies**; and an overall commitment to **just and democratic societies** *[138]*.

Objectives

Measures are required to strengthen **institutional arrangements** at all levels, using the framework of Agenda 21 *[139]* to:

- Strengthen **commitments** towards sustainable development *[139a]*;
- Balance the **integration** of economic, social and environmental dimensions *[139b]*;
- Strengthen **implementation** of Agenda 21 by mobilizing resources and capacity-building programmes, particularly for developing countries *[139c]*;

- Improve **coherence, coordination and monitoring** *[139d]*;
- Promote the **rule of law** and **strengthen governmental institutions** *[139e]*;
- Increase **effectiveness and efficiency** by limiting duplication/overlap of activities by international organizations within and outside the UN *[139f]*;
- Improve involvement of **civil society** and other **stakeholders** in implementing Agenda 21, promoting transparency and broad **public participation** *[139g]*;
- Strengthen capacities at all levels, particularly at the local level and in developing countries *[139h]*; and
- Strengthen **international cooperation** towards implementation of Agenda 21 and the WSSD *[139i]*.

International level

The **international community** *[140]* should:

- **Integrate** sustainable development goals in the work of relevant UN bodies, the Global Environment Facility (GEF) and international financial and trade institutions, taking into account national sustainable development approaches *[140a]*;
- Strengthen **collaboration**, within and between organizations in the UN system, international financial institutions, the GEF and the World Trade Organization (WTO), using the United Nations Chief Executives Board for Coordination, the United Nations Development Group, the Environment Management Group and other coordinating bodies. Step up inter-agency collaboration, especially at operational level and through partnerships *[140b]*;
- Better integrate the **three dimensions of sustainable development** policies and programmes. Promote sustainable development in the work of organizations that focus primarily on social issues. Strengthen the **social dimension** of sustainable development by emphasizing follow-up to the WSSD and by supporting social protection systems *[140c]*;
- Fully implement UNEP's decision on **international environmental governance** and invite the 57th United Nations General Assembly (UNGA) to consider the issue of universal membership for UNEP *[140d]*;
- Complete negotiations on a comprehensive **UN convention against corruption**, including on repatriating funds illicitly acquired back to countries of origin *[140e]*;
- Promote **corporate responsibility, accountability** and **exchange of best practices** through multistakeholder dialogues and other initiatives *[140f]*; and
- Act at all levels to implement the **Monterrey Consensus** *[140g]*.

The JPOI recognizes the importance of **good governance** at the international level, emphasizing the need to promote **global economic governance** by

'Real generosity towards the future lies in giving all to the present' (Albert Camus, French novelist, 1913–1960).

addressing international finance, trade, technology and investment patterns that affect the prospects of developing countries. The international community should support structural and macro-economic reform, a comprehensive solution to the external debt problem and increasing market access for developing countries. Efforts to reform the international financial 'architecture' need to be sustained with greater transparency and the participation of developing countries in decision-making. A universal, rules-based, open, non-discriminatory and equitable multilateral trading system, and meaningful trade liberalization, can substantially stimulate worldwide development, benefiting all countries *[141]*.

A vibrant and effective UN system is fundamental to international cooperation on sustainable development. This requires a firm commitment to the ideal of the United Nations, principles of international law, and the United Nations Charter, and to strengthening the UN system and other multilateral institutions and their operations. States should fulfill their commitment to negotiate and finalize a **UN convention against all forms of corruption**, including the repatriation of illicitly acquired funds, and promote cooperation to **eliminate money laundering** *[142]*.

'The United Nations once dealt only with governments. By now we know that peace and prosperity cannot be achieved without partnerships involving governments, international organizations, the business community and civil society. In today's world, we depend on each other'
(UN Secretary-General Kofi Annan, cited in WRI, 2003).

United Nations General Assembly (UNGA)

UNGA should adopt sustainable development as a key element of the overarching framework for UN activities, particularly to help achieve the MDGs and give overall political direction to implementing Agenda 21 *[143]*.

United Nations Economic and Social Council (ECOSOC)

Implementing its role as the central coordinating mechanism of the UN system, and to promote the implementation of Agenda 21 by strengthening system-wide coordination *[144]*, ECOSOC should:

- Increase its **role in overseeing system-wide coordination** and the balanced integration of the economic, social and environmental aspects of UN approaches to promote sustainable development *[144a]*;
- Organize **consultations** on themes related to Agenda 21 implementation *[144b]*;
- Make full use of its high-level coordination, operational activities and the general segments to take into account all aspects of the UN work on sustainable development. Encourage active participation of all major groups in high-level segments and the work of functional commissions *[144c]*;
- Promote greater coordination and effectiveness in the work of the **functional commissions** and other bodies responsible for implementing Agenda 21 *[144d]*;
- Transfer the work of the **Committee on Energy and Natural Resources for Development** to the CSD *[144e]*;

- Ensure a **close link** between the roles of ECOSOC in following up **WSSD** and the **Monterrey Consensus**. Explore arrangements for meetings with Bretton Woods institutions and the WTO, as set out in the Monterrey Consensus *[144f]*; and
- Intensify efforts to ensure that **gender mainstreaming** is integral to its work on Agenda 21 *[144g]*.

United Nations Commission on Sustainable Development (CSD)

The CSD should continue as the UN's high-level commission on sustainable development and serve as a forum on integrating its three aspects (economic, social and environmental). The CSD needs to be strengthened, including with an enhanced role in **reviewing and monitoring progress** on Agenda 21 and fostering **coherence** in implementation, initiatives and partnerships *[145]*.

The CSD should give greater emphasis to actions enabling implementation at all levels, including **partnerships** involving governments, international organizations and relevant stakeholders *[146]*. The CSD should:

- Review and evaluate progress and promote Agenda 21's implementation *[147a]*;
- Focus on **cross-sectoral aspects of sectoral issues**, and provide a forum on integrating policies, facilitating interactions among ministers who deal with the different dimensions of sustainable development *[147b]*;
- Address new **challenges and opportunities** on Agenda 21's implementation *[147c]*;
- Limit **negotiating sessions** to every two years *[147d]*; and
- Address a **limited number of themes** each session *[147e]*.

In facilitating implementation *[148]*, the CSD should:

- Review progress and promote further implementation of Agenda 21, identifying **constraints and making recommendations** for dealing with these *[148a]*;
- Act as a focal point for discussing partnerships, sharing lessons learned, progress and best practices *[148b]*;
- Review financial assistance, technology transfer and capacity-building, making full use of existing information and considering more effective use of **national reports and regional experience** *[148c]*;
- Provide a forum for exchanging experiences on **sustainable development planning, decision-making** and implementation of **sustainable development strategies** *[148d]*; and
- Take into account significant legal developments in sustainable development and the role of intergovernmental bodies in promoting implementation *[148e]*.

'While many viewed the official outcomes of the WSSD as modest, at best, their limitations probably reflect the difficulty of reconciling apparent conflicts between the environmental, social and economic aspects of sustainable development as nations perceive them today' (Speth, 2003).

The CSD was requested to consider and take decisions on its future work programme during its 12th session in May 2003 *[149]*. Such issues included:

- Balanced implementation of mandates of CSD contained in the General Assembly resolution 47/191 *[149a]*;
- More direct and substantial involvement of **international organizations** and **major groups** *[149b]*;
- Greater consideration of **scientific contributions** and involvement of scientific networks *[149c]*;
- Furthering the contribution of **educators** *[149d]*; and
- The scheduling and length of future meetings *[149e]*.

The CSD should take further measures to promote best practices, lessons learned and use of contemporary methods of data collection and dissemination *[150]*.

International institutions

International institutions, including the financial institutions, the WTO and the GEF, acting within their mandates, should work to *[151]*:

- Promote effective and collective support to implement Agenda 21 *[151a]*; and
- Enhance effectiveness/coordination to implement Agenda 21, the WSSD, relevant parts of the Millennium Declaration, the Monterrey Consensus and the Doha WTO Ministerial Conference *[151b]*.

The JPOI requests the United Nations Secretary-General to promote system-wide cooperation/coordination and information exchange, using the United Nations System Chief Executives Board for Coordination, and to keep ECOSOC and the CSD informed of actions being taken to implement Agenda 21 *[152]*.
The JPOI also calls for action to:

- Significantly strengthen support for United Nations Development Programme (UNDP) capacity-building, drawing on the Capacity 21 programme *[153]*;
- Strengthen cooperation between UNEP and other UN agencies/bodies, the Bretton Woods institutions and the WTO *[154]*; and
- Strengthen the contribution of UNEP, the United Nations Human Settlements Programme (UN-Habitat), UNDP and the United Nations Conference on Trade and Development (UNCTAD) to sustainable development and Agenda 21, especially in capacity-building *[155]*.

To promote effective implementation of Agenda 21 at the international level *[156]*:

'People are no longer satisfied with declarations. They demand firm action and concrete results. They expect that the nations of the world, having identified a problem, will have the vitality to act' (the late Olaf Palme, former Swedish prime minister, whose country hosted the Stockholm Conference in 1971, cited in UNEP, 2002).

- Reduce the number and length of international meetings, and allow more time for discussion of practical matters related to implementation *[156a]*;
- Encourage partnership initiatives to implement the WSSD, taking note of preparatory work for the summit *[156b]*; and
- Make full use of information and communication technologies *[156c]*.

Strengthening the international institutional framework is an evolutionary process. It is necessary to keep institutional arrangements under review, identify gaps, eliminate duplication of function and continue to strive to greater integration, efficiency and coordination *[157]*.

Regional level

Implementation of Agenda 21 and the WSSD at **regional and sub-regional** levels should be pursued through UN Regional Commissions and other regional/sub-regional bodies *[158]*, with **improved cooperation** between the regional commissions, UN funds, programmes and agencies, regional development banks and other institutions, and increased support for the development and implementation of regionally agreed sustainable development strategies and action plans *[159]*.

    UN Regional Commissions *[160]* are encouraged to:

'Action cannot be delivered by governments alone. It will require partnerships between all the relevant stakeholders, including governments, local communities, the private sector, non-governmental organizations and international agencies' (Mohammed Valli Moosa, Minister of Environmental Affairs and Tourism, Republic of South Africa, 2002).

- Promote the three pillars of sustainable development in a balanced way and enhance their **own capacity**, with external support where appropriate *[160a]*;
- Facilitate integration of sustainable development within the work of regional, sub-regional and other bodies – for example, by strengthening the exchange of information, national experience, best practice, case studies and partnerships *[160b]*;
- **Mobilize** technical assistance and funding, including for regionally and sub-regionally agreed sustainable development programmes *[160c]*; and
- Continue to promote multi-stakeholder participation and partnerships to implement Agenda 21 at regional/sub-regional levels *[160d]*.

Regionally/sub-regionally agreed sustainable development initiatives, such as the **New Partnership for African Development (NEPAD)** and the **Barbados Programme of Action on the Sustainable Development of Small Island Developing States (BPoA)** should be supported *[161]*.

National level

To strengthen implementation at the national level, **states** *[162]* should:

- Promote coherent/coordinated approaches to **institutional frameworks** for sustainable development at all national levels, including establishing or strengthening mechanisms or authorities *[162a]*; and

- Take immediate steps to progress **national strategies for sustainable development** and begin their implementation by 2005. Support strategies through international cooperation. Where applicable, these could be formulated as poverty reduction strategies, incorporating the three dimensions of sustainable development *[162b]*.

Each country has the primary responsibility for its own sustainable development and the role of national policies and development strategies cannot be overemphasized. Countries should promote sustainable development at the **national level** by:

- Enacting clear and effective **laws** and strengthening **governmental institutions**, including infrastructure and fair, transparent and accountable administrative and judicial institutions *[163]*; and
- Promoting **public participation** – for example, through access to information regarding legislation, regulations, activities, policies and programmes. Also, foster full public participation in sustainable development policy formulation and implementation, enabling women to participate fully and equally *[164]*.

The JPOI promotes **sustainable development councils** or other national/local coordinating structures to provide a high-level focus on sustainable development policies, furthered by multi-stakeholder participation *[165]*. It also calls for the **support** of country efforts to improve national/local institutional arrangements for sustainable development. This could include cross-sectoral approaches in formulating strategies for sustainable development (for example, poverty reduction strategies; aid coordination; participatory approaches and enhancing policy analysis, management and implementation capacity) and mainstreaming gender perspectives in these activities *[166]*.

The role and capacity of **local authorities** and other **stakeholders** in implementing Agenda 21 and the WSSD, and in supporting local Agenda 21, should be enhanced. In this, the JPOI encourages partnerships between local authorities, and other levels of government and stakeholders – for example, as called for in the Habitat Agenda *[167]*.

Major groups

- Enhance partnerships between governmental and **non-governmental actors**, including all **major groups** and **voluntary groups** *[168]*.
- Acknowledge the consideration being given to the possible relationship between **environment and human rights**, including the right to development, with full and transparent participation of member states of the UN and observer states *[169]*.
- Promote and support **youth participation** in sustainable development activities – for example, by supporting local **youth councils** or their equivalents *[170]*.

' Improved environmental governance will help us to deliver results – not simply for their obvious and important environmental ends, but because they have other beneficial impacts on economies, on societies and on the health of people... On this small planet, the fate of all people is bound together. Improving the well-being of any improves it for all... Sustainable development is therefore ultimately about our relationships with each other and with the planet on which we live. Future progress will not come from expressions of intent but from changes to the underlying structures that govern those relationships'
(David Andersen, Canadian Minister of the Environment and President of UNEP's Governing Council, 2002).

Institutional framework issues elsewhere in the JPOI

The Johannesburg Plan of Implementation (JPOI) is interwoven with references to issues and challenges that fall under the heading of governance: institutions, institutional structures, accountability and transparency, legal issues, partnerships, participation, stakeholders and major groups (including indigenous people, children and women). The need for good governance is stated early on (JPOI, Chapter I) and appears throughout the text. The JPOI states that efforts to strengthen the institutional framework for sustainable development should based upon the Rio principles. Chapters V and X include references to governance, with recommendations related to finance and trade, and the role of science, technology, information and education. The regional chapters, particularly Chapter VIII (Africa) refers to institutional changes required to lever current systems towards sustainable development. References to partnerships are found in every chapter of the JPOI.

Other cross-cutting themes

Other themes include:

- Governance;
- Participation;
- Finance (on international finance institutions);
- Trade (on international trade institutions);
- Stakeholders;
- Major groups;
- Youth and children;
- Indigenous people, communities and knowledge;
- Women and gender equality;
- Local authorities;
- Scientific and technological community;
- Farmers/fishers;
- Business and industry; and
- NGOs.

'Here in Johannesburg you have failed us! Signatures do not feed people. Words on paper do not stop deforestation. Where are the mechanisms? Where are the time frames? Where are the commitments?' (Youth spokeswoman Catherine Kampling in a statement during the Youth Caucus, which presented the concerns of young people to the final session of the WSSD, 2003).

TARGETS AND COMMITMENTS

* **National strategies.** Take immediate steps to make progress in the formulation and elaboration of national strategies for sustainable development and begin their implementation by 2005 *[162]*.

* **Governance.** Adopt new measures to strengthen institutional arrangements for sustainable development at international, regional, national and local levels *[139]*.

* **United Nations Commission on Sustainable Development (CSD).** Enhance the role of the CSD, including in reviewing/monitoring implementation of Agenda 21 and fostering coherence of implementation, initiatives and partnerships *[145]*.

* **Integrated approach.** Facilitate the integration of environmental, social and economic dimensions of sustainable development within the work programmes of the United Nations Regional Commissions *[160, 160a, 160d]*.

EXAMPLES OF INDICATORS FOR MEASURING PROGRESS IN IMPLEMENTATION

* Does a country have a national sustainable development strategy (United Nations Commission on Sustainable Development, or CSD)?

* Is the national sustainable development strategy being implemented? What is its degree of effectiveness (CSD)?

* Is there implementation of multilateral environmental agreements? What is the ratio between agreements legislated for and agreements ratified (CSD)?

* Do local authorities have Local Agenda 21 plans? More than 6400 local governments in 113 countries have adopted or are in the process of formulating Local Agenda 21 plans (ICLEI, 2002).

Partnership example

Partnership for principle 10 (PP10)

Leading partner: World Resources Institute (WRI)

Dates: 2002–2012

Principle 10 of the Rio Declaration (1992) commits national governments to an inclusive process of public participation in environmental decisions. It aims to improve conditions for good environmental governance at the national level and increase citizen access to environmental information, participation and justice in environmental decision-making by translating these principles into action. It also:

- Promotes transparent, inclusive and accountable decision-making at the national level.

- Provides a common forum for governments, civil society organizations, donors and other groups to work together to implement practical solutions that provide the public with access to information, participation and justice for environmentally sustainable decisions.

- Strengthens the implementation of Agenda 21 goals for inclusive and informed decision-making for sustainable development.

- Addresses the main implementation gaps in national systems for public participation identified through independent assessments, in partnership with the Access Initiative.

Common gaps include:

- Poor and insufficient access to information about water quality.

- Lack of access to information about the risks and pollution from industrial facilities.

- Poor participation in policy development in 'real' industrial sectors.

- poor participation in project-level decisions.

- Poor enabling conditions for access to justice, including high costs and limited standing.

PP10 seeks to address these gaps by:

- Addressing deficits in the framework for public participation.

- Building capacity of the government to support public participation.

- Building capacity of the public to monitor progress and use the system.

Early partners included the United Nations Development Programme (UNDP); the World Bank; the European Union (EU); European governments, including UK, Italy and Hungary, as well as Uganda and Tanzania; and a diverse range of civil society organizations.

Contact information: World Resources Institute (WRI) 10 G Street, NE (Suite 800) Washington, DC 20002 US www.pp10.org

Resources

The United Nations World Summit for Social Development, 1995, and Five-year Review, June 2000

www.un.org/esa/socdev/wssd/index.htm

This summit addressed the three core themes: poverty, unemployment and social integration. Governments agreed on the need to put people at the centre of the development process. 186 countries adopted the Copenhagen Declaration on Social Development and the Programme of Action and ten commitments covering the core themes.

United Nations Environment Programme (UNEP) Decision on International Environmental Governance (7th Session)

www.unep.org/governingbodies/gc/specialsessions/gcss_vii/Documents/ k0200009.pdf

This was a two-year review addressing the strengths and weaknesses of international environmental governance, providing recommendations for reform.

Global Ministerial Environment Forum

www.unep.org/malmo/malmo_minsterial.htm

At this meeting of environment ministers, in Sweden in May 2000, the Malmö Ministerial Declaration expressing deep concern about the increasing rate of deterioration of the environment and the natural resource base was adopted.

United Nations Economic and Social Council (ECOSOC)

Under overall authority of the United Nations General Assembly (UNGA), ECOSOC coordinates the economic and social work of the UN and the broader UN system; is the central forum for discussing international economic and social issues; plays a key role in fostering international cooperation for development; and consults with non-governmental organizations (NGOs), forming a link between the UN and civil society.

United Nations Commission on Sustainable Development (CSD)

Created in 1992 as a follow-up to UNCED, the CSD is also known as the Earth Summit. See the chapter on implementing the WSSD: The role of the United Nations Commission on sustainable development, for detailed information.

United Nations Development Programme (UNDP) and Capacity-building

www.undp.org

The UN global development network helps countries to build their own national capacity to achieve sustainable development by developing and sharing knowledge and best practices, building partnerships and mobilizing resources towards the Millennium Development Goals (MDGs).

United Nations Regional Commissions

Five commissions (for Europe, Africa, Latin America and the Caribbean, Asia and the Pacific, and Western Asia) promote economic development and strengthened economic relations in their respective regions.

New Partnership for African Development (NEPAD) (see Chapter 8, Resources)

Adopted at the 37th session of the Organization of African Unity in 2001, the New Partnership for African Development is a vision and strategic framework for Africa's renewal. NEPAD arises out of a mandate given by the Organization of African Unity to five initiating Heads of State (Algeria, Egypt, Nigeria, Senegal, South Africa) to develop an integrated socio-economic framework document for Africa.

Barbados Programme of Action on the Sustainable Development of Small Island Developing States (BPoA) (see Chapter 7, Resources)

Agreed in Barbados in 1994, the BPoA is a 14 point action plan which addresses the special development needs of Small Island developing States.

National Strategies for Sustainable Development

Defined by the Organisation for Economic Co-operation and Development (OECD)/Development Assistance Committee (DAC) as a 'strategic and participatory process of analysis, debate, capacity strengthening, planning and action towards sustainable development'. A target for implementing these plans (agreed at the 1997 Earth Summit review) is 2005.

Sustainable development councils

www.ncsdnetwork.org
National Councils for Sustainable Development (NCSD) seek to strengthen civic society participation in local and multi-stakeholder decision-making mechanisms and activities related to the implementation of the United Nations Conference on Environment and Development (UNCED) agreements. The Earth Council (an independent, international body) has, since 1992, been instrumental in promoting the creation and strengthening of NCSD.

Local Agenda 21 (LA21)

The original aim, as set by Agenda 21, was to develop a local plan for sustainable development, focusing on key issues, including poverty, health and livelihoods, as well as resource and environmental issues, by 1996, later revised to 2000. LA21 is also about the process of building partnerships at the local level between different sectors to implement the LA21 plans. It is a continuing process rather than a single activity, event or document.

UN-Habitat (United Nations Human Settlements Programme)

www.unhabitat.org/governance

Major groups (see Background to this publication, pxviii)

In recognizing the contribution that civil society makes to the achievement of sustainable development, Agenda 21 clearly defines nine major groups. These are:

- NGOs
- Business and industry
- Trade unions and their workers
- Farmers
- Indigenous people
- Local authorities
- Children and young persons
- Women
- Scientific and technical community

The WSSD went one stage further to formally recognize the role and responsibility of major groups in implementing Agenda 21 and the Johannesburg Plan of Implementation and encouraged their full participation in the follow-up to the World Summit on Sustainable Development.

CONFERENCES, AGREEMENTS AND PROCESSES

Charter of the United Nations (1945)

Universal Declaration of Human Rights (1948)

International Covenant on Economic, Social and Cultural Rights (1976)

Declaration on the Right to Development (1986)

Agenda 21, Rio Declaration, United Nations Conference on Environment and Development (UNCED) (1992)

Barbados Programme of Action on the Sustainable Development of Small Island Developing States (BPoA) (1994)

World Summit for Social Development, Copenhagen (1995)

General Assembly resolutions 47/191 (1992), 48/162 (1994) and 50/227 (1996)

Programme for the Further Implementation of Agenda 21 (1997)

World Summit for Social Development's five-year review, Geneva (2000)

Millennium Declaration (2000)

CONFERENCES, AGREEMENTS AND PROCESSES (CONTD)

⧗ Fourth World Trade Organization (WTO) Ministerial Meeting, Doha (2001)

⧗ New Partnership for African Development (NEPAD) (2001)

⧗ Monterrey Consensus, Finance for Development International Conference (2002)

⧗ Draft United Nations Convention against Corruption (2003, ongoing)

Key United Nations bodies and Bretton Woods institutions

International

⬚ Global Environment Facility (GEF)

⬚ International Monetary Fund (IMF)

⬚ United Nations Commission on Sustainable Development (CSD)

⬚ United Nations Development Group

⬚ United Nations Development Programme (UNDP)

⬚ United Nations Economic and Social Council (ECOSOC)

⬚ United Nations Environment Management Group

⬚ United Nations Environment Programme (UNEP) Governing Council/Global Ministerial Environment Forum

⬚ United Nations General Assembly (UNGA)

⬚ United Nations System Chief Executives Board for Coordination

⬚ World Bank

⬚ World Trade Organization (WTO)

Regional

⬚ Regional development banks

⬚ United Nations funds

⬚ United Nations programmes and agencies

⬚ United Nations Regional Economic Commissions

National

⬚ Local authorities

⬚ National governments

> ### Key United Nations bodies and Bretton Woods institutions (*contd*)
>
> ☼　United Nations Development Programme (UNDP) (Capacity 2015)
>
> ☼　United Nations Human Settlements Programme (UN-Habitat)
>
> ### Major groups
>
> ☼　United Nations Commission on Human Rights (UNCHR)
>
> ☼　United Nations Commission on Sustainable Development (CSD)
>
> ☼　United Nations Committee on Economic, Social and Cultural Rights
>
> ☼　United Nations Economic and Social Council (ECOSOC)
>
> ☼　United Nations High Commissioner for Human Rights
>
> ☼　United Nations Human Settlements Programme (UN-Habitat)

 # References

Anderson, D (2002) 'Beyond Brackets', *Our Planet*, UNEP, vol 13, no 2, pp11–12

DESA (United Nations Department of Economic and Social Affairs) (2002) *Johannesburg Summit 2002: Key Outcomes of the Summit*, DESA, New York, www.johannesburg summit.org/html/documents/summit_docs/2009_keyoutcomes_commitments.pdf.

Hemmati, M (2001) *Multi-Stakeholder Processes for Governance and Sustainability – Beyond Deadlock and Conflict*, Earthscan, London

ICLEI (2002) *Local Strategies for Sustainability. Presentation by the International Council for Local Environmental Initiatives (ICLEI), Special Report on Selected Side-events at WSSD PC IV*, Bali, Indonesia, 27 May–7 July 2002, International Institute for Sustainable Development and UNDP, www.iisd.ca/2002/pc4/enbots/jun04.html

Kampling, C (2003) Statement of the concerns of young people to the final session of the World Summit on Sustainable Development, reprinted in *Earthlines*, Youth and Environment Network, CEE, no 38, spring 2003

Moosa, M V (2002) 'African Renaissance', *Our Planet*, UNEP, vol 13, no 2, p13

Renner, M (2002) *The Anatomy of Resource Wars*, Worldwatch Paper 162, Worldwatch, Washington, DC

Speth, J (2003) 'Perspectives on the Johannesburg Summit', *Environment*, vol 45, no 1, pp24–29

UNDP (United Nations Development Programme) (2002) *Human Development Report 2002: Deepening Democracy in a Fragmented World,* Oxford University Press, New York

UNDP, Regional Bureau for Europe and the Commonwealth of Independent States (2003) *Environmental Governance Sourcebook*, UNDP, Bratislava

UNEP (United Nations Environment Programme) (2002) *Global Environment Outlook 3*, Earthscan, London

WRI (World Resources Institute) in collaboration with UNEP (United Nations Environment Programme), UNDP (United Nations Development Programme) and the World Bank (2003) *World Resources 2002–2004: Decisions for the Earth: Balance, Voice, and Power*, WRI, Washington, DC

Part II

Implementing The Johannesburg Plan of Implementation

WSSD Partnerships for Sustainable Development

12

 Introduction

The World Summit on Sustainable Development (WSSD) had two kinds of outcomes: negotiated texts – the Johannesburg Declaration and the Johannesburg Plan of Implementation (JPOI) – and partnerships for sustainable development. The proposal that the WSSD would act as a forum for announcing new partnerships that focused on implementation was, in part, a recognition that a great deal of work had been done in the areas of policy-making, coordination mechanisms, legal frameworks and strategies; but there was still a long way to go with practical action on the ground. Furthermore, it was recognized that governments alone can not deliver sustainable development and that a wide range of groups in society needed to be galvanized and actively brought into the process, both for their perspectives and skills, and the additional resources that they could bring. It was agreed that WSSD Partnerships for Sustainable Development, sometimes referred to as Type II Partnerships (in recognition that these were a second type of outcome from the summit), would be international in scope and aimed at contributing to implementation of intergovernmental agreements related to sustainable development, particularly the JPOI, the Millennium Development Goals (MDGs) and Agenda 21.

 Criteria for WSSD partnerships

The broad principles guiding WSSD partnerships – elaborated during preparations for the summit – were captured by the United Nations Commission on Sustainable Development (CSD) in its **Guiding Principles for Partnerships for Sustainable Development** (CSD, 2002), sometimes referred to as the Bali Guidelines.

Around half of the 500 partnerships that applied for registration at WSSD met the guidelines. These partnerships were included in the UN's website and were given the opportunity to take part in the launch and other events at the WSSD. The most common shortcomings of those that were rejected were that they were either not international in their scope or they were not new.

Partnerships: A test of trust

The matter of partnerships was intensely debated in the run up to the WSSD and in the United Nations Commission on Sustainable Development (CSD) in 2003. NGOs and a number of developing countries expressed concerns that partnerships could take some of the focus off the obligations of governments. This issue was directly addressed by the United Nations Secretary-General in his report on **Follow-up to Johannesburg and the Future Role of the CSD** (CSD, 2003a), which stated that partnerships would not be a substitute for 'government responsibilities and commitments to action'. Other issues included:

- Concerns that the objectives and focus of partnerships should be directly relevant to regional-, national- or community-level sustainable development strategies and priorities.
- There should be transparency and accountability in how partnerships are set up and operated. Some were particularly concerned about corporate responsibility and accounting when partnerships involved private-sector partners. Others were keen to ensure that arrangements did not stifle innovation or create undue reporting burdens.
- Whether there would be access to adequate and predictable funding.
- Arrangements for review and evaluation. This included concerns to identify where there were gaps in the provision of partnerships and a debate around the role of the CSD in monitoring partnerships.

 ## Advantages of partnerships

Partnerships have a number of important advantages (Calder, 2003):

- They can bring together all necessary actors to ensure that truly integrated and holistic approaches to development can be identified and implemented.
- The involvement of stakeholders can result in a more comprehensive analysis of challenges and better strategies for addressing them.
- Stakeholders bring with them different skills and perspectives. This can encourage innovation and may bring innovative sources of funding to the table.
- There is a potential for deeper and more lasting systemic change when all affected groups are involved in the design of solutions: if these encompass policy change, they can be more far reaching than project-type interventions.
- Partnerships can help coordinate resources and action with a framework of sustainable development priorities of governments and communities.
- Partnerships have the potential to go further in practical terms than can be agreed formally.

Implementing the JPOI

The Johannesburg Plan of Implementation (JPOI) identifies the CSD as the focal point within the UN for developing, monitoring and reporting on partnerships for sustainable development. At its 11th session (2003), the CSD formally agreed criteria and guidelines for partnerships that draw on the Bali Guiding Principles, as follows.

Partnerships should:

- Be developed and implemented in accordance with criteria and principles, taking into account the Bali Guidelines;
- Be voluntary, multi-stakeholder initiatives, which contribute to the implementation of Agenda 21 and the WSSD;
- Complement, not substitute, commitments to implementing the above international commitments;
- Be new, based on predictable and sustained resources, and balance the three dimensions of sustainable development in their design and implementation;
- Have sectoral geographical balance, and be transparent and accountable, exchanging relevant information with governments and stakeholders;
- Result in technology transfer and capacity-building in developing countries partnership; and
- Mobilize new resources where relevant to support these partnerships.

Additionally:

- Partnerships should be publicly announced, detailing their contribution to implementation, and be consistent with national laws and national strategies;
- Lead partners should inform national focal points for sustainable development in all relevant countries, and bear in mind guidance from governments;
- UN funds, programmes and agencies should conform to their intergovernmentally agreed mandates and not divert funds from mandated programmes to partnerships;
- Registered partnerships should take into account that registration is voluntary and is based on reporting;
- Reporting should preferably happen every two years, be transparent, participatory and credible, and should focus on the contribution to implementation; and
- The CSD secretariat should make information on partnerships widely available and produce a summary report on partnerships.

Under the work programme of the CSD, partnership fairs will be hosted every two years during the 'Review Session' (see p171). This will allow the sharing of experience and good practice, and provide a mechanism by which the contribution of partnerships to the implementation of the outcomes of Rio and the WSSD can be showcased. The fairs will also provide a platform for launching new partnerships and for networking by potential partners and funders, while 'how-to' sessions will provide practical advice and information on partnership issues, both in terms of implementation and the way in which they are dealt with within the CSD.

All interested groups have the option of developing their own partnerships in response to the WSSD. The potential for South–South partnerships needs to be further explored and successful regional partnerships expanded outwards, or transferred to, other regions. A wide range of information on CSD partnerships is available on the CSD website, including registration forms, case studies, and details and analysis of the partnerships that have been agreed.

New partnerships need to be carefully designed, with thought given to appropriate facilitation (Calder, 2003) in order to provide a clear structure for the partnership and ensure that all stakeholders feel fully engaged in the decision-making process. Most importantly, the facilitator needs to be neutral and able to act as an 'honest broker' between different elements of the partnership. Further guidance about effective stakeholder engagement has been developed by Stakeholder Forum in the book **Multi-stakeholder Processes for Governance and Sustainability: Beyond Deadlock and Conflict** (Hemmati, 2002).

Bali Guiding Principles for World Summit on Sustainable Development (WSSD) Partnerships

The following is a summary of the Bali Guiding Principles for WSSD Partnerships (CSD, 2002).

Objective of partnerships

▩ To contribute to and reinforce the implementation of the outcomes of the WSSD and help to achieve further implementation of Agenda 21 and the Millennium Development Goals (MDGs).

General principles and values

▩ Voluntary and 'self-organizing'; based on mutual respect and shared responsibility of the partners involved.

▩ Take into account the Rio Declaration's principles and values expressed in the Millennium Declaration.

Bali Guiding Principles for World Summit on Sustainable Development (WSSD) Partnerships (*contd*)

Deliver globally agreed commitments

- Commitments complement, and are anchored in, the intergovernmentally agreed outcomes of the WSSD.

- Not intended to substitute commitments made by governments.

- Deliver globally agreed commitments by mobilizing capacity for producing action on the ground.

- Help to achieve implementation of Agenda 21 and the MDGs.

Integrated approach to sustainable development

- Integrate economic, social and environmental dimensions of sustainable development.

- Approach is consistent with sustainable development strategies and poverty reduction strategies of the countries, regions and communities where their implementation takes place.

Multi-stakeholder approach

- Have a multi-stakeholder approach, preferably involving a range of significant players.

- Approach is arranged among any combination of partners, including governments, regional groups, local authorities, non-governmental organizations (NGOs), international institutions and the private sector.

- All partners are involved from an early stage, with additional partners able to join on an equal basis.

Transparency and accountability

- Developed and implemented in an open and transparent manner and in good faith.

- Ownership of the partnership and its outcomes is shared among all partners. All partners are equally accountable.

- Performance is monitored and reviewed against objectives and targets and is reported in regular intervals (self-reporting). Reports are accessible to the public.

Tangible results

- Intended outcome and benefits are defined.
- Clear objectives are set with specific measurable targets and time frames.

Bali Guiding Principles for World Summit on Sustainable Development (WSSD) Partnerships (*contd*)

☼ All partners are explicitly committed to their role in achieving the aims and objectives.

Funding arrangements

☼ Available and/or expected sources of funding are identified.

☼ At least the initial funding is assured at the time of the summit, if announced there.

New partnerships

☼ Partnerships should be *new* – that is, developed within the framework of the WSSD process.

☼ Or partnerships should provide significant added value in the context of the WSSD (for example, with more partners taken on board, replicating existing initiatives, extending these to other geographical regions, or increasing financial resources, etc).

Local involvement/international impact

☼ The Bali Guiding Principles are international in impact but seek to involve local communities in design and implementation.

Follow-up

☼ The United Nations Commission on Sustainable Development (CSD) is kept informed about activities and progress in achieving targets.

☼ The CSD should serve as a focal point for discussion of partnerships that promote sustainable development, including sharing lessons learned, progress made and best practices.

☼ Submission of partnerships after the summit will be considered in the follow-up process.

Source: CSD, 2002

 # Resources

United Nations Commission on Sustainable Development (CSD) Partnerships website

www.un.org/esa/sustdev/partnerships/partnerships.htm

This is the official CSD website, providing comprehensive information on all elements of the CSD, including past, present and future processes, events and documents.

References

Calder, F (2003) *WSSD Partnerships for Sustainable Development*, Commonwealth Secretariat, London

CSD (United Nations Commission on Sustainable Development) (2002) *Guiding Principles for Partnerships for Sustainable Development ('Type II Outcomes') to be Elaborated by Interested Parties in the Context of the World Summit on Sustainable Development: Explanatory Note by the Vice-Chairs Jan Kara and Diane Quarless*, CSD, New York, 7 June 2002

CSD (2003a) *Follow-up to Johannesburg and the Future Role of the CSD – The Implementation Track: Report of the Secretary-General*, CSD, New York, 11th Session, 28 April–9 May 2003, United Nations Economic and Social Council, E/CN.17/2003/2

CSD (2003b) *United Nations Commission on Sustainable Development Report on the 11th Session* (27 January 2003 and 28 April–9 May 2003), United Nations, New York, Economic and Social Council Official Records, Supplement No 9, E/2003/29, E/CN.17/2003/6

Hemmati, M (2002) *Multi-stakeholder Processes for Governance and Sustainability: Beyond Deadlock and Conflict*, Earthscan, London

The Role of the United Nations Commission on Sustainable Development (CSD)

13

 ## Introduction

The United Nations Commission on Sustainable Development (CSD) was born in 1993 out of the United Nations Conference on Environment and Development (UNCED) in Rio de Janeiro in 1992 – the Rio Earth Summit. The CSD exists for three principle reasons. To:

- Monitor and assess implementation of Agenda 21 and to ensure effective follow-up to the Rio Earth Summit;
- Provide review and policy guidance to help implement the outcomes of the WSSD; and
- Act as a high-level forum within the UN to coordinate discussions on sustainable development and facilitate stakeholder dialogues.

 ## Structure

The CSD is a functional commission of the United Nations Economic and Social Council (ECOSOC). It has:

- 53 member countries, elected through ECOSOC;
- A rolling membership with three-year terms of office;
- One third of members elected each year;
- A chair, which is held for one year and is rotated amongst each of the five UN regions; and
- A bureau and a secretariat provided by the United Nations Department of Economic and Social Affairs (DESA).

 ## Major groups

Broad public participation is a fundamental prerequisite of sustainable development. Agenda 21 recognizes the specific roles and responsibilities of nine major groups of civil society: women; children and youth; indigenous people and their communities; non-governmental organizations (NGOs); local authorities; workers and their trade unions; business and industry; the scientific and technological community; and farmers. The WSSD also recognizes scientists and educators.

The CSD has been heralded as one of the most progressive models of multi-stakeholder engagement in intergovermental processes in recent times. It organizes **multi-stakeholder dialogues** to ensure the direct participation of civil society and to enable major groups to substantively and formally contribute to decision-making within the CSD. As a result of the WSSD, efforts are being made to improve this process with·

- Major groups represented in interactive dialogues during high-level segments;
- Balanced gender and regional representation;
- Active involvement of stakeholders in partnerships and capacity-building activities; and
- More action-orientated multi-stakeholder dialogues.

 # First ten years: Follow-up to Rio

The CSD attempted an 'inclusive agenda' to review progress on issues related to all 47 chapters of Agenda 21 through annual sessions at which stakeholder dialogues were held and resolutions negotiated. Each year the CSD considered a seleect number of issues (for example, the themes for 1997 were tourism, oceans and seas, consumption and production patterns, and small island developing states – SIDS), as well as cross-cutting issues (such as finance), which were addressed each year. In reality, it was an overburdened agenda with unwieldy discussions and sometimes a superficial review of progress.

In June 1997, heads of government and senior representatives from over 130 countries met in New York to consider what progress had been made since Rio. This Special Session of the United Nations General Assembly (UNGA), dubbed Rio+5, failed to generate much political attention or momentum, or any real new spirit of international cooperation – though it did agree a Programme for the Further Implementation of Agenda 21. The assessment of progress since Rio recognized some positive developments – particularly at local and community levels – but pointed to growing problems of poverty, inequality and environmental degradation.

 # World Summit on Sustainable Development

At the WSSD, it was widely recognized that the CSD had not been functioning as effectively as it could, and that some changes were required if it was to fulfil its mandate to better support the international implementation of sustainable development agreements.

Reforms of the CSD called for in Chapter XI of the Johannesburg Plan of Implementation (JPOI) are:

*   Integration of the three mutually supportive dimensions of sustainable development in a balanced manner (to an extent, this means a stronger review of social concerns than had been achieved to date);
*   Monitoring and review through the exchange of experience, knowledge and views, lessons learned and best practice;
*   Improved linkages between endeavours at all levels – global, regional, national and local;
*   Coherence between implementation of Agenda 21 and associated initiatives;
*   Greater involvement at the regional level;
*   Addressing opportunities and challenges to implementation;
*   Innovative ways of working to ensure effective progress;
*   Broader participation of all stakeholders, particularly UN agencies/international financial institutions and major groups;
*   Involvement and recognition of educators and scientists;
*   A focused work programme on a limited number of issues; and
*   Negotiations limited to every two years.

 ## Follow-up to Johannesburg

The CSD met in full for the first time, after the WSSD, in April 2003 to take decisions on its organizational reform and future work programme. It adopted guidelines for Type II partnerships (see p161–164) and a future work programme (see below) that will take the CSD up to 2017.

With respect to the structure of its work programme, this is arranged in a biennial 'implementation cycle', divided into:

*   Year 1 – review session.
*   Year 2 – policy session.
*   Each cycle will address a **thematic cluster** of issues and **cross-cutting issues** [see below].
*   The CSD will address constraints and obstacles to implementation and seek opportunities and solutions to these.
*   The thematic cluster of issues will be reviewed periodically and recommendations will be made on new themes and system-wide coordination.
*   High-level segments, involving ministers from all relevant portfolios, will be organized each year to give guidance and political oversight of decision-making.

The review session

The **review session** will be informed by a 'state of implementation' report by the United Nations Secretary-General, enabling the CSD to:

- Exchange regional experiences, best practice and lessons learned and facilitate dialogues between experts, with capacity-building as a critical element; and
- Identify priority challenges, obstacles, opportunities, recommendations and lessons learned.

United Nations Regional Commissions are invited to organize Regional Implementation Meetings with the CSD secretariat to make inputs to the Secretary-General's **State of Implementation** report.

The policy session

The **policy session** will be informed by discussions during the review sessions, as well as during intergovernmental preparatory meetings. Decisions will be negotiated on practical measures to promote implementation.

UNITED NATIONS COMMISSION ON SUSTAINABLE DEVELOPMENT'S (CSD'S) MULTI-YEAR WORK PROGRAMME

Cross-cutting issues (considered each year):

- Poverty eradication
- Changing unsustainable patterns of consumption and production
- Protecting and managing the natural resource base of economic and social development
- Sustainable development in a globalizing world
- Health and sustainable development
- Sustainable development of Small Island Developing States (SIDS)
- Sustainable development for Africa
- Other regional initiatives
- Means of implementation
- Institutional framework for sustainable development
- Gender equality
- Education

UNITED NATIONS COMMISSION ON SUSTAINABLE DEVELOPMENT'S (CSD'S) MULTI-YEAR WORK PROGRAMME (CONTD)

Thematic clusters

2004/2005:

- Water
- Sanitation
- Human settlements

2006/2007:

- Energy for sustainable development
- Industrial development
- Air pollution/atmosphere
- Climate change

2008/2009:

- Agriculture
- Rural development
- Land
- Drought
- Desertification
- Africa

2010/2011:

- Transport
- Chemicals
- Waste management
- Mining
- Ten-year framework of programmes on sustainable consumption and production patterns

2012/2013:

- Forests
- Biodiversity

UNITED NATIONS COMMISSION ON SUSTAINABLE DEVELOPMENT'S (CSD'S) MULTI-YEAR WORK PROGRAMME (CONTD)

- Biotechnology
- Tourism
- Mountains

2014/2015:

- Oceans
- Marine resources
- Small island developing states (SIDS)
- Disaster management and vulnerability

2016/2017:

- Overall appraisal of implementation of Agenda 21, the programme for the further implementation of Agenda 21 and the Johannesburg Plan of Implementation (JPOI)

CONFERENCES, AGREEMENTS AND PROCESSES

- United Nations Conference on Environment and Development (UNCED), Rio de Janeiro (1992)
- 47th United Nations General Assembly (UNGA) (1992)
- 19th United Nations General Assembly Special Session (UNGASS) (1997)
- 55th UNGA (2000)
- United Nations Commission on Sustainable Development (CSD) 10 (2001–2002)
- World Summit on Sustainable Development (WSSD) (2002)
- 57th UNGA (2002)
- CSD-11 (2003)

> ## Key United Nations bodies and Bretton Woods institutions
>
> ☼ Global Environment Facility (GEF)
>
> ☼ International Monetary Fund (IMF)
>
> ☼ United Nations Department of Economic and Social Affairs (DESA)
>
> ☼ United Nations Development Programme (UNDP)
>
> ☼ United Nations Economic and Social Council (ECOSOC)
>
> ☼ United Nations Environment Programme (UNEP)
>
> ☼ United Nations General Assembly (UNGA)
>
> ☼ World Bank
>
> ☼ World Trade Organization (WTO)

 # Resources

United Nations Commission on Sustainable Development (CSD)

www.un.org/esa/sustdev/
This is the official website on all elements of the CSD: past, present and future sessions, events and documents.

19th Special Session of the United Nations General Assembly (UNGA)

www.un.org/documents/ga/res/spec/aress19-2.htm
This session adopted the programme for the Further Implementation of Agenda 21, in September 1997, with the purpose of re-energizing commitments to achieving the goals and targets made during the Rio Earth Summit in 1992.

 # References

CSD (United Nations Commission on Sustainable Development) (2003a) *Follow-up to Johannesburg and the Future Role of the CSD – The Implementation Track: Report of the Secretary-General*, CSD, New York, 11th Session, 28 April–9 May 2003, United Nations Economic and Social Council, E/CN.17/2003/2

CSD (2003b) *United Nations Commission on Sustainable Development Report on the 11th Session* (27 January 2003 and 28 April–9 May 2003), United Nations, New York, Economic and Social Council Official Records, Supplement No 9, E/2003/29, E/CN.17/2003/6

A/RES/47/191 (1992) *Institutional Arrangements to Follow Up the United Nations Conference on Environment and Development*, www.un.org/documents/ga/hcs/47/a47r191.htm

A/RES/S-19/2 (1997) *Programme for the Further Implementation of Agenda 21*,
www.un.org/documents/ga/hcs/spec/arkss19-2.htm

A/RES/55/199 (2000) *Ten-year Review of Progress Achieved in the Implementation of
the Outcome of the United Nations Conference on Environment and Development*,
www.nyo.unep.org/pdfs/55199.pdf

A/RES/57/235 (2003) *World Summit on Sustainable Development*

Plan of Implementation of the World Summit on Sustainable Development[*]

Annex A ————

I Introduction

1. The United Nations Conference on Environment and Development, held in Rio de Janeiro in 1992,[1] provided the fundamental principles and the programme of action for achieving sustainable development. We strongly reaffirm our commitment to the Rio principles,[2] the full implementation of Agenda 21[2] and the Programme for the Further Implementation of Agenda 21.[3] We also commit ourselves to achieving the internationally agreed development goals, including those contained in the United Nations Millennium Declaration[4] and in the outcomes of the major United Nations conferences and international agreements since 1992.

2. The present plan of implementation will further build on the achievements made since the United Nations Conference on Environment and Development and expedite the realization of the remaining goals. To this end, we commit ourselves to undertaking concrete actions and measures at all levels and to enhancing international cooperation, taking into account the Rio principles, including, inter alia, the principle of common but differentiated responsibilities as set out in principle 7 of the Rio Declaration on Environment and Development.[5] These efforts will also promote the integration of the three components of sustainable development – economic development, social development and environmental protection – as interdependent and mutually reinforcing pillars. Poverty eradication, changing unsustainable patterns of production and consumption and protecting and managing the natural resource base of economic and social development are overarching objectives of, and essential requirements for, sustainable development.

3. We recognize that the implementation of the outcomes of the Summit should benefit all, particularly women, youth, children and vulnerable groups. Furthermore, the implementation should involve all relevant actors through partnerships, especially between Governments of the North and South, on the one hand, and between Governments and major groups, on the other, to achieve the widely shared goals of sustainable development. As reflected in the Monterrey Consensus,[6] such partnerships are key to pursuing sustainable development in a globalizing world.

4. Good governance within each country and at the international level is essential for sustainable development. At the domestic level, sound environmental, social and economic policies, democratic institutions responsive to the needs of the people, the rule of law, anti-corruption measures, gender equality and an enabling environment for investment are the basis for sustainable development. As a result of globalization, external factors have become critical in determining the success

or failure of developing countries in their national efforts. The gap between developed and developing countries points to the continued need for a dynamic and enabling international economic environment supportive of international cooperation, particularly in the areas of finance, technology transfer, debt and trade and full and effective participation of developing countries in global decision-making, if the momentum for global progress towards sustainable development is to be maintained and increased.

5. Peace, security, stability and respect for human rights and fundamental freedoms, including the right to development, as well as respect for cultural diversity, are essential for achieving sustainable development and ensuring that sustainable development benefits all.

6. We acknowledge the importance of ethics for sustainable development and, therefore, emphasize the need to consider ethics in the implementation of Agenda 21.

II Poverty eradication

7. Eradicating poverty is the greatest global challenge facing the world today and an indispensable requirement for sustainable development, particularly for developing countries. Although each country has the primary responsibility for its own sustainable development and poverty eradication and the role of national policies and development strategies cannot be overemphasized, concerted and concrete measures are required at all levels to enable developing countries to achieve their sustainable development goals as related to the internationally agreed poverty-related targets and goals, including those contained in Agenda 21, the relevant outcomes of other United Nations conferences and the United Nations Millennium Declaration. This would include actions at all levels to:

   (a) Halve, by the year 2015, the proportion of the world's people whose income is less than 1 dollar a day and the proportion of people who suffer from hunger and, by the same date, to halve the proportion of people without access to safe drinking water;

   (b) Establish a world solidarity fund to eradicate poverty and to promote social and human development in the developing countries pursuant to modalities to be determined by the General Assembly, while stressing the voluntary nature of the contributions and the need to avoid duplication of existing United Nations funds, and encouraging the role of the private sector and individual citizens relative to Governments in funding the endeavours;

   (c) Develop national programmes for sustainable development and local and community development, where appropriate within country-owned poverty reduction strategies, to promote the empowerment of people living in poverty and their organizations. These programmes should reflect their priorities and enable them to increase access to productive resources, public services and institutions – in particular, land, water, employment opportunities, credit, education and health;

   (d) Promote women's equal access to and full participation in, on the basis of equality with men, decision-making at all levels, mainstreaming gender perspectives in all policies and strategies, eliminating all forms of violence and discrimination against women and improving the status, health and economic welfare of women and girls through full and equal access to economic opportunity, land, credit, education and healthcare services;

(e) Develop policies and ways and means to improve access by indigenous people and their communities to economic activities and increase their employment through, where appropriate, measures such as training, technical assistance and credit facilities. Recognize that traditional and direct dependence on renewable resources and ecosystems, including sustainable harvesting, continues to be essential to the cultural, economic and physical well-being of indigenous people and their communities;

(f) Deliver basic health services for all and reduce environmental health threats, taking into account the special needs of children and the linkages between poverty, health and environment, with provision of financial resources, technical assistance and knowledge transfer to developing countries and countries with economies in transition;

(g) Ensure that children everywhere, boys and girls alike, will be able to complete a full course of primary schooling and will have equal access to all levels of education;

(h) Provide access to agricultural resources for people living in poverty, especially women and indigenous communities, and promote, as appropriate, land tenure arrangements that recognize and protect indigenous and common property resource management systems;

(i) Build basic rural infrastructure, diversify the economy and improve transportation and access to markets, market information and credit for the rural poor to support sustainable agriculture and rural development;

(j) Transfer basic sustainable agricultural techniques and knowledge, including natural resource management, to small- and medium-scale farmers, fishers and the rural poor, especially in developing countries, including through multi-stakeholder approaches and public–private partnerships aimed at increasing agriculture production and food security;

(k) Increase food availability and affordability, including through harvest and food technology and management, as well as equitable and efficient distribution systems, by promoting, for example, community-based partnerships linking urban and rural people and enterprises;

(l) Combat desertification and mitigate the effects of drought and floods through measures such as improved use of climate and weather information and forecasts, early warning systems, land and natural resource management, agricultural practices and ecosystem conservation in order to reverse current trends and minimize degradation of land and water resources, including through the provision of adequate and predictable financial resources to implement the United Nations Convention to Combat Desertification in Those Countries Experiencing Serious Drought and/or Desertification, particularly in Africa,[7] as one of the tools for poverty eradication;

(m) Increase access to sanitation to improve human health and reduce infant and child mortality, prioritizing water and sanitation in national sustainable development strategies and poverty reduction strategies where they exist.

8. The provision of clean drinking water and adequate sanitation is necessary to protect human health and the environment. In this respect, we agree to halve, by the year 2015, the proportion of people who are unable to reach or to afford safe drinking water (as outlined in the Millennium Declaration) and the proportion of

people who do not have access to basic sanitation, which would include actions at all levels to:

(a) Develop and implement efficient household sanitation systems;

(b) Improve sanitation in public institutions, especially schools;

(c) Promote safe hygiene practices;

(d) Promote education and outreach focused on children, as agents of behavioural change;

(e) Promote affordable and socially and culturally acceptable technologies and practices;

(f) Develop innovative financing and partnership mechanisms;

(g) Integrate sanitation into water resources management strategies.

9. Take joint actions and improve efforts to work together at all levels to improve access to reliable and affordable energy services for sustainable development sufficient to facilitate the achievement of the Millennium development goals, including the goal of halving the proportion of people in poverty by 2015, and as a means to generate other important services that mitigate poverty, bearing in mind that access to energy facilitates the eradication of poverty. This would include actions at all levels to:

(a) Improve access to reliable, affordable, economically viable, socially acceptable and environmentally sound energy services and resources, taking into account national specificities and circumstances, through various means, such as enhanced rural electrification and decentralized energy systems, increased use of renewables, cleaner liquid and gaseous fuels and enhanced energy efficiency, by intensifying regional and international cooperation in support of national efforts, including through capacity-building, financial and technological assistance and innovative financing mechanisms, including at the micro and meso levels, recognizing the specific factors for providing access to the poor;

(b) Improve access to modern biomass technologies and fuelwood sources and supplies and commercialize biomass operations, including the use of agricultural residues, in rural areas and where such practices are sustainable;

(c) Promote a sustainable use of biomass and, as appropriate, other renewable energies through improvement of current patterns of use, such as management of resources, more efficient use of fuelwood and new or improved products and technologies;

(d) Support the transition to the cleaner use of liquid and gaseous fossil fuels, where considered more environmentally sound, socially acceptable and cost-effective;

(e) Develop national energy policies and regulatory frameworks that will help to create the necessary economic, social and institutional conditions in the energy sector to improve access to reliable, affordable, economically viable, socially acceptable and environmentally sound energy services for sustainable development and poverty eradication in rural, peri-urban and urban areas;

(f) Enhance international and regional cooperation to improve access to reliable, affordable, economically viable, socially acceptable and environmentally sound energy services, as an integral part of poverty reduction programmes, by facilitating the creation of enabling environments and addressing capacity-building needs, with special attention to rural and isolated areas, as appropriate;

(g) Assist and facilitate on an accelerated basis, with the financial and technical assistance of developed countries, including through public–private partnerships, the access of the poor to reliable, affordable, economically viable, socially acceptable and environmentally sound energy services, taking into account the instrumental role of developing national policies on energy for sustainable development, bearing in mind that in developing countries sharp increases in energy services are required to improve the standards of living of their populations and that energy services have positive impacts on poverty eradication and improve standards of living.

10. Strengthen the contribution of industrial development to poverty eradication and sustainable natural resource management. This would include actions at all levels to:

(a) Provide assistance and mobilize resources to enhance industrial productivity and competitiveness, as well as industrial development, in developing countries, including the transfer of environmentally sound technologies on preferential terms, as mutually agreed;

(b) Provide assistance to increase income-generating employment opportunities, taking into account the Declaration on Fundamental Principles and Rights at Work of the International Labour Organization;[8]

(c) Promote the development of micro-, small- and medium-sized enterprises, including by means of training, education and skill enhancement, with a special focus on agro-industry as a provider of livelihoods for rural communities;

(d) Provide financial and technological support, as appropriate, to rural communities of developing countries to enable them to benefit from safe and sustainable livelihood opportunities in small-scale mining ventures;

(e) Provide support to developing countries for the development of safe low-cost technologies that provide or conserve fuel for cooking and water heating;

(f) Provide support for natural resource management for creating sustainable livelihoods for the poor.

11. By 2020, achieve a significant improvement in the lives of at least 100 million slum dwellers, as proposed in the Cities without slums initiative. This would include actions at all levels to:

(a) Improve access to land and property, to adequate shelter and to basic services for the urban and rural poor, with special attention to female heads of household;

(b) Use low-cost and sustainable materials and appropriate technologies for the construction of adequate and secure housing for the poor, with financial and technological assistance to developing countries, taking into account their culture, climate, specific social conditions and vulnerability to natural disasters;

(c) Increase decent employment, credit and income for the urban poor, through appropriate national policies, promoting equal opportunities for women and men;

(d) Remove unnecessary regulatory and other obstacles for microenterprises and the informal sector;

(e) Support local authorities in elaborating slum upgrading programmes within the framework of urban development plans and facilitate access, particularly for the poor, to information on housing legislation.

12. Take immediate and effective measures to eliminate the worst forms of child labour as defined in International Labour Organization Convention 182, and elaborate

and implement strategies for the elimination of child labour that is contrary to accepted international standards.

13. Promote international cooperation to assist developing countries, upon request, in addressing child labour and its root causes, inter alia, through social and economic policies aimed at poverty conditions, while stressing that labour standards should not be used for protectionist trade purposes.

III Changing unsustainable patterns of consumption and production

14. Fundamental changes in the way societies produce and consume are indispensable for achieving global sustainable development. All countries should promote sustainable consumption and production patterns, with the developed countries taking the lead and with all countries benefiting from the process, taking into account the Rio principles, including, inter alia, the principle of common but differentiated responsibilities as set out in principle 7 of the Rio Declaration on Environment and Development. Governments, relevant international organizations, the private sector and all major groups should play an active role in changing unsustainable consumption and production patterns. This would include the actions at all levels set out below.

15. Encourage and promote the development of a 10-year framework of programmes in support of regional and national initiatives to accelerate the shift towards sustainable consumption and production to promote social and economic development within the carrying capacity of ecosystems by addressing and, where appropriate, delinking economic growth and environmental degradation through improving efficiency and sustainability in the use of resources and production processes and reducing resource degradation, pollution and waste. All countries should take action, with developed countries taking the lead, taking into account the development needs and capabilities of developing countries, through mobilization, from all sources, of financial and technical assistance and capacity-building for developing countries. This would require actions at all levels to:

(a) Identify specific activities, tools, policies, measures and monitoring and assessment mechanisms, including, where appropriate, life-cycle analysis and national indicators for measuring progress, bearing in mind that standards applied by some countries may be inappropriate and of unwarranted economic and social cost to other countries, in particular developing countries;

(b) Adopt and implement policies and measures aimed at promoting sustainable patterns of production and consumption, applying, inter alia, the polluter-pays principle described in principle 16 of the Rio Declaration on Environment and Development;

(c) Develop production and consumption policies to improve the products and services provided, while reducing environmental and health impacts, using, where appropriate, science-based approaches, such as life-cycle analysis;

(d) Develop awareness-raising programmes on the importance of sustainable production and consumption patterns, particularly among youth and the relevant segments in all countries, especially in developed countries, through, inter alia, education, public and consumer information, advertising and other media, taking into account local, national and regional cultural values;

(e) Develop and adopt, where appropriate, on a voluntary basis, effective, transparent, verifiable, non-misleading and non-discriminatory consumer information tools to provide information relating to sustainable consumption and production, including human health and safety aspects. These tools should not be used as disguised trade barriers;

(f) Increase eco-efficiency, with financial support from all sources, where mutually agreed, for capacity-building, technology transfer and exchange of technology with developing countries and countries with economies in transition, in cooperation with relevant international organizations.

16. Increase investment in cleaner production and eco-efficiency in all countries through, inter alia, incentives and support schemes and policies directed at establishing appropriate regulatory, financial and legal frameworks. This would include actions at all levels to:

(a) Establish and support cleaner production programmes and centres and more efficient production methods by providing, inter alia, incentives and capacity-building to assist enterprises, especially small- and medium-sized enterprises, particularly in developing countries, in improving productivity and sustainable development;

(b) Provide incentives for investment in cleaner production and eco-efficiency in all countries, such as state-financed loans, venture capital, technical assistance and training programmes for small- and medium-sized companies, while avoiding trade-distorting measures inconsistent with the rules of the World Trade Organization;

(c) Collect and disseminate information on cost-effective examples in cleaner production, eco-efficiency and environmental management and promote the exchange of best practices and know-how on environmentally sound technologies between public and private institutions;

(d) Provide training programmes to small- and medium-sized enterprises on the use of information and communication technologies.

17. Integrate the issue of production and consumption patterns into sustainable development policies, programmes and strategies, including, where applicable, into poverty reduction strategies.

18. Enhance corporate environmental and social responsibility and accountability. This would include actions at all levels to:

(a) Encourage industry to improve social and environmental performance through voluntary initiatives, including environmental management systems, codes of conduct, certification and public reporting on environmental and social issues, taking into account such initiatives as the International Organization for Standardization standards and Global Reporting Initiative guidelines on sustainability reporting, bearing in mind principle 11 of the Rio Declaration on Environment and Development;

(b) Encourage dialogue between enterprises and the communities in which they operate and other stakeholders;

(c) Encourage financial institutions to incorporate sustainable development considerations into their decision-making processes;

(d) Develop workplace-based partnerships and programmes, including training and education programmes.

19. Encourage relevant authorities at all levels to take sustainable development considerations into account in decision-making, including on national and local

development planning, investment in infrastructure, business development and public procurement. This would include actions at all levels to:

(a) Provide support for the development of sustainable development strategies and programmes, including in decision-making on investment in infrastructure and business development;

(b) Continue to promote the internalization of environmental costs and the use of economic instruments, taking into account the approach that the polluter should, in principle, bear the costs of pollution, with due regard to the public interest and without distorting international trade and investment;

(c) Promote public procurement policies that encourage development and diffusion of environmentally sound goods and services;

(d) Provide capacity-building and training to assist relevant authorities with regard to the implementation of the initiatives listed in the present paragraph;

(e) Use environmental impact assessment procedures.

* * *

20. Call upon Governments as well as relevant regional and international organizations and other relevant stakeholders to implement, taking into account national and regional specificities and circumstances, the recommendations and conclusions adopted by the Commission on Sustainable Development concerning energy for sustainable development at its ninth session, including the issues and options set out below, bearing in mind that in view of the different contributions to global environmental degradation, States have common but differentiated responsibilities. This would include actions at all levels to:

(a) Take further action to mobilize the provision of financial resources, technology transfer, capacity-building and the diffusion of environmentally sound technologies according to the recommendations and conclusions of the Commission on Sustainable Development, as contained in section A, paragraph 3, and Section D, paragraph 30, of its decision 9/1[9] on energy for sustainable development;

(b) Integrate energy considerations, including energy efficiency, affordability and accessibility, into socio-economic programmes, especially into policies of major energy-consuming sectors, and into the planning, operation and maintenance of long-lived energy consuming infrastructures, such as the public sector, transport, industry, agriculture, urban land use, tourism and construction sectors;

(c) Develop and disseminate alternative energy technologies with the aim of giving a greater share of the energy mix to renewable energies, improving energy efficiency and greater reliance on advanced energy technologies, including cleaner fossil fuel technologies;

(d) Combine, as appropriate, the increased use of renewable energy resources, more efficient use of energy, greater reliance on advanced energy technologies, including advanced and cleaner fossil fuel technologies, and the sustainable use of traditional energy resources, which could meet the growing need for energy services in the longer term to achieve sustainable development;

(e) Diversify energy supply by developing advanced, cleaner, more efficient, affordable and cost-effective energy technologies, including fossil fuel technologies and renewable energy technologies, hydro included, and their transfer to developing countries on concessional terms as mutually agreed. With a sense of urgency, substantially increase the global share of renewable energy sources with the objective of increasing its contribution to total energy supply, recognizing the role of national and voluntary regional targets as well as initiatives, where they exist, and ensuring that energy policies are supportive to developing countries' efforts to eradicate poverty, and regularly evaluate available data to review progress to this end;

(f) Support efforts, including through provision of financial and technical assistance to developing countries, with the involvement of the private sector, to reduce flaring and venting of gas associated with crude oil production;

(g) Develop and utilize indigenous energy sources and infrastructures for various local uses and promote rural community participation, including local Agenda 21 groups, with the support of the international community, in developing and utilizing renewable energy technologies to meet their daily energy needs to find simple and local solutions;

(h) Establish domestic programmes for energy efficiency, including, as appropriate, by accelerating the deployment of energy efficiency technologies, with the necessary support of the international community;

(i) Accelerate the development, dissemination and deployment of affordable and cleaner energy efficiency and energy conservation technologies, as well as the transfer of such technologies, in particular to developing countries, on favourable terms, including on concessional and preferential terms, as mutually agreed;

(j) Recommend that international financial institutions and other agencies' policies support developing countries, as well as countries with economies in transition, in their own efforts to establish policy and regulatory frameworks which create a level playing field between the following: renewable energy, energy efficiency, advanced energy technologies, including advanced and cleaner fossil fuel technologies, and centralized, distributed and decentralized energy systems;

(k) Promote increased research and development in the field of various energy technologies, including renewable energy, energy efficiency and advanced energy technologies, including advanced and cleaner fossil fuel technologies, both nationally and through international collaboration; strengthen national and regional research and development institutions/centres on reliable, affordable, economically viable, socially acceptable and environmentally sound energy for sustainable development;

(l) Promote networking between centres of excellence on energy for sustainable development, including regional networks, by linking competent centres on energy technologies for sustainable development that could support and promote efforts at capacity-building and technology transfer activities, particularly of developing countries, as well as serve as information clearing houses;

(m) Promote education to provide information for both men and women about available energy sources and technologies;

(n) Utilize financial instruments and mechanisms, in particular the Global Environment Facility, within its mandate, to provide financial resources to developing countries, in particular least developed countries and small island developing States, to meet their capacity needs for training, technical know-how and strengthening national institutions in reliable, affordable, economically viable, socially acceptable and environmentally sound energy, including promoting energy efficiency and conservation, renewable energy and advanced energy technologies, including advanced and cleaner fossil fuel technologies;

(o) Support efforts to improve the functioning, transparency and information about energy markets with respect to both supply and demand, with the aim of achieving greater stability and predictability, and to ensure consumer access to reliable, affordable, economically viable, socially acceptable and environmentally sound energy services;

(p) Policies to reduce market distortions would promote energy systems compatible with sustainable development through the use of improved market signals and by removing market distortions, including restructuring taxation and phasing out harmful subsidies, where they exist, to reflect their environmental impacts, with such policies taking fully into account the specific needs and conditions of developing countries, with the aim of minimizing the possible adverse impacts on their development;

(q) Take action, where appropriate, to phase out subsidies in this area that inhibit sustainable development, taking fully into account the specific conditions and different levels of development of individual countries and considering their adverse effect, particularly on developing countries;

(r) Governments are encouraged to improve the functioning of national energy markets in such a way that they support sustainable development, overcome market barriers and improve accessibility, taking fully into account that such policies should be decided by each country, and that its own characteristics and capabilities and level of development should be considered, especially as reflected in national sustainable development strategies, where they exist;

(s) Strengthen national and regional energy institutions or arrangements for enhancing regional and international cooperation on energy for sustainable development, in particular to assist developing countries in their domestic efforts to provide reliable, affordable, economically viable, socially acceptable and environmentally sound energy services to all sections of their populations;

(t) Countries are urged to develop and implement actions within the framework of the ninth session of the Commission on Sustainable Development, including through public–private partnerships, taking into account the different circumstances of countries, based on lessons learned by Governments, international institutions and stakeholders, including business and industry, in the field of access to energy, including renewable energy and energy-efficiency and advanced energy technologies, including advanced and cleaner fossil fuel technologies;

(u) Promote cooperation between international and regional institutions and bodies dealing with different aspects of energy for sustainable development within their existing mandate, bearing in mind paragraph 46(h) of the Programme of Action for the Further Implementation of Agenda 21, strengthening, as appropriate, regional and national activities for the promotion of education and capacity-building regarding energy for sustainable development;

(v) Strengthen and facilitate, as appropriate, regional cooperation arrangements for promoting cross-border energy trade, including the interconnection of electricity grids and oil and natural gas pipelines;

(w) Strengthen and, where appropriate, facilitate dialogue forums among regional, national and international producers and consumers of energy.

* * *

21. Promote an integrated approach to policy-making at the national, regional and local levels for transport services and systems to promote sustainable development, including policies and planning for land use, infrastructure, public transport systems and goods delivery networks, with a view to providing safe, affordable and efficient transportation, increasing energy efficiency, reducing pollution, congestion and adverse health effects and limiting urban sprawl, taking into account national priorities and circumstances. This would include actions at all levels to:
    (a) Implement transport strategies for sustainable development, reflecting specific regional, national and local conditions, to improve the affordability, efficiency and convenience of transportation, as well as urban air quality and health and reduce greenhouse gas emissions, including through the development of better vehicle technologies that are more environmentally sound, affordable and socially acceptable;
    (b) Promote investment and partnerships for the development of sustainable, energy efficient multi-modal transportation systems, including public mass transportation systems and better transportation systems in rural areas, with technical and financial assistance for developing countries and countries with economies in transition.

* * *

22. Prevent and minimize waste and maximize reuse, recycling and use of environmentally friendly alternative materials, with the participation of government authorities and all stakeholders, in order to minimize adverse effects on the environment and improve resource efficiency, with financial, technical and other assistance for developing countries. This would include actions at all levels to:
    (a) Develop waste management systems, with the highest priority placed on waste prevention and minimization, reuse and recycling, and environmentally sound disposal facilities, including technology to recapture the energy contained in waste, and encourage small-scale waste-recycling initiatives that support urban and rural waste management and provide income-generating opportunities, with international support for developing countries;
    (b) Promote waste prevention and minimization by encouraging production of reusable consumer goods and biodegradable products and developing the infrastructure required.

* * *

23. Renew the commitment, as advanced in Agenda 21, to sound management of chemicals throughout their life cycle and of hazardous wastes for sustainable development, as well as for the protection of human health and the environment, inter alia, aiming to achieve, by 2020, that chemicals are used and produced in ways that lead to the minimization of significant adverse effects on human health and the environment, using transparent science-based risk assessment procedures and science-based risk management procedures, taking into account the precautionary approach, as set out in principle 15 of the Rio Declaration on Environment and Development, and support developing countries in strengthening

their capacity for the sound management of chemicals and hazardous wastes by providing technical and financial assistance. This would include actions at all levels to:

(a) Promote the ratification and implementation of relevant international instruments on chemicals and hazardous waste, including the Rotterdam Convention on Prior Informed Consent Procedures for Certain Hazardous Chemicals and Pesticides in International Trade[10] so that it can enter into force by 2003 and the Stockholm Convention on Persistent Organic Pollutants[11] so that it can enter into force by 2004, and encourage and improve coordination, as well as supporting developing countries in their implementation;

(b) Further develop a strategic approach to international chemicals management based on the Bahia Declaration and Priorities for Action beyond 2000 of the Intergovernmental Forum on Chemical Safety[12] by 2005, and urge that the United Nations Environment Programme, the Intergovernmental Forum, other international organizations dealing with chemical management and other relevant international organizations and actors closely cooperate in this regard, as appropriate;

(c) Encourage countries to implement the new globally harmonized system for the classification and labelling of chemicals as soon as possible with a view to having the system fully operational by 2008;

(d) Encourage partnerships to promote activities aimed at enhancing environmentally sound management of chemicals and hazardous wastes, implementing multilateral environmental agreements, raising awareness of issues relating to chemicals and hazardous waste, and encouraging the collection and use of additional scientific data;

(e) Promote efforts to prevent international illegal trafficking of hazardous chemicals and hazardous wastes and to prevent damage resulting from the transboundary movement and disposal of hazardous wastes in a manner consistent with obligations under relevant international instruments, such as the Basel Convention on the Control of Transboundary Movements of Hazardous Wastes and Their Disposal;[13]

(f) Encourage development of coherent and integrated information on chemicals, such as through national pollutant release and transfer registers;

(g) Promote reduction of the risks posed by heavy metals that are harmful to human health and the environment, including through a review of relevant studies, such as the United Nations Environment Programme global assessment of mercury and its compounds.

IV Protecting and managing the natural resource base of economic and social development

24. Human activities are having an increasing impact on the integrity of ecosystems that provide essential resources and services for human well-being and economic activities. Managing the natural resources base in a sustainable and integrated manner is essential for sustainable development. In this regard, to reverse the current trend in natural resource degradation as soon as possible, it is necessary to implement strategies which should include targets adopted at the national and,

where appropriate, regional levels to protect ecosystems and to achieve integrated management of land, water and living resources, while strengthening regional, national and local capacities. This would include actions at all levels as set out below.

25. Launch a programme of actions, with financial and technical assistance, to achieve the Millennium development goal on safe drinking water. In this respect, we agree to halve, by the year 2015, the proportion of people who are unable to reach or to afford safe drinking water, as outlined in the Millennium Declaration, and the proportion of people without access to basic sanitation, which would include actions at all levels to:

    (a) Mobilize international and domestic financial resources at all levels, transfer technology, promote best practice and support capacity-building for water and sanitation infrastructure and services development, ensuring that such infrastructure and services meet the needs of the poor and are gender sensitive;

    (b) Facilitate access to public information and participation, including by women, at all levels in support of policy and decision-making related to water resources management and project implementation;

    (c) Promote priority action by Governments, with the support of all stakeholders, in water management and capacity-building at the national level and, where appropriate, at the regional level, and promote and provide new and additional financial resources and innovative technologies to implement Chapter 18 of Agenda 21;

    (d) Intensify water pollution prevention to reduce health hazards and protect ecosystems by introducing technologies for affordable sanitation and industrial and domestic wastewater treatment by mitigating the effects of groundwater contamination and by establishing, at the national level, monitoring systems and effective legal frameworks;

    (e) Adopt prevention and protection measures to promote sustainable water use and to address water shortages.

26. Develop integrated water resources management and water efficiency plans by 2005, with support to developing countries, through actions at all levels to:

    (a) Develop and implement national/regional strategies, plans and programmes with regard to integrated river basin, watershed and groundwater management and introduce measures to improve the efficiency of water infrastructure to reduce losses and increase recycling of water;

    (b) Employ the full range of policy instruments, including regulation, monitoring, voluntary measures, market and information-based tools, land-use management and cost recovery of water services, without cost recovery objectives becoming a barrier to access to safe water by poor people, and adopt an integrated water basin approach;

    (c) Improve the efficient use of water resources and promote their allocation among competing uses in a way that gives priority to the satisfaction of basic human needs and balances the requirement of preserving or restoring ecosystems and their functions, in particular in fragile environments, with human domestic, industrial and agriculture needs, including safeguarding drinking water quality;

    (d) Develop programmes for mitigating the effects of extreme water-related events.

(e)   Support the diffusion of technology and capacity-building for non-conventional water resources and conservation technologies to developing countries and regions facing water scarcity conditions or subject to drought and desertification, through technical and financial support and capacity-building;

(f)   Support, where appropriate, efforts and programmes for energy-efficient, sustainable and cost-effective desalination of seawater, water recycling and water harvesting from coastal fogs in developing countries through such measures as technological, technical and financial assistance and other modalities;

(g)   Facilitate the establishment of public–private partnerships and other forms of partnership that give priority to the needs of the poor within stable and transparent national regulatory frameworks provided by Governments, while respecting local conditions, involving all concerned stakeholders, and monitoring the performance and improving accountability of public institutions and private companies.

27.   Support developing countries and countries with economies in transition in their efforts to monitor and assess the quantity and quality of water resources, including through the establishment and/or further development of national monitoring networks and water resources databases and the development of relevant national indicators.

28.   Improve water resource management and scientific understanding of the water cycle through cooperation in joint observation and research, and for this purpose encourage and promote knowledge-sharing and provide capacity-building and the transfer of technology, as mutually agreed, including remote-sensing and satellite technologies, particularly to developing countries and countries with economies in transition.

29.   Promote effective coordination among the various international and intergovernmental bodies and processes working on water-related issues, both within the United Nations system and between the United Nations and international financial institutions, drawing on the contributions of other international institutions and civil society to inform intergovernmental decision-making; closer coordination should also be promoted to elaborate and support proposals and undertake activities related to the International Year of Freshwater 2003, and beyond.

*   *   *

30.   Oceans, seas, islands and coastal areas form an integrated and essential component of the Earth's ecosystem and are critical for global food security and for sustaining economic prosperity and the well-being of many national economies, particularly in developing countries. Ensuring the sustainable development of the oceans requires effective coordination and cooperation, including at the global and regional levels, between relevant bodies, and actions at all levels to:

(a)   Invite States to ratify or accede to and implement the United Nations Convention on the Law of the Sea of 1982,[14] which provides the overall legal framework for ocean activities;

(b)   Promote the implementation of Chapter 17 of Agenda 21, which provides the programme of action for achieving the sustainable development of oceans, coastal areas and seas through its programme areas of integrated management and sustainable development of coastal areas, including exclusive economic zones; marine environmental protection; sustainable use and conservation of marine living resources; addressing critical uncertainties for the management of the marine environment and climate change; strengthening international, including regional, cooperation and coordination; and sustainable development of small islands;

(c) Establish an effective, transparent and regular inter-agency coordination mechanism on ocean and coastal issues within the United Nations system;

(d) Encourage the application by 2010 of the ecosystem approach, noting the Reykjavik Declaration on Responsible Fisheries in the Marine Ecosystem[15] and decision V/6 of the Conference of Parties to the Convention on Biological Diversity (CBD);[16]

(e) Promote integrated, multidisciplinary and multi-sectoral coastal and ocean management at the national level and encourage and assist coastal States in developing ocean policies and mechanisms on integrated coastal management;

(f) Strengthen regional cooperation and coordination between the relevant regional organizations and programmes, the regional seas programmes of the United Nations Environment Programme, regional fisheries management organizations and other regional science, health and development organizations;

(g) Assist developing countries in coordinating policies and programmes at the regional and sub-regional levels aimed at the conservation and sustainable management of fishery resources and implement integrated coastal area management plans, including through the promotion of sustainable coastal and small-scale fishing activities and, where appropriate, the development of related infrastructure;

(h) Take note of the work of the open-ended informal consultative process established by the United Nations General Assembly in its resolution 54/33 in order to facilitate the annual review by the Assembly of developments in ocean affairs and the upcoming review of its effectiveness and utility to be held at its 57th session under the terms of the above-mentioned resolution.

31. To achieve sustainable fisheries, the following actions are required at all levels:

(a) Maintain or restore stocks to levels that can produce the maximum sustainable yield with the aim of achieving these goals for depleted stocks on an urgent basis and, where possible, not later than 2015;

(b) Ratify or accede to and effectively implement the relevant United Nations and, where appropriate, associated regional fisheries agreements or arrangements, noting in particular the Agreement for the Implementation of the Provisions of the United Nations Convention on the Law of the Sea of 10 December 1982 relating to the Conservation and Management of Straddling Fish Stocks and Highly Migratory Fish Stocks[17] and the 1993 Agreement to Promote Compliance with International Conservation and Management Measures by Fishing Vessels on the High Seas;[18]

(c) Implement the 1995 Code of Conduct for Responsible Fisheries,[19] taking note of the special requirements of developing countries as noted in its article 5, and the relevant international plans of action and technical guidelines of the Food and Agriculture Organization of the United Nations;

(d) Urgently develop and implement national and, where appropriate, regional plans of action, to put into effect the international plans of action of the Food and Agriculture Organization of the United Nations, in particular the International Plan of Action for the Management of Fishing Capacity[20] by

2005 and the International Plan of Action to Prevent, Deter and Eliminate Illegal, Unreported and Unregulated Fishing[21] by 2004. Establish effective monitoring, reporting and enforcement, and control of fishing vessels, including by flag States, to further the International Plan of Action to Prevent, Deter and Eliminate Illegal, Unreported and Unregulated Fishing;

(e) Encourage relevant regional fisheries management organizations and arrangements to give due consideration to the rights, duties and interests of coastal States and the special requirements of developing States when addressing the issue of the allocation of share of fishery resources for straddling stocks and highly migratory fish stocks, mindful of the provisions of the United Nations Convention on the Law of the Sea and the Agreement for the Implementation of the Provisions of the United Nations Convention on the Law of the Sea of 10 December 1982 relating to the Conservation and Management of Straddling Fish Stocks and Highly Migratory Fish Stocks, on the high seas and within exclusive economic zones;

(f) Eliminate subsidies that contribute to illegal, unreported and unregulated fishing and to over-capacity, while completing the efforts undertaken at the World Trade Organization to clarify and improve its disciplines on fisheries subsidies, taking into account the importance of this sector to developing countries;

(g) Strengthen donor coordination and partnerships between international financial institutions, bilateral agencies and other relevant stakeholders to enable developing countries, in particular the least developed countries and small island developing States and countries with economies in transition, to develop their national, regional and sub-regional capacities for infrastructure and integrated management and the sustainable use of fisheries;

(h) Support the sustainable development of aquaculture, including small-scale aquaculture, given its growing importance for food security and economic development.

32. In accordance with Chapter 17 of Agenda 21, promote the conservation and management of the oceans through actions at all levels, giving due regard to the relevant international instruments to:

(a) Maintain the productivity and biodiversity of important and vulnerable marine and coastal areas, including in areas within and beyond national jurisdiction;

(b) Implement the work programme arising from the Jakarta Mandate on the Conservation and Sustainable Use of Marine and Coastal Biological Diversity of the Convention on Biological Diversity,[22] including through the urgent mobilization of financial resources and technological assistance and the development of human and institutional capacity, particularly in developing countries;

(c) Develop and facilitate the use of diverse approaches and tools, including the ecosystem approach, the elimination of destructive fishing practices, the establishment of marine protected areas consistent with international law and based on scientific information, including representative networks by 2012 and time/area closures for the protection of nursery grounds and periods, proper coastal land-use and watershed planning, and the integration of marine and coastal areas management into key sectors;

(d) Develop national, regional and international programmes for halting the loss of marine biodiversity, including in coral reefs and wetlands;

(e) Implement the Ramsar Convention,[23] including its joint work programme, with the Convention on Biological Diversity[24] and the programme of action called for by the International Coral Reef Initiative to strengthen joint management plans and international networking for wetland ecosystems in coastal zones, including coral reefs, mangroves, seaweed beds and tidal mud flats.

33. Advance implementation of the Global Programme of Action for the Protection of the Marine Environment from Land-based Activities[25] and the Montreal Declaration on the Protection of the Marine Environment from Land-based Activities,[26] with particular emphasis during the period from 2002 to 2006 on municipal wastewater, the physical alteration and destruction of habitats and nutrients by actions at all levels to:

(a) Facilitate partnerships, scientific research and diffusion of technical knowledge; mobilize domestic, regional and international resources; and promote human and institutional capacity-building, paying particular attention to the needs of developing countries;

(b) Strengthen the capacity of developing countries in the development of their national and regional programmes and mechanisms to mainstream the objectives of the Global Programme of Action and to manage the risks and impacts of ocean pollution;

(c) Elaborate regional programmes of action and improve the links with strategic plans for the sustainable development of coastal and marine resources, noting, in particular, areas that are subject to accelerated environmental changes and development pressures;

(d) Make every effort to achieve substantial progress by the next Global Programme of Action conference in 2006 to protect the marine environment from land-based activities.

34. Enhance maritime safety and protection of the marine environment from pollution by actions at all levels to:

(a) Invite States to ratify or accede to and implement the conventions and protocols and other relevant instruments of the International Maritime Organization relating to the enhancement of maritime safety and protection of the marine environment from marine pollution and environmental damage caused by ships, including the use of toxic anti-fouling paints, and urge the International Maritime Organization (IMO) to consider stronger mechanisms to secure the implementation of IMO instruments by flag States;

(b) Accelerate the development of measures to address invasive alien species in ballast water. Urge the International Maritime Organization to finalize its draft International Convention on the Control and Management of Ships' Ballast Water and Sediments.

35. Governments, taking into account their national circumstances, are encouraged, recalling paragraph 8 of resolution GC (44)/RES/17 of the General Conference of the International Atomic Energy Agency, and taking into account the very serious potential for environment and human health impacts of radioactive wastes, to make efforts to examine and further improve measures and internationally agreed regulations regarding safety, while stressing the importance of having effective liability mechanisms in place relevant to international maritime transportation and other transboundary movement of radioactive material, radioactive waste and spent fuel, including, inter alia, arrangements for prior notification and consultations done in accordance with relevant international instruments.

36. Improve the scientific understanding and assessment of marine and coastal ecosystems as a fundamental basis for sound decision-making through actions at all levels to:

(a) Increase scientific and technical collaboration, including integrated assessment at the global and regional levels, including the appropriate transfer of marine science and marine technologies and techniques for the conservation and management of living and non-living marine resources and expanding ocean-observing capabilities for the timely prediction and assessment of the state of marine environment;

(b) Establish by 2004 a regular process under the United Nations for global reporting and assessment of the state of the marine environment, including socio-economic aspects, both current and foreseeable, building on existing regional assessments;

(c) Build capacity in marine science, information and management, through, inter alia, promoting the use of environmental impact assessments and environmental evaluation and reporting techniques for projects or activities that are potentially harmful to the coastal and marine environments and their living and non-living resources;

(d) Strengthen the ability of the Intergovernmental Oceanographic Commission of the United Nations Educational, Scientific and Cultural Organization, the Food and Agriculture Organization of the United Nations and other relevant international and regional and sub-regional organizations to build national and local capacity in marine science and the sustainable management of oceans and their resources.

* * *

37. An integrated, multi-hazard, inclusive approach to address vulnerability, risk assessment and disaster management, including prevention, mitigation, preparedness, response and recovery, is an essential element of a safer world in the 21st century. Actions are required at all levels to:

(a) Strengthen the role of the International Strategy for Disaster Reduction and encourage the international community to provide the necessary financial resources to its Trust Fund;

(b) Support the establishment of effective regional, sub-regional and national strategies and scientific and technical institutional support for disaster management;

(c) Strengthen the institutional capacities of countries and promote international joint observation and research through improved surface-based monitoring and increased use of satellite data, dissemination of technical and scientific knowledge, and the provision of assistance to vulnerable countries;

(d) Reduce the risks of flooding and drought in vulnerable countries by, inter alia, promoting wetland and watershed protection and restoration, improved land-use planning, improving and applying more widely techniques and methodologies for assessing the potential adverse effects of climate change on wetlands and, as appropriate, assisting countries that are particularly vulnerable to those effects;

(e) Improve techniques and methodologies for assessing the effects of climate change, and encourage the continuing assessment of those adverse effects by the Intergovernmental Panel on Climate Change;

(f) Encourage the dissemination and use of traditional and indigenous knowledge to mitigate the impact of disasters and promote community-based disaster management planning by local authorities, including through training activities and raising public awareness;

(g) Support the ongoing voluntary contribution of, as appropriate, non-governmental organizations, the scientific community and other partners in the management of natural disasters according to agreed, relevant guidelines;

(h) Develop and strengthen early warning systems and information networks in disaster management, consistent with the International Strategy for Disaster Reduction;

(i) Develop and strengthen capacity at all levels to collect and disseminate scientific and technical information, including the improvement of early warning systems for predicting extreme weather events, especially El Niño/La Niña, through the provision of assistance to institutions devoted to addressing such events, including the International Centre for the Study of the El Niño phenomenon;

(j) Promote cooperation for the prevention and mitigation of, preparedness for, response to and recovery from major technological and other disasters with an adverse impact on the environment in order to enhance the capabilities of affected countries to cope with such situations.

* * *

38. Change in the Earth's climate and its adverse effects are a common concern of humankind. We remain deeply concerned that all countries, particularly developing countries, including the least developed countries and small island developing States, face increased risks of negative impacts of climate change and recognize that, in this context, the problems of poverty, land degradation, access to water and food and human health remain at the centre of global attention. The United Nations Framework Convention on Climate Change[27] is the key instrument for addressing climate change, a global concern, and we reaffirm our commitment to achieving its ultimate objective of stabilization of greenhouse gas concentrations in the atmosphere at a level that would prevent dangerous anthropogenic interference with the climate system, within a time frame sufficient to allow ecosystems to adapt naturally to climate change, to ensure that food production is not threatened and to enable economic development to proceed in a sustainable manner, in accordance with our common but differentiated responsibilities and respective capabilities. Recalling the United Nations Millennium Declaration, in which heads of State and Government resolved to make every effort to ensure the entry into force of the Kyoto Protocol to the United Nations Framework Convention on Climate Change,[28] preferably by the tenth anniversary of the United Nations Conference on Environment and Development in 2002, and to embark on the required reduction of emissions of greenhouse gases, States that have ratified the Kyoto Protocol strongly urge States that have not already done so to ratify it in a timely manner. Actions at all levels are required to:

(a) Meet all the commitments and obligations under the United Nations Framework Convention on Climate Change;

(b) Work cooperatively towards achieving the objectives of the Convention;

(c) Provide technical and financial assistance and capacity-building to developing countries and countries with economies in transition in accordance with commitments under the Convention, including the Marrakesh Accords;[29]

(d) Build and enhance scientific and technological capabilities, inter alia, through continuing support to the Intergovernmental Panel on Climate Change for the exchange of scientific data and information, especially in developing countries;

(e) Develop and transfer technological solutions;

(f) Develop and disseminate innovative technologies with regard to key sectors of development, particularly energy, and of investment in this regard, including through private-sector involvement, market-oriented approaches and supportive public policies and international cooperation;

(g) Promote the systematic observation of the Earth's atmosphere, land and oceans by improving monitoring stations, increasing the use of satellites and appropriate integration of these observations to produce high-quality data that could be disseminated for the use of all countries, in particular developing countries;

(h) Enhance the implementation of national, regional and international strategies to monitor the Earth's atmosphere, land and oceans, including, as appropriate, strategies for integrated global observations, inter alia, with the cooperation of relevant international organizations, especially the specialized agencies, in cooperation with the Convention;

(i) Support initiatives to assess the consequences of climate change, such as the Arctic Council initiative, including the environmental, economic and social impacts on local and indigenous communities.

39. Enhance cooperation at the international, regional and national levels to reduce air pollution, including transboundary air pollution, acid deposition and ozone depletion, bearing in mind the Rio principles, including, inter alia, the principle that, in view of the different contributions to global environmental degradation, States have common but differentiated responsibilities, with actions at all levels to:

(a) Strengthen capacities of developing countries and countries with economies in transition to measure, reduce and assess the impacts of air pollution, including health impacts, and provide financial and technical support for these activities;

(b) Facilitate implementation of the Montreal Protocol on Substances that Deplete the Ozone Layer by ensuring adequate replenishment of its fund by 2003/2005;

(c) Further support the effective regime for the protection of the ozone layer established in the Vienna Convention for the Protection of the Ozone Layer and the Montreal Protocol, including its compliance mechanism;

(d) Improve access by developing countries to affordable, accessible, cost-effective, safe and environmentally sound alternatives to ozone-depleting substances by 2010, and assist them in complying with the phase-out schedule under the Montreal Protocol, bearing in mind that ozone depletion and climate change are scientifically and technically interrelated;

(e) Take measures to address illegal traffic in ozone-depleting substances.

* * *

40. Agriculture plays a crucial role in addressing the needs of a growing global population and is inextricably linked to poverty eradication, especially in developing countries. Enhancing the role of women at all levels and in all aspects of rural development, agriculture, nutrition and food security is imperative. Sustainable

agriculture and rural development are essential to the implementation of an integrated approach to increasing food production and enhancing food security and food safety in an environmentally sustainable way. This would include actions at all levels to:

(a) Achieve the Millennium Declaration target to halve by the year 2015 the proportion of the world's people who suffer from hunger and realize the right to a standard of living adequate for the health and well-being of themselves and their families, including food, including by promoting food security and fighting hunger in combination with measures which address poverty, consistent with the outcome of the World Food Summit and, for States' Parties, with their obligations under Article 11 of the International Covenant on Economic, Social and Cultural Rights;[30]

(b) Develop and implement integrated land management and water-use plans that are based on sustainable use of renewable resources and on integrated assessments of socio-economic and environmental potentials and strengthen the capacity of Governments, local authorities and communities to monitor and manage the quantity and quality of land and water resources;

(c) Increase understanding of the sustainable use, protection and management of water resources to advance long-term sustainability of freshwater, coastal and marine environments;

(d) Promote programmes to enhance in a sustainable manner the productivity of land and the efficient use of water resources in agriculture, forestry, wetlands, artisanal fisheries and aquaculture, especially through indigenous and local community-based approaches;

(e) Support the efforts of developing countries to protect oases from silt, land degradation and increasing salinity by providing appropriate technical and financial assistance;

(f) Enhance the participation of women in all aspects and at all levels relating to sustainable agriculture and food security;

(g) Integrate existing information systems on land-use practices by strengthening national research and extension services and farmer organizations to trigger farmer-to-farmer exchange on good practices, such as those related to environmentally sound, low-cost technologies, with the assistance of relevant international organizations;

(h) Enact, as appropriate, measures that protect indigenous resource management systems and support the contribution of all appropriate stakeholders, men and women alike, in rural planning and development;

(i) Adopt policies and implement laws that guarantee well-defined and enforceable land- and water-use rights and promote legal security of tenure, recognizing the existence of different national laws and/or systems of land access and tenure, and provide technical and financial assistance to developing countries as well as countries with economies in transition that are undertaking land tenure reform in order to enhance sustainable livelihoods;

(j) Reverse the declining trend in public-sector finance for sustainable agriculture, provide appropriate technical and financial assistance, and promote private-sector investment and support efforts in developing countries and countries with economies in transition to strengthen agricultural research and natural resource management capacity and dissemination of research results to the farming communities;

(k) Employ market-based incentives for agricultural enterprises and farmers to monitor and manage water use and quality, inter alia, by applying such methods as small-scale irrigation and wastewater recycling and reuse;

(l) Enhance access to existing markets and develop new markets for value-added agricultural products;

(m) Increase brown-field redevelopment in developed countries and countries with economies in transition, with appropriate technical assistance where contamination is a serious problem;

(n) Enhance international cooperation to combat the illicit cultivation of narcotic plants, taking into account their negative social, economic and environmental impacts;

(o) Promote programmes for the environmentally sound, effective and efficient use of soil fertility improvement practices and agricultural pest control;

(p) Strengthen and improve coordination of existing initiatives to enhance sustainable agricultural production and food security;

(q) Invite countries that have not done so to ratify the International Treaty on Plant Genetic Resources for Food and Agriculture;[31]

(r) Promote the conservation and sustainable use and management of traditional and indigenous agricultural systems, and strengthen indigenous models of agricultural production.

* * *

41. Strengthen the implementation of the United Nations Convention to Combat Desertification in Those Countries Experiencing Serious Drought and/or Desertification, particularly in Africa,[7] to address causes of desertification and land degradation in order to maintain and restore land, and to address poverty resulting from land degradation. This would include actions at all levels to:

(a) Mobilize adequate and predictable financial resources, transfer of technologies and capacity-building at all levels;

(b) Formulate national action programmes to ensure timely and effective implementation of the Convention and its related projects, with the support of the international community, including through decentralized projects at the local level;

(c) Encourage the United Nations Framework Convention on Climate Change, the Convention on Biological Diversity and the Convention to Combat Desertification to continue exploring and enhancing synergies, with due regard to their respective mandates, in the elaboration and implementation of plans and strategies under the respective Conventions;

(d) Integrate measures to prevent and combat desertification, as well as to mitigate the effects of drought through relevant policies and programmes, such as land, water and forest management, agriculture, rural development, early warning systems, environment, energy, natural resources, health and education, and poverty eradication and sustainable development strategies;

(e) Provide affordable local access to information to improve monitoring and early warning related to desertification and drought;

(f) Call on the Second Assembly of the Global Environment Facility (GEF) to take action on the recommendations of the GEF Council concerning the designation of land degradation (desertification and deforestation) as a focal area of GEF as a means of GEF support for the successful implementation of the

Convention to Combat Desertification; and consequently, consider making GEF a financial mechanism of the Convention, taking into account the prerogatives and decisions of the Conference of the Parties to the Convention, while recognizing the complementary roles of GEF and the Global Mechanism of the convention in providing and mobilizing resources for the elaboration and implementation of action programmes;

(g) Improve the sustainability of grassland resources through strengthening management and law enforcement and providing financial and technical support by the international community to developing countries.

* * *

42. Mountain ecosystems support particular livelihoods and include significant watershed resources, biological diversity and unique flora and fauna. Many are particularly fragile and vulnerable to the adverse effects of climate change and need specific protection. Actions at all levels are required to:

(a) Develop and promote programmes, policies and approaches that integrate environmental, economic and social components of sustainable mountain development and strengthen international cooperation for its positive impacts on poverty eradication programmes, especially in developing countries;

(b) Implement programmes to address, where appropriate, deforestation, erosion, land degradation, loss of biodiversity, disruption of water flows and retreat of glaciers;

(c) Develop and implement, where appropriate, gender-sensitive policies and programmes, including public and private investments that help eliminate inequities facing mountain communities;

(d) Implement programmes to promote diversification and traditional mountain economies, sustainable livelihoods and small-scale production systems, including specific training programmes and better access to national and international markets, communications and transport planning, taking into account the particular sensitivity of mountains;

(e) Promote full participation and involvement of mountain communities in decisions that affect them and integrate indigenous knowledge, heritage and values in all development initiatives;

(f) Mobilize national and international support for applied research and capacity-building, provide financial and technical assistance for the effective implementation of the sustainable development of mountain ecosystems in developing countries and countries with economies in transition, and address the poverty among people living in mountains through concrete plans, projects and programmes, with sufficient support from all stakeholders, taking into account the spirit of the International Year of Mountains 2002.

* * *

43. Promote sustainable tourism development, including non-consumptive and ecotourism, taking into account the spirit of the International Year of Ecotourism 2002, the United Nations Year for Cultural Heritage in 2002, the World Ecotourism Summit 2002 and its Quebec Declaration, and the Global Code of Ethics for Tourism as adopted by the World Tourism Organization in order to increase the benefits from tourism resources for the population in host communities while maintaining the cultural and environmental integrity of the host communities and

enhancing the protection of ecologically sensitive areas and natural heritages. Promote sustainable tourism development and capacity-building in order to contribute to the strengthening of rural and local communities. This would include actions at all levels to:

(a) Enhance international cooperation, foreign direct investment and partnerships with both private and public sectors, at all levels;

(b) Develop programmes, including education and training programmes, that encourage people to participate in ecotourism, enable indigenous and local communities to develop and benefit from ecotourism, and enhance stakeholder cooperation in tourism development and heritage preservation in order to improve the protection of the environment, natural resources and cultural heritage;

(c) Provide technical assistance to developing countries and countries with economies in transition to support sustainable tourism business development and investment and tourism awareness programmes, to improve domestic tourism and to stimulate entrepreneurial development;

(d) Assist host communities in managing visits to their tourism attractions for their maximum benefit, while ensuring the least negative impacts on and risks for their traditions, culture and environment, with the support of the World Tourism Organization and other relevant organizations;

(e) Promote the diversification of economic activities, including through the facilitation of access to markets and commercial information, and participation of emerging local enterprises, especially small- and medium-sized enterprises.

* * *

44. Biodiversity, which plays a critical role in overall sustainable development and poverty eradication, is essential to our planet, human well-being and to the livelihood and cultural integrity of people. However, biodiversity is currently being lost at unprecedented rates due to human activities; this trend can only be reversed if the local people benefit from the conservation and sustainable use of biological diversity, in particular in countries of origin of genetic resources, in accordance with article 15 of the Convention on Biological Diversity. The Convention is the key instrument for the conservation and sustainable use of biological diversity and the fair and equitable sharing of benefits arising from use of genetic resources. A more efficient and coherent implementation of the three objectives of the Convention and the achievement, by 2010, of a significant reduction in the current rate of loss of biological diversity will require the provision of new and additional financial and technical resources to developing countries, and includes actions at all levels to:

(a) Integrate the objectives of the Convention into global, regional and national sectoral and cross-sectoral programmes and policies, in particular in the programmes and policies of the economic sectors of countries and international financial institutions;

(b) Promote the ongoing work under the Convention on the sustainable use on biological diversity, including on sustainable tourism, as a cross-cutting issue relevant to different ecosystems, sectors and thematic areas;

(c) Encourage effective synergies between the Convention and other multilateral environmental agreements, inter alia, through the development of joint plans and programmes, with due regard to their respective mandates, regarding common responsibilities and concerns;

(d) Implement the Convention and its provisions, including active follow-up of its work programmes and decisions through national, regional and global action programmes, in particular the national biodiversity strategies and action plans, and strengthen their integration into relevant cross-sectoral strategies, programmes and policies, including those related to sustainable development and poverty eradication, including initiatives which promote community-based sustainable use of biological diversity;

(e) Promote the wide implementation and further development of the ecosystem approach, as being elaborated in the ongoing work of the Convention;

(f) Promote concrete international support and partnership for the conservation and sustainable use of biodiversity, including in ecosystems, at World Heritage sites and for the protection of endangered species, in particular through the appropriate channelling of financial resources and technology to developing countries and countries with economies in transition;

(g) To effectively conserve and sustainably use biodiversity, promote and support initiatives for hot spot areas and other areas essential for biodiversity and promote the development of national and regional ecological networks and corridors;

(h) Provide financial and technical support to developing countries, including capacity-building, in order to enhance indigenous and community-based biodiversity conservation efforts;

(i) Strengthen national, regional and international efforts to control invasive alien species, which are one of the main causes of biodiversity loss, and encourage the development of effective work programme on invasive alien species at all levels;

(j) Subject to national legislation, recognize the rights of local and indigenous communities who are holders of traditional knowledge, innovations and practices, and, with the approval and involvement of the holders of such knowledge, innovations and practices, develop and implement benefit-sharing mechanisms on mutually agreed terms for the use of such knowledge, innovations and practices;

(k) Encourage and enable all stakeholders to contribute to the implementation of the objectives of the Convention and, in particular, recognize the specific role of youth, women and indigenous and local communities in conserving and using biodiversity in a sustainable way;

(l) Promote the effective participation of indigenous and local communities in decision- and policy-making concerning the use of their traditional knowledge;

(m) Encourage technical and financial support to developing countries and countries with economies in transition in their efforts to develop and implement, as appropriate, inter alia, national sui generis systems and traditional systems according to national priorities and legislation, with a view to conserving and the sustainable use of biodiversity;

(n) Promote the wide implementation of and continued work on the Bonn Guidelines on Access to Genetic Resources and Fair and Equitable Sharing of Benefits arising out of their Utilization as an input to assist the Parties when developing and drafting legislative, administrative or policy measures on access and benefit-sharing, as well as contract and other arrangements under mutually agreed terms for access and benefit-sharing;

(o) Negotiate within the framework of the Convention on Biological Diversity, bearing in mind the Bonn Guidelines, an international regime to promote and safeguard the fair and equitable sharing of benefits arising out of the utilization of genetic resources;

(p) Encourage successful conclusion of existing processes under the auspices of the Intergovernmental Committee on Intellectual Property and Genetic Resources, Traditional Knowledge and Folklore of the World Intellectual Property Organization, and in the ad hoc open-ended working group on article 8(j) and related provisions of the Convention;

(q) Promote practicable measures for access to the results and benefits arising from biotechnologies based upon genetic resources, in accordance with articles 15 and 19 of the Convention, including through enhanced scientific and technical cooperation on biotechnology and biosafety, including the exchange of experts, training human resources and developing research-oriented institutional capacities;

(r) With a view to enhancing synergy and mutual supportiveness, taking into account the decisions under the relevant agreements, promote the discussions, without prejudging their outcome, with regard to the relationships between the Convention and agreements related to international trade and intellectual property rights, as outlined in the Doha Ministerial Declaration;[32]

(s) Promote the implementation of the programme of work of the Global Taxonomy Initiative;

(t) Invite all States that have not already done so to ratify the Convention, the Cartagena Protocol on Biosafety to the Convention[33] and other biodiversity-related agreements, and invite those that have done so to promote their effective implementation at the national, regional and international levels and to support developing countries and countries with economies in transition technically and financially in this regard.

* * *

45. Forests and trees cover nearly one third of the Earth's surface. Sustainable forest management of both natural and planted forests and for timber and non-timber products is essential to achieving sustainable development, as well as a critical means to eradicate poverty, significantly reduce deforestation, halt the loss of forest biodiversity and land and resource degradation, and improve food security and access to safe drinking water and affordable energy; in addition, it highlights the multiple benefits of both natural and planted forests and trees and contributes to the well-being of the planet and humanity. The achievement of sustainable forest management, nationally and globally, including through partnerships among interested Governments and stakeholders, including the private sector, indigenous and local communities and non-governmental organizations, is an essential goal of sustainable development. This would include actions at all levels to:

(a) Enhance political commitment to achieve sustainable forest management by endorsing it as a priority on the international political agenda, taking full account of the linkages between the forest sector and other sectors through integrated approaches;

(b) Support the United Nations Forum on Forests, with the assistance of the Collaborative Partnership on Forests, as key intergovernmental mechanisms to facilitate and coordinate the implementation of sustainable forest management at the national, regional and global levels, thus contributing, inter alia, to the conservation and sustainable use of forest biodiversity;

(c) Take immediate action on domestic forest law enforcement and illegal international trade in forest products, including in forest biological resources, with the support of the international community, and provide human and institutional capacity-building related to the enforcement of national legislation in those areas;

(d) Take immediate action at the national and international levels to promote and facilitate the means to achieve sustainable timber harvesting and to facilitate the provision of financial resources and the transfer and development of environmentally sound technologies, and thereby address unsustainable timber-harvesting practices;

(e) Develop and implement initiatives to address the needs of those parts of the world that currently suffer from poverty and the highest rates of deforestation and where international cooperation would be welcomed by affected Governments;

(f) Create and strengthen partnerships and international cooperation to facilitate the provision of increased financial resources, the transfer of environmentally sound technologies, trade, capacity-building, forest law enforcement and governance at all levels and integrated land and resource management to implement sustainable forest management, including the proposals for action of the Intergovernmental Panel on Forests/Intergovernmental Forum on Forests;

(g) Accelerate implementation of the proposals for action of the Intergovernmental Panel on Forests/Intergovernmental Forum on Forests by countries and by the Collaborative Partnership on Forests and intensify efforts on reporting to the United Nations Forum on Forests to contribute to an assessment of progress in 2005;

(h) Recognize and support indigenous and community-based forest management systems to ensure their full and effective participation in sustainable forest management;

(i) Implement the expanded action-oriented work programme of the Convention on Biological Diversity on all types of forest biological diversity, in close cooperation with the Forum, Partnership members and other forest-related processes and conventions, with the involvement of all relevant stakeholders.

* * *

46. Mining, minerals and metals are important to the economic and social development of many countries. Minerals are essential for modern living. Enhancing the contribution of mining, minerals and metals to sustainable development includes actions at all levels to:

(a) Support efforts to address the environmental, economic, health and social impacts and benefits of mining, minerals and metals throughout their life cycle, including workers' health and safety, and use a range of partnerships, furthering existing activities at the national and international levels among interested Governments, intergovernmental organizations, mining companies and workers and other stakeholders to promote transparency and accountability for sustainable mining and minerals development;

(b) Enhance the participation of stakeholders, including local and indigenous communities and women, to play an active role in minerals, metals and mining development throughout the life cycles of mining operations, including after closure for rehabilitation purposes, in accordance with national regulations and taking into account significant transboundary impacts;

(c) Foster sustainable mining practices through the provision of financial, technical and capacity-building support to developing countries and countries with economies in transition for the mining and processing of minerals, including small-scale mining, and, where possible and appropriate, improve value-added processing, upgrade scientific and technological information and reclaim and rehabilitate degraded sites.

V Sustainable development in a globalizing world

47. Globalization offers opportunities and challenges for sustainable development. We recognize that globalization and interdependence are offering new opportunities for trade, investment and capital flows and advances in technology, including information technology, for the growth of the world economy, development and the improvement of living standards around the world. At the same time, there remain serious challenges, including serious financial crises, insecurity, poverty, exclusion and inequality within and among societies. The developing countries and countries with economies in transition face special difficulties in responding to those challenges and opportunities. Globalization should be fully inclusive and equitable, and there is a strong need for policies and measures at the national and international levels, formulated and implemented with the full and effective participation of developing countries and countries with economies in transition, to help them to respond effectively to those challenges and opportunities. This will require urgent action at all levels to:

(a) Continue to promote open, equitable, rules-based, predictable and non-discriminatory multilateral trading and financial systems that benefit all countries in the pursuit of sustainable development. Support the successful completion of the work programme contained in the Doha Ministerial Declaration and the implementation of the Monterrey Consensus. Welcome the decision contained in the Doha Ministerial Declaration to place the needs and interests of developing countries at the heart of the work programme of the Declaration, including through enhanced market access for products of interest to developing countries;

(b) Encourage ongoing efforts by international financial and trade institutions to ensure that decision-making processes and institutional structures are open and transparent;

(c) Enhance the capacities of developing countries, including the least developed countries, landlocked developing countries and small island developing States, to benefit from liberalized trade opportunities through international cooperation and measures aimed at improving productivity, commodity diversification and competitiveness, community-based entrepreneurial capacity and transportation and communication infrastructure development;

(d) Support the International Labour Organization and encourage its ongoing work on the social dimension of globalization, as stated in paragraph 64 of the Monterrey Consensus;

(e) Enhance the delivery of coordinated, effective and targeted trade-related technical assistance and capacity-building programmes, including taking advantage of existing and future market access opportunities, and examining the relationship between trade, environment and development.

48. Implement the outcomes of the Doha Ministerial Conference by the members of the World Trade Organization, further strengthen trade-related technical assistance and capacity-building and ensure the meaningful, effective and full participation of developing countries in multilateral trade negotiations by placing their needs and interests at the heart of the work programme of the World Trade Organization.

49. Actively promote corporate responsibility and accountability, based on the Rio principles, including through the full development and effective implementation of intergovernmental agreements and measures, international initiatives and public–private partnerships and appropriate national regulations, and support continuous improvement in corporate practices in all countries.

50. Strengthen the capacities of developing countries to encourage public/private initiatives that enhance the ease of access, accuracy, timeliness and coverage of information on countries and financial markets. Multilateral and regional financial institutions could provide further assistance for these purposes.

51. Strengthen regional trade and cooperation agreements, consistent with the multilateral trading system, among developed and developing countries and countries with economies in transition, as well as among developing countries, with the support of international finance institutions and regional development banks, as appropriate, with a view to achieving the objectives of sustainable development.

52. Assist developing countries and countries with economies in transition in narrowing the digital divide, creating digital opportunities and harnessing the potential of information and communication technologies for development through technology transfer on mutually agreed terms and the provision of financial and technical support and, in this context, support the World Summit on the Information Society.

VI Health and sustainable development

53. The Rio Declaration on Environment and Development states that human beings are at the centre of concerns for sustainable development, and that they are entitled to a healthy and productive life, in harmony with nature. The goals of sustainable development can only be achieved in the absence of a high prevalence of debilitating diseases, while obtaining health gains for the whole population requires poverty eradication. There is an urgent need to address the causes of ill health, including environmental causes, and their impact on development, with particular emphasis on women and children, as well as vulnerable groups of society, such as people with disabilities, elderly persons and indigenous people.

54. Strengthen the capacity of healthcare systems to deliver basic health services to all in an efficient, accessible and affordable manner aimed at preventing, controlling and treating diseases, and to reduce environmental health threats, in conformity with human rights and fundamental freedoms and consistent with national laws and cultural and religious values, and taking into account the reports of relevant

United Nations conferences and summits and of special sessions of the General Assembly. This would include actions at all levels to:

(a) Integrate the health concerns, including those of the most vulnerable populations, into strategies, policies and programmes for poverty eradication and sustainable development;

(b) Promote equitable and improved access to affordable and efficient healthcare services, including prevention, at all levels of the health system, essential and safe drugs at affordable prices, immunization services and safe vaccines and medical technology;

(c) Provide technical and financial assistance to developing countries and countries with economies in transition to implement the Health for All Strategy, including health information systems and integrated databases on development hazards;

(d) Improve the development and management of human resources in healthcare services;

(e) Promote and develop partnerships to enhance health education with the objective of achieving improved health literacy on a global basis by 2010, with the involvement of United Nations agencies, as appropriate;

(f) Develop programmes and initiatives to reduce, by the year 2015, mortality rates for infants and children under five by two-thirds, and maternal mortality rates by three-quarters, of the prevailing rate in 2000, and reduce disparities between and within developed and developing countries as quickly as possible, with particular attention to eliminating the pattern of disproportionate and preventable mortality among girl infants and children;

(g) Target research efforts and apply research results to priority public health issues, in particular those affecting susceptible and vulnerable populations, through the development of new vaccines, reducing exposures to health risks, building on equal access to healthcare services, education, training and medical treatment and technology, and addressing the secondary effects of poor health;

(h) Promote the preservation, development and use of effective traditional medicine knowledge and practices, where appropriate, in combination with modern medicine, recognizing indigenous and local communities as custodians of traditional knowledge and practices, while promoting effective protection of traditional knowledge, as appropriate, consistent with international law;

(i) Ensure equal access of women to healthcare services, giving particular attention to maternal and emergency obstetric care;

(j) Address effectively, for all individuals of appropriate age, the promotion of healthy living, including their reproductive and sexual health, consistent with the commitments and outcomes of recent United Nations conferences and summits, including the World Summit for Children, the United Nations Conference on Environment and Development, the International Conference on Population and Development, the World Summit for Social Development and the Fourth World Conference on Women, and their respective reviews and reports;

(k) Launch international capacity-building initiatives, as appropriate, that assess health and environment linkages and use the knowledge gained to create more effective national and regional policy responses to environmental threats to human health;

(l) Transfer and disseminate, on mutually agreed terms, including through public–private multi-sector partnerships, with international financial support, technologies for safe water, sanitation and waste management for rural and urban areas in developing countries and countries with economies in transition, taking into account country-specific conditions and gender equality, including specific technology needs of women;

(m) Strengthen and promote programmes of the International Labour Organization and World Health Organization to reduce occupational deaths, injuries and illnesses, and link occupational health with public health promotion as a means of promoting public health and education;

(n) Improve availability and access for all to sufficient, safe, culturally acceptable and nutritionally adequate food, increase consumer health protection, address issues of micro-nutrient deficiency and implement existing internationally agreed commitments and relevant standards and guidelines;

(o) Develop or strengthen, where applicable, preventive, promotive and curative programmes to address non-communicable diseases and conditions, such as cardiovascular diseases, cancer, diabetes, chronic respiratory diseases, injuries, violence and mental health disorders and associated risk factors, including alcohol, tobacco, unhealthy diets and lack of physical activity.

55. Implement, within the agreed time frames, all commitments agreed in the Declaration of Commitment on HIV/AIDS[34] adopted by the General Assembly at its 26th Special Session, emphasizing, in particular, the reduction of HIV prevalence among young men and women aged 15 to 24 by 25 per cent in the most affected countries by 2005, and globally by 2010, as well as combat malaria, tuberculosis and other diseases by, inter alia:

(a) Implementing national preventive and treatment strategies, regional and international cooperation measures and the development of international initiatives to provide special assistance to children orphaned by HIV/AIDS;

(b) Fulfilling commitments for the provision of sufficient resources to support the Global Fund to Fight AIDS, Tuberculosis and Malaria, while promoting access to the fund by countries most in need;

(c) Protecting the health of workers and promoting occupational safety, by, inter alia, taking into account, as appropriate, the voluntary Code of Practice on HIV/AIDS and the World of Work of the International Labour Organization to improve conditions of the workplace;

(d) Mobilizing adequate public, and encouraging private, financial resources for research and development on diseases of the poor, such as HIV/AIDS, malaria and tuberculosis, directed at biomedical and health research, as well as new vaccine and drug development.

56. Reduce respiratory diseases and other health impacts resulting from air pollution, with particular attention to women and children, by:

(a) Strengthening regional and national programmes, including through public–private partnerships, with technical and financial assistance to developing countries;

(b) Supporting the phasing-out of lead in gasoline;

(c) Strengthening and supporting efforts for the reduction of emissions through the use of cleaner fuels and modern pollution control techniques;

(d) Assisting developing countries in providing affordable energy to rural communities, particularly to reduce dependence on traditional fuel sources for cooking and heating, which affect the health of women and children.

57. Phase out lead in lead-based paints and in other sources of human exposure, work to prevent, in particular, children's exposure to lead and strengthen monitoring and surveillance efforts and the treatment of lead poisoning.

VII Sustainable development of small island developing States

58. Small island developing States are a special case both for environment and development. Although they continue to take the lead in the path towards sustainable development in their countries, they are increasingly constrained by the interplay of adverse factors clearly underlined in Agenda 21, the Programme of Action for the Sustainable Development of Small Island Developing States[35] and the decisions adopted at the 22nd Special Session of the General Assembly. This would include actions at all levels to:

   (a) Accelerate national and regional implementation of the Programme of Action, with adequate financial resources, including through Global Environment Facility focal areas, transfer of environmentally sound technologies and assistance for capacity-building from the international community;

   (b) Implement further sustainable fisheries management and improve financial returns from fisheries by supporting and strengthening relevant regional fisheries management organizations, as appropriate, such as the recently established Caribbean Regional Fisheries Mechanism and such agreements as the Convention on the Conservation and Management of Highly Migratory Fish Stocks in the Western and Central Pacific Ocean;

   (c) Assist small island developing States, including through the elaboration of specific initiatives, in delimiting and managing in a sustainable manner their coastal areas and exclusive economic zones and the continental shelf, including, where appropriate, the continental shelf areas beyond 200 miles from coastal baselines, as well as relevant regional management initiatives within the context of the United Nations Convention on the Law of the Sea and the regional seas programmes of the United Nations Environment Programme;

   (d) Provide support, including for capacity-building, for the development and further implementation of:

      (i) small island developing States-specific components within programmes of work on marine and coastal biological diversity;

      (ii) freshwater programmes for small island developing states, including through the Global Environment Facility focal areas.

   (e) Effectively reduce, prevent and control waste and pollution and their health-related impacts by undertaking initiatives by 2004 aimed at implementing the Global Programme of Action for the Protection of the Marine Environment from Land-based Activities in small island developing States;

   (f) Work to ensure that, in the ongoing negotiations and elaboration of the World Trade Organization work programme on trade in small economies, due account is taken of small island developing States, which have severe structural handicaps in integrating into the global economy, within the context of the Doha development agenda;

(g) Develop community-based initiatives on sustainable tourism by 2004 and build the capacities necessary to diversify tourism products, while protecting culture and traditions and effectively conserving and managing natural resources;

(h) Extend assistance to small island developing States in support of local communities and appropriate national and regional organizations of small island developing States for comprehensive hazard and risk management, disaster prevention, mitigation and preparedness, and help relieve the consequences of disasters, extreme weather events and other emergencies;

(i) Support the finalization and subsequent early operationalization, on agreed terms, of economic, social and environmental vulnerability indices and related indicators as tools for the achievement of the sustainable development of the small island developing States;

(j) Assist small island developing States in mobilizing adequate resources and partnerships for their adaptation needs relating to the adverse effects of climate change, sea level rise and climate variability, consistent with commitments under the United Nations Framework Convention on Climate Change, where applicable;

(k) Support efforts by small island developing States to build capacities and institutional arrangements to implement intellectual property regimes.

59. Support the availability of adequate, affordable and environmentally sound energy services for the sustainable development of small island developing States by, inter alia:

(a) Strengthening ongoing and supporting new efforts on energy supply and services, by 2004, including through the United Nations system and partnership initiatives;

(b) Developing and promoting efficient use of sources of energy, including indigenous sources and renewable energy, and building the capacities of small island developing States for training, technical know-how and strengthening national institutions in the area of energy management.

60. Provide support to small island developing States to develop capacity and strengthen:

(a) healthcare services for promoting equitable access to healthcare;

(b) health systems for making available necessary drugs and technology in a sustainable and affordable manner to fight and control communicable and non-communicable diseases, in particular HIV/AIDS, tuberculosis, diabetes, malaria and dengue fever;

(c) efforts to reduce and manage waste and pollution and building capacity for maintaining and managing systems to deliver water and sanitation services, in both rural and urban areas;

(d) efforts to implement initiatives aimed at poverty eradication, which have been outlined in section 2, 'Poverty eradication'.

61. Undertake a full and comprehensive review of the implementation of the Barbados Programme of Action on the Sustainable Development of Small Island Developing States in 2004, in accordance with the provisions set forth in General Assembly

resolution S-22/2, and in this context requests the General Assembly at its 57th session to consider convening an international meeting for the sustainable development of small island developing States.

VIII Sustainable development for Africa

62. Since the United Nations Conference on Environment and Development, sustainable development has remained elusive for many African countries. Poverty remains a major challenge and most countries on the continent have not benefited fully from the opportunities of globalization, further exacerbating the continent's marginalization. Africa's efforts to achieve sustainable development have been hindered by conflicts, insufficient investment, limited market access opportunities and supply-side constraints, unsustainable debt burdens, historically declining levels of official development assistance and the impact of HIV/AIDS. The World Summit on Sustainable Development should reinvigorate the commitment of the international community to address these special challenges and give effect to a new vision based on concrete actions for the implementation of Agenda 21 in Africa. The New Partnership for African Development (NEPAD) is a commitment by African leaders to the people of Africa. It recognizes that partnerships among African countries themselves and between them and with the international community are key elements of a shared and common vision to eradicate poverty; and furthermore, it aims to place their countries, both individually and collectively, on a path of sustained economic growth and sustainable development, while participating actively in the world economy and body politic. It provides a framework for sustainable development on the continent to be shared by all Africa's people. The international community welcomes NEPAD and pledges its support to the implementation of this vision, including through utilization of the benefits of South–South cooperation supported, inter alia, by the Tokyo International Conference on African Development. It also pledges support for other existing development frameworks that are owned and driven nationally by African countries and that embody poverty reduction strategies, including poverty reduction strategy papers. Achieving sustainable development includes actions at all levels to:

(a) Create an enabling environment at the regional, sub-regional, national and local levels in order to achieve sustained economic growth and sustainable development and support African efforts for peace, stability and security, the resolution and prevention of conflicts, democracy, good governance, respect for human rights and fundamental freedoms, including the right to development and gender equality;

(b) Support the implementation of the vision of NEPAD and other established regional and sub-regional efforts, including through financing, technical cooperation and institutional cooperation and human and institutional capacity-building at the regional, sub-regional and national levels, consistent with national policies, programmes and nationally owned and led strategies for poverty reduction and sustainable development, such as, where applicable, poverty reduction strategy papers;

(c) Promote technology development, transfer and diffusion to Africa and further develop technology and knowledge available in African centres of excellence;

(d) Support African countries in developing effective science and technology institutions and research activities capable of developing and adapting to world class technologies;

(e) Support the development of national programmes and strategies to promote education within the context of nationally owned and led strategies for poverty reduction and strengthen research institutions in education in order to increase the capacity to fully support the achievement of internationally agreed development goals related to education, including those contained in the Millennium Declaration on ensuring that, by 2015, children everywhere, boys and girls alike, will be able to complete a full course of primary schooling and that girls and boys will have equal access to all levels of education relevant to national needs;

(f) Enhance the industrial productivity, diversity and competitiveness of African countries through a combination of financial and technological support for the development of key infrastructure, access to technology, networking of research centres, adding value to export products, skills development and enhancing market access in support of sustainable development;

(g) Enhance the contribution of the industrial sector, in particular mining, minerals and metals, to the sustainable development of Africa by supporting the development of effective and transparent regulatory and management frameworks and value addition, broad-based participation, social and environmental responsibility and increased market access in order to create an attractive and conducive environment for investment;

(h) Provide financial and technical support to strengthen the capacity of African countries to undertake environmental legislative policy and institutional reform for sustainable development and to undertake environmental impact assessments and, as appropriate, to negotiate and implement multilateral environment agreements;

(i) Develop projects, programmes and partnerships with relevant stakeholders and mobilize resources for the effective implementation of the outcome of the African Process for the Protection and Development of the Marine and Coastal Environment;

(j) Deal effectively with energy problems in Africa, including through initiatives to:

(i) Establish and promote programmes, partnerships and initiatives to support Africa's efforts to implement NEPAD objectives on energy, which seek to secure access for at least 35 per cent of the African population within 20 years, especially in rural areas;

(ii) Provide support to implement other initiatives on energy, including the promotion of cleaner and more efficient use of natural gas and increased use of renewable energy, and to improve energy efficiency and access to advanced energy technologies, including cleaner fossil fuel technologies, particularly in rural and peri-urban areas;

(k) Assist African countries in mobilizing adequate resources for their adaptation needs relating to the adverse effects of climate change, extreme weather events, sea level rise and climate variability, and assist in developing national climate change strategies and mitigation programmes, and continue to take actions to mitigate the adverse effects on climate change in Africa consistent with the United Nations Framework Convention on Climate Change;

(l)   Support African efforts to develop affordable transport systems and infrastructure that promote sustainable development and connectivity in Africa;

(m) Further to paragraph 42 above, address the poverty affecting mountain communities in Africa;

(n)   Provide financial and technical support for afforestation and reforestation in Africa and to build capacity for sustainable forest management, including combating deforestation and measures to improve the policy and legal framework of the forest sector.

63. Provide financial and technical support for Africa's efforts to implement the Convention to Combat Desertification at the national level and to integrate indigenous knowledge systems into land and natural resources management practices, as appropriate, and improve extension services to rural communities and promote better land and watershed management practices, including through improved agricultural practices that address land degradation, in order to develop capacity for the implementation of national programmes.

64. Mobilize financial and other support to develop and strengthen health systems that aim to:

(a)   Promote equitable access to healthcare services;

(b)   Make available necessary drugs and technology in a sustainable and affordable manner to fight and control communicable diseases, including HIV/AIDS, malaria and tuberculosis, and trypanosomiasis, as well as non-communicable diseases, including those caused by poverty;

(c)   Build capacity of medical and paramedical personnel;

(d)   Promote indigenous medical knowledge, as appropriate, including traditional medicine;

(e)   Research and control Ebola disease.

65. Deal effectively with natural disasters and conflicts, including their humanitarian and environmental impacts, recognizing that conflicts in Africa have hindered, and in many cases obliterated, both the gains and efforts aimed at sustainable development, with the most vulnerable members of society, particularly women and children, being the most impacted victims, through efforts and initiatives, at all levels, to:

(a)   Provide financial and technical assistance to strengthen the capacities of African countries, including institutional and human capacity, including at the local level, for effective disaster management, including observation and early warning systems, assessments, prevention, preparedness, response and recovery;

(b)   Provide support to African countries to enable them to better deal with the displacement of people as a result of natural disasters and conflicts and put in place rapid response mechanisms;

(c)   Support Africa's efforts for the prevention and resolution, management and mitigation of conflicts and its early response to emerging conflict situations to avert tragic humanitarian consequences;

(d)   Provide support to refugee host countries in rehabilitating infrastructure and environment, including ecosystems and habitats, that were damaged in the process of receiving and settling refugees.

66. Promote integrated water resources development and optimize the upstream and downstream benefits therefrom, the development and effective management of

water resources across all uses and the protection of water quality and aquatic ecosystems, including through initiatives at all levels, to:

(a) Provide access to potable domestic water, hygiene education and improved sanitation and waste management at the household level through initiatives to encourage public and private investment in water supply and sanitation that give priority to the needs of the poor within stable and transparent national regulatory frameworks provided by Governments, while respecting local conditions involving all concerned stakeholders and monitoring the performance and improving the accountability of public institutions and private companies; and develop critical water supply, reticulation and treatment infrastructure, and build capacity to maintain and manage systems to deliver water and sanitation services in both rural and urban areas;

(b) Develop and implement integrated river basin and watershed management strategies and plans for all major water bodies, consistent with paragraph 25 above;

(c) Strengthen regional, sub-regional and national capacities for data collection and processing and for planning, research, monitoring, assessment and enforcement, as well as arrangements for water resource management;

(d) Protect water resources, including groundwater and wetland ecosystems, against pollution, and, in cases of the most acute water scarcity, support efforts for developing non-conventional water resources, including the energy-efficient, cost-effective and sustainable desalination of seawater, rainwater harvesting and recycling of water.

67. Achieve significantly improved sustainable agricultural productivity and food security in furtherance of the agreed Millennium development goals, including those contained in the Millennium Declaration, in particular to halve by 2015 the proportion of people who suffer from hunger, including through initiatives at all levels to:

(a) Support the development and implementation of national policies and programmes, including research programmes and development plans of African countries to regenerate their agricultural sector and sustainably develop their fisheries, and increase investment in infrastructure, technology and extension services, according to country needs. African countries should be in the process of developing and implementing food security strategies, within the context of national poverty eradication programmes, by 2005;

(b) Promote and support efforts and initiatives to secure equitable access to land tenure and clarify resource rights and responsibilities through land and tenure reform processes that respect the rule of law and are enshrined in national law, and provide access to credit for all, especially women, and that enable economic and social empowerment and poverty eradication, as well as efficient and ecologically sound utilization of land, and that enable women producers to become decision-makers and owners in the sector, including the right to inherit land;

(c) Improve market access for goods, including goods originating from African countries, in particular least developed countries, within the framework of the Doha Ministerial Declaration, without prejudging the outcome of the World Trade Organization negotiations, as well as within the framework of preferential agreements;

(d) Provide support for African countries to improve regional trade and economic integration between African countries. Attract and increase investment in regional market infrastructure;

(e) Support livestock development programmes aimed at progressive and effective control of animal diseases.

68. Achieve sound management of chemicals, with particular focus on hazardous chemicals and wastes, inter alia, through initiatives to assist African countries in elaborating national chemical profiles and regional and national frameworks and strategies for chemical management and establishing chemical focal points.

69. Bridge the digital divide and create digital opportunity in terms of access infrastructure and technology transfer and application through integrated initiatives for Africa. Create an enabling environment to attract investment, accelerate existing and new programmes and projects to connect essential institutions and stimulate the adoption of information communication technologies in government and commerce programmes and other aspects of national economic and social life.

70. Support Africa's efforts to attain sustainable tourism that contributes to social, economic and infrastructure development through the following measures:

(a) Implementing projects at the local, national and sub-regional levels, with specific emphasis on marketing African tourism products, such as adventure tourism, ecotourism and cultural tourism;

(b) Establishing and supporting national and cross-border conservation areas to promote ecosystem conservation according to the ecosystem approach, and to promote sustainable tourism;

(c) Respecting local traditions and cultures and promoting the use of indigenous knowledge in natural resource management and ecotourism;

(d) Assisting host communities in managing their tourism projects for maximum benefit, while limiting negative impact on their traditions, culture and environment;

(e) Support the conservation of Africa's biological diversity, the sustainable use of its components and the fair and equitable sharing of the benefits arising out of the utilization of genetic resources, in accordance with commitments that countries have under biodiversity-related agreements to which they are parties, including such agreements as the Convention on Biological Diversity and the Convention on International Trade in Endangered Species of Wild Fauna and Flora, as well as regional biodiversity agreements.

71. Support African countries in their efforts to implement the Habitat Agenda and the Istanbul Declaration through initiatives to strengthen national and local institutional capacities in the areas of sustainable urbanization and human settlements, provide support for adequate shelter and basic services and the development of efficient and effective governance systems in cities and other human settlements and strengthen, inter alia, the joint programme on managing water for African cities of the United Nations Human Settlements Programme and the United Nations Environment Programme.

IX Other regional initiatives

72. Important initiatives have been developed within other United Nations regions and regional, sub-regional and transregional forums to promote sustainable development. The international community welcomes these efforts and the results already achieved, calls for actions at all levels for their further development, while encouraging inter-regional, intra-regional and international cooperation in this respect, and expresses its support for their further development and implementation by the countries of the regions.

A. Sustainable development in Latin America and the Caribbean

73. The Initiative of Latin America and the Caribbean on Sustainable Development is an undertaking by the leaders of that region that, building on the Platform for Action on the Road to Johannesburg, 2002,[36] which was approved in Rio de Janeiro in October 2001, recognizes the importance of regional actions towards sustainable development and takes into account the region's singularities, shared visions and cultural diversity. It is targeted towards the adoption of concrete actions in different areas of sustainable development, such as biodiversity, water resources, vulnerabilities and sustainable cities, social aspects, including health and poverty, economic aspects, including energy, and institutional arrangements, including capacity-building, indicators and participation of civil society, taking into account ethics for sustainable development.

74. The Initiative envisages the development of actions among countries in the region that may foster South–South cooperation and may count with the support of groups of countries, as well as multilateral and regional organizations, including financial institutions. As a framework for cooperation, the Initiative is open to partnerships with governments and all major groups.

B. Sustainable development in Asia and the Pacific

75. Bearing in mind the target of halving the number of people who live in poverty by the year 2015, as provided in the Millennium Declaration, the Phnom Penh Regional Platform on Sustainable Development for Asia and the Pacific[37] recognized that the region contains over half of the world's population and the largest number of the world's people living in poverty. Hence, sustainable development in the region is critical to achieving sustainable development at the global level.

76. The Regional Platform identified seven initiatives for follow-up action: capacity-building for sustainable development; poverty reduction for sustainable development; cleaner production and sustainable energy; land management and biodiversity conservation; protection and management of and access to freshwater resources; oceans, coastal and marine resources and sustainable development of small island developing States; and action on atmosphere and climate change. Follow-up actions of these initiatives will be taken through national strategies and relevant regional and sub-regional initiatives, such as the Regional Action Programme for Environmentally Sound and Sustainable Development and the Kitakyushu Initiative for a Clean Environment, adopted at the Fourth Ministerial

Conference on Environment and Development in Asia and the Pacific organized by the Economic and Social Commission for Asia and the Pacific.

C. Sustainable development in the West Asia region

77.　The West Asia region is known for its scarce water and limited fertile land resources. The region has made progress to a more knowledge-based production of higher value-added commodities.

78.　The regional preparatory meeting endorsed the following priorities: poverty alleviation; relief of debt burden; and sustainable management of natural resources, including, inter alia, integrated water resources management, implementation of programmes to combat desertification, integrated coastal zone management and land and water pollution control.

D. Sustainable development in the Economic Commission for Europe region

79.　The Economic Commission for Europe regional ministerial meeting for the World Summit on Sustainable Development recognized that the region has a major role to play and responsibilities in global efforts to achieve sustainable development by concrete actions. The region recognized that different levels of economic development in countries of the region may require the application of different approaches and mechanisms to implement Agenda 21. In order to address the three pillars of sustainable development in a mutually reinforcing way, the region identified its priority actions for sustainable development for the Economic Commission for Europe region in its Ministerial Statement to the Summit.[38]

80.　In furtherance of the region's commitment to sustainable development, there are ongoing efforts at the regional, sub-regional and transregional levels, including, inter alia, the Environment for Europe process; the fifth Economic Commission for Europe ministerial conference, to be held in Kiev in May 2003; the development of an environmental strategy for the 12 countries of Eastern Europe; the Caucasus and Central Asia; the Central Asian Agenda 21; work of the Organisation for Economic Co-operation and Development on sustainable development; the European Union sustainable development strategy; and regional and sub-regional conventions and processes relevant to sustainable development, including, inter alia, the Convention on Access to Information, Public Participation in Decision-Making and Access to Justice in Environmental Matters (Aarhus Convention), the Alpine Convention, the North American Commission for Environmental Cooperation, the International Boundary Waters Treaty Act, the Iqaluit Declaration of the Arctic Council, the Baltic Agenda 21 and the Mediterranean Agenda 21.

X Means of implementation

81.　The implementation of Agenda 21 and the achievement of the internationally agreed development goals, including those contained in the Millennium Declaration as well as in the present plan of action, require a substantially increased effort, both by countries themselves and by the rest of the international community, based on the recognition that each country has primary responsibility for its own development and that the role of national policies and development strategies cannot be overemphasized, taking fully into account the Rio principles, including, in particular, the principle of common but differentiated responsibilities, which states:

> *"States shall cooperate in a spirit of global partnership to conserve, protect and restore the health and integrity of the Earth's ecosystem. In view of the different contributions to global environmental degradation, States have common but differentiated responsibilities. The developed countries acknowledge the responsibility that they bear in the international pursuit of sustainable development in view of the pressures their societies place on the global environment and of the technologies and financial resources they command."*

The internationally agreed development goals, including those contained in the Millennium Declaration and Agenda 21, as well as in the present plan of action, will require significant increases in the flow of financial resources as elaborated in the Monterrey Consensus, including through new and additional financial resources, in particular to developing countries, to support the implementation of national policies and programmes developed by them, improved trade opportunities, access to and transfer of environmentally sound technologies on a concessional or preferential basis, as mutually agreed, education and awareness-raising, capacity-building and information for decision-making and scientific capabilities within the agreed time frame required to meet these goals and initiatives. Progress to this end will require that the international community implement the outcomes of major United Nations conferences, such as the programmes of action adopted at the Third United Nations Conference on the Least Developed Countries[39] and the Global Conference on the Sustainable Development of Small Island Developing States, and relevant international agreements since 1992, particularly those of the International Conference on Financing for Development and the Fourth Ministerial Conference of the World Trade Organization, including building on them as part of a process of achieving sustainable development.

82. Mobilizing and increasing the effective use of financial resources and achieving the national and international economic conditions needed to fulfil internationally agreed development goals, including those contained in the Millennium Declaration, to eliminate poverty, improve social conditions and raise living standards and protect our environment, will be our first step to ensuring that the 21st century becomes the century of sustainable development for all.

83. In our common pursuit of growth, poverty eradication and sustainable development, a critical challenge is to ensure the necessary internal conditions for mobilizing domestic savings, both public and private, sustaining adequate levels of productive investment and increasing human capacity. A crucial task is to enhance the efficacy, coherence and consistency of macro-economic policies. An enabling domestic environment is vital for mobilizing domestic resources, increasing productivity, reducing capital flight, encouraging the private sector and attracting and making effective use of international investment and assistance. Efforts to create such an environment should be supported by the international community.

84. Facilitate greater flows of foreign direct investment so as to support the sustainable development activities, including the development of infrastructure, of developing countries, and enhance the benefits that developing countries can draw from foreign direct investment, with particular actions to:

(a) Create the necessary domestic and international conditions to facilitate significant increases in the flow of foreign direct investment to developing countries, in particular the least developed countries, which is critical to sustainable development, particularly foreign direct investment flows for infrastructure development and other priority areas in developing countries to supplement the domestic resources mobilized by them;

(b) Encourage foreign direct investment in developing countries and countries with economies in transition through export credits that could be instrumental to sustainable development.

85. Recognize that a substantial increase in official development assistance and other resources will be required if developing countries are to achieve the internationally agreed development goals and objectives, including those contained in the Millennium Declaration. To build support for official development assistance, we will cooperate to further improve policies and development strategies, both nationally and internationally, to enhance aid effectiveness, with actions to:

(a) Make available the increased commitments in official development assistance announced by several developed countries at the International Conference on Financing for Development. Urge the developed countries that have not done so to make concrete efforts towards the target of 0.7 per cent of gross national product as official development assistance to developing countries and effectively implement their commitment on such assistance to the least developed countries as contained in paragraph 83 of the Programme of Action for the Least Developed Countries for the Decade 2001–2010,[40] which was adopted in Brussels on 20 May 2001. We also encourage developing countries to build on progress achieved in ensuring that official development assistance is used effectively to help achieve development goals and targets in accordance with the outcome of the International Conference on Financing for Development. We acknowledge the efforts of all donors, commend those donors whose contributions exceed, reach or are increasing towards the targets, and underline the importance of undertaking to examine the means and time frames for achieving the targets and goals;

(b) Encourage recipient and donor countries, as well as international institutions, to make official development assistance more efficient and effective for poverty eradication, sustained economic growth and sustainable development. In this regard, intensify efforts by the multilateral and bilateral financial and development institutions, in accordance with paragraph 43 of the Monterrey Consensus, in particular to harmonize their operational procedures at the highest standards so as to reduce transaction costs and make disbursement and delivery of official development assistance more flexible and more responsive to the needs of developing countries, taking into account national development needs and objectives under the ownership of recipient countries, and to use development frameworks that are owned and driven by developing countries and that embody poverty reduction strategies, including poverty reduction strategy papers, as vehicles for aid delivery, upon request.

86. Make full and effective use of existing financial mechanisms and institutions, including through actions at all levels to:

(a) Strengthen ongoing efforts to reform the existing international financial architecture to foster a transparent, equitable and inclusive system that is able to provide for the effective participation of developing countries in the international economic decision-making processes and institutions, as well as for their effective and equitable participation in the formulation of financial standards and codes;

(b) Promote, inter alia, measures in source and destination countries to improve transparency and information about financial flows to contribute to stability in the international financial environment. Measures that mitigate the impact of excessive volatility of short-term capital flows are important and must be considered;

(c) Work to ensure that the funds are made available on a timely, more assured and predictable basis to international organizations and agencies, where appropriate, for their sustainable development activities, programmes and projects;

(d) Encourage the private sector, including transnational corporations, private foundations and civil society institutions, to provide financial and technical assistance to developing countries;

(e) Support new and existing public/private-sector financing mechanisms for developing countries and countries with economies in transition to benefit, in particular, small entrepreneurs and small, medium-sized and community-based enterprises and to improve their infrastructure, while ensuring the transparency and accountability of such mechanisms.

87. Welcome the successful and substantial third replenishment of the Global Environment Facility, which will enable it to address the funding requirements of new focal areas and existing ones and continue to be responsive to the needs and concerns of its recipient countries, in particular developing countries, and further encourage the Global Environment Facility to leverage additional funds from key public and private organizations, improve the management of funds through more speedy and streamlined procedures and simplify its project cycle.

88. Explore ways of generating new public and private innovative sources of finance for development purposes, provided that those sources do not unduly burden developing countries, noting the proposal to use special drawing rights allocations for development purposes, as set forth in paragraph 44 of the Monterrey Consensus.

89. Reduce unsustainable debt burden through such actions as debt relief and, as appropriate, debt cancellation and other innovative mechanisms geared to comprehensively address the debt problems of developing countries, in particular the poorest and most heavily indebted ones. Therefore, debt relief measures should, where appropriate, be pursued vigorously and expeditiously, including within the Paris and London Clubs and other relevant forums, in order to contribute to debt sustainability and facilitate sustainable development, while recognizing that debtors and creditors must share responsibility for preventing and resolving unsustainable debt situations, and that external debt relief can play a key role in liberating resources that can then be directed towards activities consistent with attaining sustainable growth and development. Therefore, we support paragraphs 47 to 51 of the Monterrey Consensus dealing with external debt. Debt relief arrangements should seek to avoid imposing any unfair burdens on other developing countries. There should be an increase in the use of grants for the poorest, debt-vulnerable countries. Countries are encouraged to develop national comprehensive strategies to monitor and manage external liabilities as a key element in reducing national vulnerabilities. In this regard, actions are required to:

(a) Implement speedily, effectively and fully the enhanced heavily lindebted poor countries (HIPC) initiative, which should be fully financed through additional resources, taking into consideration, as appropriate, measures to address any fundamental changes in the economic circumstances of those developing countries with unsustainable debt burden caused by natural catastrophes, severe terms-of-trade shocks or affected by conflict, taking into account initiatives which have been undertaken to reduce outstanding indebtedness;

(b) Encourage participation in the HIPC initiative of all creditors that have not yet done so;

(c) Bring international debtors and creditors together in relevant international forums to restructure unsustainable debt in a timely and efficient manner, taking into account the need to involve the private sector in the resolution of crises due to indebtedness, where appropriate;

(d) Acknowledge the problems of the debt sustainability of some non-HIPC low-income countries, in particular those facing exceptional circumstances;

(e) Encourage exploring innovative mechanisms to comprehensively address the debt problems of developing countries, including middle-income countries and countries with economies in transition. Such mechanisms may include debt-for-sustainable-development swaps;

(f) Encourage donor countries to take steps to ensure that resources provided for debt relief do not detract from official development assistance resources intended for developing countries.

90. Recognizing the major role that trade can play in achieving sustainable development and in eradicating poverty, we encourage members of the World Trade Organization (WTO) to pursue the work programme agreed at their Fourth Ministerial Conference. In order for developing countries, especially the least developed among them, to secure their share in the growth of world trade commensurate with the needs of their economic development, we urge WTO members to take the following actions:

(a) Facilitate the accession of all developing countries, particularly the least developed countries, as well as countries with economies in transition, that apply for membership in WTO, in accordance with the Monterrey Consensus;

(b) Support the work programme adopted at the Doha Ministerial Conference as an important commitment on the part of developed and developing countries to mainstream appropriate trade policies in their respective development policies and programmes;

(c) Implement substantial trade-related technical assistance and capacity-building measures and support the Doha Development Agenda Global Trust Fund, established after the Doha Ministerial Conference, as an important step forward in ensuring a sound and predictable basis for WTO-related technical assistance and capacity-building;

(d) Implement the New Strategy for Technical Cooperation for Capacity-Building, Growth and Integration endorsed in the Doha Declaration;

(e) Fully support the implementation of the Integrated Framework for Trade-Related Technical Assistance to Least Developed Countries and urge development partners to significantly increase contributions to the Trust Fund for the framework, in accordance with the Doha Ministerial Declaration.

91. In accordance with the Doha Declaration, as well as with relevant decisions taken at Doha, we are determined to take concrete action to address issues and concerns

raised by developing countries regarding the implementation of some WTO agreements and decisions, including the difficulties and resource constraints faced by them in fulfilling those agreements.

92. Call upon members of the World Trade Organization to fulfil the commitments made in the Doha Ministerial Declaration, notably in terms of market access, in particular for products of export interest to developing countries, especially least developed countries, by implementing the following actions, taking into account paragraph 45 of the Doha Ministerial Declaration:

   (a) Review all special and differential treatment provisions with a view to strengthening them and making them more precise, effective and operational in accordance with paragraph 44 of the Doha Ministerial Declaration;

   (b) Aim to reduce or, as appropriate, eliminate tariffs on non-agricultural products, including the reduction or elimination of tariff peaks, high tariffs and tariff escalation, as well as non-tariff barriers, in particular on products of export interest to developing countries. Product coverage should be comprehensive and without a priori exclusions. The negotiations shall take fully into account the special needs and interests of developing and least developed countries, including through less than full reciprocity in reduction commitments, in accordance with the Doha Ministerial Declaration;

   (c) Fulfil, without prejudging the outcome of the negotiations, the commitment for comprehensive negotiations initiated under article 20 of the Agreement on Agriculture, as referred to in the Doha Ministerial Declaration,[41] aiming at substantial improvements in market access, reductions of with a view to phasing out all forms of export subsidies, and substantial reductions in trade-distorting domestic support, while agreeing that the provisions for special and differential treatment for developing countries shall be an integral part of all elements of the negotiations and shall be embodied in the schedules of concession and commitments and, as appropriate, in the rules and disciplines to be negotiated so as to be operationally effective and to enable developing countries to effectively take account of their development needs, including food security and rural development. Take note of the non-trade concerns reflected in the negotiating proposals submitted by members of the World Trade Organization and confirm that non-trade concerns will be taken into account in the negotiations as provided for in the Agreement on Agriculture, in accordance with the Doha Ministerial Declaration.

93. Call on developed countries that have not already done so to work towards the objective of duty-free and quota-free access for all least developed countries' exports, as envisaged in the Programme of Action for the Least Developed Countries for the Decade 2001–2010.

94. Commit to actively pursue the work programme of the World Trade Organization to address the trade-related issues and concerns affecting the fuller integration of small, vulnerable economies into the multilateral trading system in a manner commensurate with their special circumstances and in support of their efforts towards sustainable development, in accordance with paragraph 35 of the Doha Declaration.

95. Build the capacity of commodity-dependent countries to diversify exports through, inter alia, financial and technical assistance, international assistance for economic diversification and sustainable resource management, and address the instability of commodity prices and declining terms of trade, as well as strengthen the

activities covered by the second account of the Common Fund for Commodities to support sustainable development.

96. Enhance the benefits for developing countries, as well as countries with economies in transition, from trade liberalization, including through public–private partnerships, through, inter alia, action at all levels, including through financial support for technical assistance, the development of technology and capacity-building to developing countries to:

(a) Enhance trade infrastructure and strengthen institutions;

(b) Increase developing country capacity to diversify and increase exports to cope with the instability of commodity prices and declining terms of trade;

(c) Increase the value added of developing country exports.

97. Continue to enhance the mutual supportiveness of trade, environment and development with a view to achieving sustainable development through actions at all levels to:

(a) Encourage the WTO Committee on Trade and Environment and the WTO Committee on Trade and Development, within their respective mandates, to each act as a forum to identify and debate developmental and environmental aspects of the negotiations in order to help achieve an outcome which benefits sustainable development in accordance with the commitments made under the Doha Ministerial Declaration;

(b) Support the completion of the work programme of the Doha Ministerial Declaration on subsidies so as to promote sustainable development and enhance the environment, and encourage reform of subsidies that have considerable negative effects on the environment and are incompatible with sustainable development;

(c) Encourage efforts to promote cooperation on trade, environment and development, including in the field of providing technical assistance to developing countries, between the secretariats of WTO, UNCTAD, UNDP, UNEP, and other relevant international environmental and development and regional organizations;

(d) Encourage the voluntary use of environmental impact assessments as an important national-level tool to better identify trade, environment and development interlinkages. Further encourage countries and international organizations with experience in this field to provide technical assistance to developing countries for these purposes.

98. Promote mutual supportiveness between the multilateral trading system and the multilateral environmental agreements, consistent with sustainable development goals, in support of the work programme agreed through WTO, while recognizing the importance of maintaining the integrity of both sets of instruments.

99. Complement and support the Doha Ministerial Declaration and the Monterrey Consensus by undertaking further action at the national, regional and international levels, including through public/private partnerships, to enhance the benefits, in particular for developing countries as well as for countries with economies in transition, of trade liberalization, through, inter alia, actions at all levels to:

(a) Establish and strengthen existing trade and cooperation agreements, consistent with the multilateral trading system, with a view to achieving sustainable development;

(b) Support voluntary WTO-compatible market-based initiatives for the creation and expansion of domestic and international markets for environmentally friendly goods and services, including organic products, which maximize environmental and developmental benefits through, inter alia, capacity-building and technical assistance to developing countries;

(c) Support measures to simplify and make more transparent domestic regulations and procedures that affect trade so as to assist exporters, particularly those from developing countries.

100. Address the public health problems affecting many developing and least developed countries, especially those resulting from HIV/AIDS, tuberculosis, malaria and other epidemics, while noting the importance of the Doha Declaration on the Agreement on Trade-Related Aspects of Intellectual Property Rights (TRIPS Agreement) and public health,[42] in which it was agreed that the TRIPS Agreement does not and should not prevent WTO members from taking measures to protect public health. Accordingly, while reiterating our commitment to the TRIPS Agreement, we reaffirm that the Agreement can and should be interpreted and implemented in a manner supportive of WTO members' right to protect public health and, in particular, to promote access to medicines for all.

101. States should cooperate to promote a supportive and open international economic system that would lead to economic growth and sustainable development in all countries to better address the problems of environmental degradation. Trade policy measures for environmental purposes should not constitute a means of arbitrary or unjustifiable discrimination or a disguised restriction on international trade. Unilateral actions to deal with environmental challenges outside the jurisdiction of the importing country should be avoided. Environmental measures addressing transboundary or global environmental problems should, as far as possible, be based on an international consensus.

102. Take steps with a view to the avoidance of, and refrain from, any unilateral measure not in accordance with international law and the Charter of the United Nations that impedes the full achievement of economic and social development by the population of the affected countries, in particular women and children, that hinders their well-being or that creates obstacles to the full enjoyment of their human rights, including the right of everyone to a standard of living adequate for their health and well-being and their right to food, medical care and the necessary social services. Ensure that food and medicine are not used as tools for political pressure.

103. Take further effective measures to remove obstacles to the realization of the right of peoples to self-determination, in particular peoples living under colonial and foreign occupation, which continue to adversely affect their economic and social development and are incompatible with the dignity and worth of the human person and must be combated and eliminated. People under foreign occupation must be protected in accordance with the provisions of international humanitarian law.

104. In accordance with the Declaration on Principles of International Law concerning Friendly Relations and Cooperation among States in accordance with the Charter of the United Nations,[43] this shall not be construed as authorizing or encouraging any action which would dismember or impair, totally or in part, the territorial integrity or political unity of sovereign and independent States conducting themselves in compliance with the principle of equal rights and self-determination

of peoples and thus possessed of a Government representing the whole people belonging to the territory without distinction of any kind.

* * *

105. Promote, facilitate and finance, as appropriate, access to and the development, transfer and diffusion of environmentally sound technologies and corresponding know-how, in particular to developing countries and countries with economies in transition on favourable terms, including on concessional and preferential terms, as mutually agreed, as set out in Chapter 34 of Agenda 21, including through urgent actions at all levels to:

(a) Provide information more effectively;

(b) Enhance existing national institutional capacity in developing countries to improve access to and the development, transfer and diffusion of environmentally sound technologies and corresponding know-how;

(c) Facilitate country-driven technology needs assessments;

(d) Establish legal and regulatory frameworks in both supplier and recipient countries that expedite the transfer of environmentally sound technologies in a cost-effective manner by both public and private sectors and support their implementation;

(e) Promote the access and transfer of technology related to early warning systems and to mitigation programmes to developing countries affected by natural disasters.

106. Improve the transfer of technologies to developing countries, in particular at the bilateral and regional levels, including through urgent actions at all levels to:

(a) Improve interaction and collaboration, stakeholder relationships and networks between and among universities, research institutions, government agencies and the private sector;

(b) Develop and strengthen networking of related institutional support structures, such as technology and productivity centres, research, training and development institutions, and national and regional cleaner production centres;

(c) Create partnerships conducive to investment and technology transfer, development and diffusion to assist developing countries, as well as countries with economies in transition, in sharing best practices and promoting programmes of assistance, and encourage collaboration between corporations and research institutes to enhance industrial efficiency, agricultural productivity, environmental management and competitiveness;

(d) Provide assistance to developing countries, as well as to countries with economies in transition, in accessing environmentally sound technologies that are publicly owned or in the public domain, as well as available knowledge in the public domain on science and technology, and in accessing the know-how and expertise required in order for them to make independent use of this knowledge in pursuing their development goals;

(e) Support existing mechanisms and, where appropriate, establish new mechanisms for the development, transfer and diffusion of environmentally sound technologies to developing countries and economies in transition.

* * *

107. Assist developing countries in building capacity to access a larger share of multilateral and global research and development programmes. In this regard, strengthen and, where appropriate, create centres for sustainable development in developing countries.

108. Build greater capacity in science and technology for sustainable development, with action to improve collaboration and partnerships on research and development and their widespread application among research institutions, universities, the private sector, governments, non-governmental organizations and networks, as well as between and among scientists and academics of developing and developed countries, and in this regard encourage networking with and between centres of scientific excellence in developing countries.

109. Improve policy- and decision-making at all levels through, inter alia, improved collaboration between natural and social scientists, and between scientists and policy-makers, including through urgent actions at all levels to:

    (a) Increase the use of scientific knowledge and technology and increase the beneficial use of local and indigenous knowledge in a manner respectful of the holders of that knowledge and consistent with national law;

    (b) Make greater use of integrated scientific assessments, risk assessments and interdisciplinary and intersectoral approaches;

    (c) Continue to support and collaborate with international scientific assessments supporting decision-making, including the Intergovernmental Panel on Climate Change, with the broad participation of developing country experts;

    (d) Assist developing countries in developing and implementing science and technology policies;

    (e) Establish partnerships between scientific, public and private institutions, including by integrating the advice of scientists into decision-making bodies to ensure a greater role for science, technology development and engineering sectors;

    (f) Promote and improve science-based decision-making and reaffirm the precautionary approach as set out in principle 15 of the Rio Declaration on Environment and Development, which states:

        "In order to protect the environment, the precautionary approach shall be widely applied by States according to their capabilities. Where there are threats of serious or irreversible damage, lack of full scientific certainty shall not be used as a reason for postponing cost-effective measures to prevent environmental degradation."

110. Assist developing countries, through international cooperation, in enhancing their capacity in their efforts to address issues pertaining to environmental protection, including in their formulation and implementation of policies for environmental management and protection, including through urgent actions at all levels to:

    (a) Improve their use of science and technology for environmental monitoring, assessment models, accurate databases and integrated information systems;

    (b) Promote and, where appropriate, improve their use of satellite technologies for quality data collection, verification and updating, and further improve aerial and ground-based observations in support of their efforts to collect quality, accurate, long-term, consistent and reliable data;

    (c) Set up and, where appropriate, further develop national statistical services capable of providing sound data on science education and research and development activities that are necessary for effective science and technology policy-making.

111. Establish regular channels between policy-makers and the scientific community to request and receive science and technology advice for the implementation of Agenda 21 and create and strengthen networks for science and education for sustainable development, at all levels, with the aim of sharing knowledge, experience and best practices and building scientific capacities, particularly in developing countries.

112. Use information and communication technologies, where appropriate, as tools to increase the frequency of communication and the sharing of experience and knowledge and to improve the quality of and access to information and communications technology in all countries, building on the work facilitated by the United Nations Information and Communications Technology Task Force and the efforts of other relevant international and regional forums.

113. Support publicly funded research and development entities to engage in strategic alliances for the purpose of enhancing research and development to achieve cleaner production and product technologies through, inter alia, the mobilization from all sources of adequate financial and technical resources, including new and additional resources, and encourage the transfer and diffusion of those technologies, in particular to developing countries.

114. Examine issues of global public interest through open, transparent and inclusive workshops to promote a better public understanding of such questions.

115. Further resolve to take concerted action against international terrorism, which causes serious obstacles to sustainable development.

* * *

116. Education is critical for promoting sustainable development. It is therefore essential to mobilize necessary resources, including financial resources at all levels, by bilateral and multilateral donors, including the World Bank and the regional development banks, by civil society and by foundations to complement the efforts by national governments to pursue the following goals and actions:

    (a) Meet the Millennium development goal of achieving universal primary education, ensuring that, by 2015, children everywhere, boys and girls alike, will be able to complete a full course of primary schooling;

    (b) Provide all children, particularly those living in rural areas and those living in poverty, especially girls, with the access and opportunity to complete a full course of primary education.

117. Provide financial assistance and support to education, research, public awareness programmes and developmental institutions in developing countries and countries with economies in transition in order to:

    (a) Sustain their educational infrastructures and programmes, including those related to environment and public health education;

    (b) Consider means of avoiding the frequent, serious financial constraints faced by many institutions of higher learning, including universities around the world, particularly in developing countries and countries in transition.

118. Address the impact of HIV/AIDS on the educational system in those countries seriously affected by the pandemic.

119. Allocate national and international resources for basic education as proposed by the Dakar Framework for Action on Education for All and for improved integration

of sustainable development into education and in bilateral and multilateral development programmes, and improve integration between publicly funded research and development and development programmes.

120. Eliminate gender disparity in primary and secondary education by 2005, as provided in the Dakar Framework for Action on Education for All, and at all levels of education no later than 2015, to meet the development goals contained in the Millennium Declaration, with action to ensure, inter alia, equal access to all levels and forms of education, training and capacity-building by gender mainstreaming, and by creating a gender-sensitive educational system.

121. Integrate sustainable development into education systems at all levels of education in order to promote education as a key agent for change.

122. Develop, implement, monitor and review education action plans and programmes at the national, sub-national and local levels, as appropriate, that reflect the Dakar Framework for Action on Education for All and that are relevant to local conditions and needs leading to the achievement of community development and make education for sustainable development a part of those plans.

123. Provide all community members with a wide range of formal and non-formal continuing educational opportunities, including volunteer community service programmes, in order to end illiteracy and emphasize the importance of lifelong learning and promote sustainable development.

124. Support the use of education to promote sustainable development, including through urgent actions at all levels to:

    (a) Integrate information and communications technology in school curriculum development to ensure its access by both rural and urban communities and provide assistance, particularly to developing countries, inter alia, for the establishment of an appropriate enabling environment required for such technology;

    (b) Promote, as appropriate, affordable and increased access to programmes for students, researchers and engineers from developing countries in the universities and research institutions of developed countries in order to promote the exchange of experience and capacity that will benefit all partners;

    (c) Continue to implement the work programme of the Commission on Sustainable Development on education for sustainable development;

    (d) Recommend to the United Nations General Assembly that it consider adopting a decade of education for sustainable development, starting in 2005.

* * *

125. Enhance and accelerate human, institutional and infrastructure capacity-building initiatives and promote partnerships in that regard that respond to the specific needs of developing countries in the context of sustainable development.

126. Support local, national, sub-regional and regional initiatives with action to develop, use and adapt knowledge and techniques and to enhance local, national, sub-regional and regional centres of excellence for education, research and training in order to strengthen the knowledge capacity of developing countries and countries with economies in transition through, inter alia, the mobilization from all sources of adequate financial and other resources, including new and additional resources.

127. Provide technical and financial assistance to developing countries, including through the strengthening of capacity-building efforts, such as the United Nations Development Programme Capacity 21 programme, to:

(a) Assess their own capacity development needs and opportunities at the individual, institutional and societal levels;

(b) Design programmes for capacity-building and support for local, national and community-level programmes that focus on meeting the challenges of globalization more effectively and attaining the internationally agreed development goals, including those contained in the Millennium Declaration;

(c) Develop the capacity of civil society, including youth, to participate, as appropriate, in designing, implementing and reviewing sustainable development policies and strategies at all levels;

(d) Build and, where appropriate, strengthen national capacities for carrying out effective implementation of Agenda 21.

* * *

128. Ensure access, at the national level, to environmental information and judicial and administrative proceedings in environmental matters, as well as public participation in decision-making, so as to further principle 10 of the Rio Declaration on Environment and Development, taking into full account principles 5, 7 and 11 of the Declaration.

129. Strengthen national and regional information and statistical and analytical services relevant to sustainable development policies and programmes, including data disaggregated by sex, age and other factors, and encourage donors to provide financial and technical support to developing countries to enhance their capacity to formulate policies and implement programmes for sustainable development.

130. Encourage further work on indicators for sustainable development by countries at the national level, including integration of gender aspects, on a voluntary basis, in line with national conditions and priorities.

131. Promote further work on indicators, in conformity with paragraph 3 of decision 9/4 of the Commission on Sustainable Development.[44]

132. Promote the development and wider use of earth observation technologies, including satellite remote sensing, global mapping and geographic information systems, to collect quality data on environmental impacts, land use and land-use changes, including through urgent actions at all levels to:

(a) Strengthen cooperation and coordination among global observing systems and research programmes for integrated global observations, taking into account the need for building capacity and sharing of data from ground-based observations, satellite remote sensing and other sources among all countries;

(b) Develop information systems that make the sharing of valuable data possible, including the active exchange of Earth observation data;

(c) Encourage initiatives and partnerships for global mapping.

133. Support countries, particularly developing countries, in their national efforts to:

(a) Collect data that are accurate, long-term, consistent and reliable;

(b) Use satellite and remote-sensing technologies for data collection and further improvement of ground-based observations;

(c) Access, explore and use geographic information by utilizing the technologies of satellite remote sensing, satellite global positioning, mapping and geographic information systems.

134. Support efforts to prevent and mitigate the impacts of natural disasters, including through urgent actions at all levels to:

(a) Provide affordable access to disaster-related information for early warning purposes;

(b) Translate available data, particularly from global meteorological observation systems, into timely and useful products.

135. Develop and promote the wider application of environmental impact assessments, inter alia, as a national instrument, as appropriate, to provide essential decision-support information on projects that could cause significant adverse effects to the environment.

136. Promote and further develop methodologies at policy, strategy and project levels for sustainable development decision-making at the local and national levels, and where relevant at the regional level. In this regard, emphasize that the choice of the appropriate methodology to be used in countries should be adequate to their country-specific conditions and circumstances, should be on a voluntary basis and should conform to their development priority needs.

XI Institutional framework for sustainable development

137. An effective institutional framework for sustainable development at all levels is key to the full implementation of Agenda 21, the follow-up to the outcomes of the World Summit on Sustainable Development and meeting emerging sustainable development challenges. Measures aimed at strengthening such a framework should build on the provisions of Agenda 21, as well as the Programme for the Further Implementation of Agenda 21 of 1997 and the principles of the Rio Declaration on Environment and Development, and should promote the achievement of the internationally agreed development goals, including those contained in the Millennium Declaration, taking into account the Monterrey Consensus and relevant outcomes of other major United Nations conferences and international agreements since 1992. It should be responsive to the needs of all countries, taking into account the specific needs of developing countries, including the means of implementation. It should lead to the strengthening of international bodies and organizations dealing with sustainable development, while respecting their existing mandates, as well as to the strengthening of relevant regional, national and local institutions.

138. Good governance is essential for sustainable development. Sound economic policies, solid democratic institutions responsive to the needs of the people and improved infrastructure are the basis for sustained economic growth, poverty eradication and employment creation. Freedom, peace and security, domestic stability, respect for human rights, including the right to development, and the rule of law, gender equality, market-oriented policies, and an overall commitment to just and democratic societies are also essential and mutually reinforcing.

A. Objectives

139. Measures to strengthen institutional arrangements on sustainable development, at all levels, should be taken within the framework of Agenda 21,[45] build on developments since the United Nations Conference on Environment and Development and lead to the achievement of, inter alia, the following objectives:

(a) Strengthening commitments to sustainable development;

(b) Integration of the economic, social and environmental dimensions of sustainable development in a balanced manner;

(c) Strengthening of the implementation of Agenda 21, including through the mobilization of financial and technological resources, as well as capacity-building programmes, particularly for developing countries;

(d) Strengthening coherence, coordination and monitoring;

(e) Promoting the rule of law and strengthening of governmental institutions;

(f) Increasing effectiveness and efficiency through limiting overlap and duplication of activities of international organizations, within and outside the United Nations system, based on their mandates and comparative advantages;

(g) Enhancing participation and effective involvement of civil society and other relevant stakeholders in the implementation of Agenda 21, as well as promoting transparency and broad public participation;

(h) Strengthening capacities for sustainable development at all levels, including the local level, in particular those of developing countries;

(i) Strengthening international cooperation aimed at reinforcing the implementation of Agenda 21 and the outcomes of the Summit.

B. Strengthening the institutional framework for sustainable development at the international level

140. The international community should:

(a) Enhance the integration of sustainable development goals as reflected in Agenda 21 and support for implementation of Agenda 21 and the outcomes of the Summit into the policies, work programmes and operational guidelines of relevant United Nations agencies, programmes and funds, the Global Environment Facility and international financial and trade institutions, within their mandates, while stressing that their activities should take full account of national programmes and priorities, particularly those of developing countries, as well as, where appropriate, countries with economies in transition, to achieve sustainable development;

(b) Strengthen collaboration within and between the United Nations system, international financial institutions, the Global Environment Facility and the World Trade Organization, utilizing the United Nations System Chief Executives Board for Coordination, the United Nations Development Group, the Environment Management Group and other inter-agency coordinating bodies. Strengthened inter-agency collaboration should be pursued in all relevant contexts, with special emphasis on the operational level and involving partnership arrangements on specific issues, to support, in particular, the efforts of developing countries in implementing Agenda 21;

(c) Strengthen and better integrate the three dimensions of sustainable development policies and programmes and promote the full integration of sustainable development objectives into programmes and policies of bodies that have a primary focus on social issues. In particular, the social dimension of sustainable development should be strengthened, inter alia, by emphasizing follow-up to the outcomes of the World Summit for Social Development and its five-year review, and taking into account their reports, and by support to social protection systems;

(d) Fully implement the outcomes of the decision on international environmental governance adopted by the Governing Council of the United Nations Environment Programme at its seventh Special Session[46] and invite the General Assembly at its 57th session to consider the important but complex issue of establishing universal membership for the Governing Council/Global Ministerial Environment Forum;

(e) Engage actively and constructively in ensuring the timely completion of the negotiations on a comprehensive United Nations convention against corruption, including the question of repatriation of funds illicitly acquired to countries of origin;

(f) Promote corporate responsibility and accountability and the exchange of best practices in the context of sustainable development, including, as appropriate, through multi-stakeholder dialogue, such as through the Commission on Sustainable Development, and other initiatives;

(g) Take concrete action to implement the Monterrey Consensus at all levels.

141. Good governance at the international level is fundamental for achieving sustainable development. In order to ensure a dynamic and enabling international economic environment, it is important to promote global economic governance through addressing the international finance, trade, technology and investment patterns that have an impact on the development prospects of developing countries. To this effect, the international community should take all necessary and appropriate measures, including ensuring support for structural and macro-economic reform, a comprehensive solution to the external debt problem and increasing market access for developing countries. Efforts to reform the international financial architecture need to be sustained with greater transparency and the effective participation of developing countries in decision-making processes. A universal, rules-based, open, non-discriminatory and equitable multilateral trading system, as well as meaningful trade liberalization, can substantially stimulate development worldwide, benefiting countries at all stages of development.

142. A vibrant and effective United Nations system is fundamental to the promotion of international cooperation for sustainable development and to a global economic system that works for all. To this effect, a firm commitment to the ideals of the United Nations, the principles of international law and those enshrined in the Charter of the United Nations, as well as to strengthening the United Nations system and other multilateral institutions and promoting the improvement of their operations, is essential. States should also fulfil their commitment to negotiate and finalize as soon as possible a United Nations convention against corruption in all its aspects, including the question of repatriation of funds illicitly acquired to countries of origin and also to promoting stronger cooperation to eliminate money laundering.

C. Role of the General Assembly

143. The General Assembly of the United Nations should adopt sustainable development as a key element of the overarching framework for United Nations activities, particularly for achieving the internationally agreed development goals, including those contained in the Millennium Declaration, and should give overall political direction to the implementation of Agenda 21 and its review.

D. Role of the Economic and Social Council

144. Pursuant to the relevant provisions of the Charter of the United Nations, the provisions of Agenda 21 regarding the Economic and Social Council and General Assembly resolutions 48/162 and 50/227, which reaffirmed the Council as the central mechanism for the coordination of the United Nations system and its specialized agencies and supervision of subsidiary bodies, in particular its functional commissions, and to promote the implementation of Agenda 21 by strengthening system-wide coordination, the Council should:

    (a) Increase its role in overseeing system-wide coordination and the balanced integration of economic, social and environmental aspects of United Nations policies and programmes aimed at promoting sustainable development;

    (b) Organize periodic consideration of sustainable development themes in regard to the implementation of Agenda 21, including the means of implementation. Recommendations in regard to such themes could be made by the Commission on Sustainable Development;

    (c) Make full use of its high-level, coordination, operational activities and the general segments to effectively take into account all relevant aspects of the work of the United Nations on sustainable development. In this context, the Council should encourage the active participation of major groups in its high-level segment and the work of its relevant functional commissions, in accordance with the respective rules of procedure;

    (d) Promote greater coordination, complementarity, effectiveness and efficiency of activities of its functional commissions and other subsidiary bodies that are relevant to the implementation of Agenda 21;

    (e) Terminate the work of the Committee on Energy and Natural Resources for Development and transfer its work to the Commission on Sustainable Development;

    (f) Ensure that there is a close link between the role of the Council in the follow-up to the Summit and its role in the follow-up to the Monterrey Consensus, in a sustained and coordinated manner. To that end, the Council should explore ways to develop arrangements relating to its meetings with the Bretton Woods institutions and the World Trade Organization, as set out in the Monterrey Consensus;

    (g) Intensify its efforts to ensure that gender mainstreaming is an integral part of its activities concerning the coordinated implementation of Agenda 21.

E. Role and function of the Commission on Sustainable Development

145. The Commission on Sustainable Development should continue to be the high-level commission on sustainable development within the United Nations system and serve as a forum for consideration of issues related to integration of the three dimensions of sustainable development. Although the role, functions and mandate of the Commission as set out in relevant parts of Agenda 21 and adopted in General Assembly resolution 47/191 continue to be relevant, the Commission needs to be strengthened, taking into account the role of relevant institutions and organizations. An enhanced role of the Commission should include reviewing and

monitoring progress in the implementation of Agenda 21 and fostering coherence of implementation, initiatives and partnerships.

146. Within that context, the Commission should place more emphasis on actions that enable implementation at all levels, including promoting and facilitating partnerships involving Governments, international organizations and relevant stakeholders for the implementation of Agenda 21.

147. The Commission should:
    (a) Review and evaluate progress and promote further implementation of Agenda 21;
    (b) Focus on the cross-sectoral aspects of specific sectoral issues and provide a forum for better integration of policies, including through interaction among Ministers dealing with the various dimensions and sectors of sustainable development through the high-level segments;
    (c) Address new challenges and opportunities related to the implementation of Agenda 21;
    (d) Focus on actions related to implementation of Agenda 21, limiting negotiations in the sessions of the Commission to every two years;
    (e) Limit the number of themes addressed in each session.

148. In relation to its role in facilitating implementation, the CSD should emphasize the following:
    (a) Review progress and promote the further implementation of Agenda 21. In this context, the Commission should identify constraints on implementation and make recommendations to overcome those constraints;
    (b) Serve as a focal point for the discussion of partnerships that promote sustainable development, including sharing lessons learned, progress made and best practices;
    (c) Review issues related to financial assistance and transfer of technology for sustainable development, as well as capacity-building, while making full use of existing information. In this regard, the Commission on Sustainable Development could give consideration to more effective use of national reports and regional experience and to this end make appropriate recommendations;
    (d) Provide a forum for analysis and exchange of experience on measures that assist sustainable development planning, decision-making and the implementation of sustainable development strategies. In this regard, the Commission could give consideration to more effective use of national and regional reports;
    (e) Take into account significant legal developments in the field of sustainable development, with due regard to the role of relevant intergovernmental bodies in promoting the implementation of Agenda 21 relating to international legal instruments and mechanisms.

149. With regard to the practical modalities and programme of work of the Commission, specific decisions on those issues should be taken by the Commission at its next session, when the Commission's thematic work programme will be elaborated. In particular, the following issues should be considered:
    (a) Giving a balanced consideration to implementation of all of the mandates of the Commission contained in General Assembly resolution 47/191;
    (b) Continuing to provide for more direct and substantive involvement of international organizations and major groups in the work of the Commission;

(c) Give greater consideration to the scientific contributions to sustainable development through, for example, drawing on the scientific community and encouraging national, regional and international scientific networks to be involved in the Commission;

(d) Further the contribution of educators to sustainable development, including, where appropriate, in the activities of the Commission;

(e) Take into account the scheduling and duration of intersessional meetings.

150. Undertake further measures to promote best practices and lessons learned in sustainable development, and, in addition, promote the use of contemporary methods of data collection and dissemination, including broader use of information technologies.

F. Role of international institutions

151. Stress the need for international institutions both within and outside the United Nations system, including international financial institutions, the World Trade Organization and the Global Environment Facility, to enhance, within their mandates, their cooperative efforts to:

(a) Promote effective and collective support to the implementation of Agenda 21 at all levels;

(b) Enhance the effectiveness and coordination of international institutions to implement Agenda 21, the outcomes of the World Summit on Sustainable Development, relevant sustainable development aspects of the Millennium Declaration, the Monterrey Consensus and the outcome of the Fourth Ministerial Meeting of the World Trade Organization, held in Doha in November 2001.

152. Request the Secretary-General of the United Nations, utilizing the United Nations System Chief Executives Board for Coordination, including through informal collaborative efforts, to further promote system-wide interagency cooperation and coordination on sustainable development, to take appropriate measures to facilitate exchange of information, and to continue to keep the Economic and Social Council and the Commission informed of actions being taken to implement Agenda 21.

153. Significantly strengthen support for the capacity-building programmes of the United Nations Development Programme for sustainable development, building on the experience gained from the Capacity 21 programme, as important mechanisms for supporting local and national development capacity-building efforts, in particular in developing countries.

154. Strengthen cooperation between the United Nations Environment Programme and other United Nations bodies and specialized agencies, the Bretton Woods institutions and the World Trade Organization, within their mandates.

155. The United Nations Environment Programme, the United Nations Centre for Human Settlements, the United Nations Development Programme and the United Nations Conference on Trade and Development, within their mandates, should strengthen their contribution to sustainable development programmes and the implementation of Agenda 21 at all levels, particularly in the area of promoting capacity-building.

156. To promote effective implementation of Agenda 21 at the international level, the following should also be undertaken:

(a) Streamline the international sustainable development meeting calendar and, as appropriate, reduce the number of meetings, the length of meetings and the amount of time spent on negotiated outcomes in favour of more time spent on practical matters related to implementation;

(b) Encourage partnership initiatives for implementation by all relevant actors to support the outcome of the World Summit on Sustainable Development. In this context, further development of partnerships and partnership follow-up should take note of the preparatory work for the Summit;

(c) Make full use of developments in the field of information and communication technologies.

157. Strengthening of the international institutional framework for sustainable development is an evolutionary process. It is necessary to keep relevant arrangements under review; identify gaps; eliminate duplication of functions; and continue to strive for greater integration, efficiency and coordination of the economic, social and environmental dimensions of sustainable development aiming at the implementation of Agenda 21.

G. Strengthening institutional arrangements for sustainable development at the regional level

158. Implementation of Agenda 21 and the outcomes of the Summit should be effectively pursued at the regional and sub-regional levels, through the regional commissions and other regional and sub-regional institutions and bodies.

159. Intra-regional coordination and cooperation on sustainable development should be improved among the regional commissions, United Nations Funds, programmes and agencies, regional development banks and other regional and sub-regional institutions and bodies. This should include, as appropriate, support for development, enhancement and implementation of agreed regional sustainable development strategies and action plans, reflecting national and regional priorities.

160. In particular, taking into account relevant provisions of Agenda 21, the regional commissions, in collaboration with other regional and subregional bodies, should:

(a) Promote the integration of the three dimensions of sustainable development into their work in a balanced way, including through implementation of Agenda 21. To this end, the regional commissions should enhance their capacity through internal action and be provided, as appropriate, with external support;

(b) Facilitate and promote a balanced integration of the economic, social and environmental dimensions of sustainable development into the work of regional, sub-regional and other bodies – for example, by facilitating and strengthening the exchange of experiences, including national experience, best practices, case studies and partnership experience related to the implementation of Agenda 21;

(c) Assist in the mobilization of technical and financial assistance, and facilitate the provision of adequate financing for the implementation of regionally and sub-regionally agreed sustainable development programmes and projects, including addressing the objective of poverty eradication;

(d) Continue to promote multi-stakeholder participation and encourage partnerships to support the implementation of Agenda 21 at the regional and sub-regional levels.

161. Regionally and sub-regionally agreed sustainable development initiatives and programmes, such as the New Partnership for African Development (NEPAD) and

the interregional aspects of the globally agreed Programme of Action on the Sustainable Development of Small Island Developing States, should be supported.

H. Strengthening institutional frameworks for sustainable development at the national level

162. States should:

(a) Continue to promote coherent and coordinated approaches to institutional frameworks for sustainable development at all national levels, including through, as appropriate, the establishment or strengthening of existing authorities and mechanisms necessary for policy-making, coordination and implementation and enforcement of laws;

(b) Take immediate steps to make progress in the formulation and elaboration of national strategies for sustainable development and begin their implementation by 2005. To this end, as appropriate, strategies should be supported through international cooperation, taking into account the special needs of developing countries, in particular the least developed countries. Such strategies, which, where applicable, could be formulated as poverty reduction strategies that integrate economic, social and environmental aspects of sustainable development, should be pursued in accordance with each country's national priorities.

163. Each country has the primary responsibility for its own sustainable development, and the role of national policies and development strategies cannot be overemphasized. All countries should promote sustainable development at the national level by, inter alia, enacting and enforcing clear and effective laws that support sustainable development. All countries should strengthen governmental institutions, including by providing necessary infrastructure and by promoting transparency, accountability and fair administrative and judicial institutions.

164. All countries should also promote public participation, including through measures that provide access to information regarding legislation, regulations, activities, policies and programmes. They should also foster full public participation in sustainable development policy formulation and implementation. Women should be able to participate fully and equally in policy formulation and decision-making.

165. Further promote the establishment or enhancement of sustainable development councils and/or coordination structures at the national level, including at the local level, in order to provide a high-level focus on sustainable development policies. In that context, multi-stakeholder participation should be promoted.

166. Support efforts by all countries, particularly developing countries, as well as countries with economies in transition, to enhance national institutional arrangements for sustainable development, including at the local level. This could include promoting cross-sectoral approaches in the formulation of strategies and plans for sustainable development, such as, where applicable, poverty reduction strategies, aid coordination, encouraging participatory approaches and enhancing policy analysis, management capacity and implementation capacity, including mainstreaming a gender perspective in all those activities.

167. Enhance the role and capacity of local authorities as well as stakeholders in implementing Agenda 21 and the outcomes of the Summit and in strengthening the continuing support for local Agenda 21 programmes and associated initiatives

and partnerships and encourage, in particular, partnerships among and between local authorities and other levels of government and stakeholders to advance sustainable development as called for in, inter alia, the Habitat Agenda.[47]

I. Participation of major groups

168. Enhance partnerships between governmental and non-governmental actors, including all major groups, as well as volunteer groups, on programmes and activities for the achievement of sustainable development at all levels.

169. Acknowledge the consideration being given to the possible relationship between environment and human rights, including the right to development, with full and transparent participation of Member States of the United Nations and observer States.

170. Promote and support youth participation in programmes and activities relating to sustainable development through, for example, supporting local youth councils or their equivalent, and by encouraging their establishment where they do not exist.

Notes

* The text has been reproduced fully from the original UN document, A/CONF.199/20. Please refer to http://www.un.org/esa/sustdev/ for full details of references cited.

1 *Report of the United Nations Conference on Environment and Development, Rio de Janeiro, 3–14 June 1992* (United Nations publication, Sales No E.93.I.8 and corrigenda)

2 Ibid, vol I: *Resolutions Adopted by the Conference*, resolution 1, annexes I and II

3 General Assembly resolution S-19/2, annex

4 General Assembly resolution 55/2

5 Report of the *United Nations Conference on Environment and Development, Rio de Janeiro, 3–14 June 1992* (United Nations publication, Sales No E.93.I.8 and corrigenda), vol I: *Resolutions Adopted by the Conference*, resolution 1, annex I

6 *Report of the International Conference on Financing for Development, Monterrey, Mexico, 18–22 March 2002* (United Nations, publication, Sales No E.02.II.A.7), Chapter 1, resolution 1, annex

7 United Nations, Treaty Series, vol 1954, no 33480

8 See *ILO Declaration on Fundamental Principles and Rights at Work and its Follow-up Adopted by the International Labour Conference at its Eighty-sixth Session, Geneva, 16 June 1998*, (Geneva, International Labour Office)

9 *Official Records of the Economic and Social Council, 2001, Supplement No 9* (E/2001/29), chap I.B

10 UNEP/FAO/PIC/CONF.5, annex III

11 www.chem.unep.ch/sc

12 Intergovernmental Forum on Chemical Safety (IFCS), Third Session, *Forum III Final Report* (IFCS/Forum III/23w) annex 6

13 United Nations *Treaty Series*, vol 1673, no 28911

14 *Official Records of the Third United Nations Conference on the Law of the Sea*, vol XVII, United Nations, publication, Sales No E.84.V.3, Document A/CONF.62/122

15 See Food and Agriculture Organization of the United Nations document C200/INF/25, appendix I

16 See UNEP/CBD/COP/5/23, annex III

17 See *International Fisheries Instruments* (United Nations, publication, Sales No E.98.V.11) sect I; see also A/CONF.164/37

18 Ibid

19 Ibid, sect III

20 Rome, Food and Agriculture Organization of the United Nations, 1999,

21 Ibid, 2001

22 See A/51/312, annex II, decision II/10

23 *Ramsar Convention on Wetlands of International Importance Especially as Waterfowl Habitat* (United Nations, Treaty Series, vol 996, no 14583)

24 See United Nations Environment Programme, *Convention on Biological Diversity* (Environmental Law and Institution Programme Activity Centre) June 1992

25 A/51/116, annex II

26 See E/CN.17/2002/PC.2/15

27 A/AC.237/18 (Part II)/Add.1 and Corr.1, annex I

28 FCCC/CP/1997/7/Add.1, decision 1/CP.3, annex

29 FCCC/CP/2001/13 and Add.1–4

30 See General Assembly resolution 2200 A (XXI), annex

31 *Report of the Conference of the Food and Agriculture Organization of the United Nations, Thirty-first Session, Rome, 2–13 November 2001* (C2001/REP) Appendix D

32 See A/C.2/56/7, annex

33 http://www.biodiv.org/biosafety/protocol.asp

34 General Assembly resolution S-26/2, annex

35 *Report of the Global Conference on the Sustainable Development of Small Island Developing States, Bridgetown, Barbados, 25 April–6 May 1994* (United Nations, publication, Sales No E.94.I.18 and corrigenda) chap I, resolution 1, annex II

36 E/CN.17/2002/PC.2/5/Add.2

37 E/CN.17/2002/PC.2/8

38 ECE/ACC.22/2001/2, annex I

39 A/CONF.192/13

40 A/CONF.191/11

41 A/C.2/56/2, annex, paras 13 and 14

42 Ibid, paras 17–19

43 General Assembly resolution 2625 (XXV), annex

44 See *Official Records of the Economic and Social Council (2001) Supplement No 9* (E/2001/29), chap I.B

45 References in the present chapter to Agenda 21 are deemed to include Agenda 21, the Programme for the Further Implementation of Agenda 21 and the outcomes of the Summit

46 UNEP/GCSS.VII/6, annex I

47 A/CONF.165/14, chap 1, resolution 1, annex II

Johannesburg Declaration on Sustainable Development[*]

Annex B

From our origins to the future

1. We, the representatives of the peoples of the world, assembled at the World Summit on Sustainable Development in Johannesburg, South Africa, from 2 to 4 September 2002, reaffirm our commitment to sustainable development.
2. We commit ourselves to building a humane, equitable and caring global society, cognizant of the need for human dignity for all.
3. At the beginning of this Summit, the children of the world spoke to us in a simple yet clear voice that the future belongs to them, and accordingly challenged all of us to ensure that through our actions they will inherit a world free of the indignity and indecency occasioned by poverty, environmental degradation and patterns of unsustainable development.
4. As part of our response to these children, who represent our collective future, all of us, coming from every corner of the world, informed by different life experiences, are united and moved by a deeply felt sense that we urgently need to create a new and brighter world of hope.
5. Accordingly, we assume a collective responsibility to advance and strengthen the interdependent and mutually reinforcing pillars of sustainable development – economic development, social development and environmental protection – at the local, national, regional and global levels.
6. From this continent, the cradle of humanity, we declare, through the Plan of Implementation of the World Summit on Sustainable Development and the present Declaration, our responsibility to one another, to the greater community of life and to our children.
7. Recognizing that humankind is at a crossroads, we have united in a common resolve to make a determined effort to respond positively to the need to produce a practical and visible plan to bring about poverty eradication and human development.

From Stockholm to Rio de Janeiro to Johannesburg

8. Thirty years ago, in Stockholm, we agreed on the urgent need to respond to the problem of environmental deterioration.[1] Ten years ago, at the United Nations Conference on Environment and Development, held in Rio de Janeiro,[2] we agreed that the protection of the environment and social and economic development are fundamental to sustainable development, based on the Rio Principles. To achieve such development, we adopted the global programme entitled Agenda 21[3] and the Rio Declaration on Environment and Development,[3] to which we reaffirm our

commitment. The Rio Conference was a significant milestone that set a new agenda for sustainable development.

9. Between Rio and Johannesburg, the world's nations have met in several major conferences under the auspices of the United Nations, including the International Conference on Financing for Development,[4] as well as the Doha Ministerial Conference.[5] These conferences defined for the world a comprehensive vision for the future of humanity.

10. At the Johannesburg Summit, we have achieved much in bringing together a rich tapestry of peoples and views in a constructive search for a common path towards a world that respects and implements the vision of sustainable development. The Johannesburg Summit has also confirmed that significant progress has been made towards achieving a global consensus and partnership among all the people of our planet.

The challenges we face

11. We recognize that poverty eradication, changing consumption and production patterns and protecting and managing the natural resource base for economic and social development are overarching objectives of, and essential requirements for, sustainable development.

12. The deep fault line that divides human society between the rich and the poor and the ever-increasing gap between the developed and developing worlds pose a major threat to global prosperity, security and stability.

13. The global environment continues to suffer. Loss of biodiversity continues, fish stocks continue to be depleted, desertification claims more and more fertile land, the adverse effects of climate change are already evident, natural disasters are more frequent and more devastating, and developing countries more vulnerable, and air, water and marine pollution continue to rob millions of a decent life.

14. Globalization has added a new dimension to these challenges. The rapid integration of markets, mobility of capital and significant increases in investment flows around the world have opened new challenges and opportunities for the pursuit of sustainable development. But the benefits and costs of globalization are unevenly distributed, with developing countries facing special difficulties in meeting this challenge.

15. We risk the entrenchment of these global disparities, and unless we act in a manner that fundamentally changes their lives the poor of the world may lose confidence in their representatives and the democratic systems to which we remain committed, seeing their representatives as nothing more than sounding brass or tinkling cymbals.

Our commitment to sustainable development

16. We are determined to ensure that our rich diversity, which is our collective strength, will be used for constructive partnership for change and for the achievement of the common goal of sustainable development.

17. Recognizing the importance of building human solidarity, we urge the promotion of dialogue and cooperation among the world's civilizations and peoples, irrespective of race, disabilities, religion, language, culture or tradition.

18. We welcome the focus of the Johannesburg Summit on the indivisibility of human dignity and are resolved, through decisions on targets, timetables and partnerships, to speedily increase access to such basic requirements as clean water, sanitation, adequate shelter, energy, healthcare, food security and the protection of biodiversity. At the same time, we will work together to help one another gain access to financial resources, benefit from the opening of markets, ensure capacity-building, use modern technology to bring about development and make sure that there is technology transfer, human resource development, education and training to banish underdevelopment forever.

19. We reaffirm our pledge to place particular focus on, and give priority attention to, the fight against the worldwide conditions that pose severe threats to the sustainable development of our people, which include chronic hunger; malnutrition; foreign occupation; armed conflict; illicit drug problems; organized crime; corruption; natural disasters; illicit arms trafficking; trafficking in persons; terrorism; intolerance and incitement to racial, ethnic, religious and other hatreds; xenophobia; and endemic, communicable and chronic diseases, in particular HIV/AIDS, malaria and tuberculosis.

20. We are committed to ensuring that women's empowerment, emancipation and gender equality are integrated in all the activities encompassed within Agenda 21, the Millennium development goals[6] and the Plan of Implementation of the Summit.

21. We recognize the reality that global society has the means and is endowed with the resources to address the challenges of poverty eradication and sustainable development confronting all humanity. Together, we will take extra steps to ensure that these available resources are used to the benefit of humanity.

22. In this regard, to contribute to the achievement of our development goals and targets, we urge developed countries that have not done so to make concrete efforts to reach the internationally agreed levels of official development assistance.

23. We welcome and support the emergence of stronger regional groupings and alliances, such as the New Partnership for Africa's Development, to promote regional cooperation, improved international cooperation and sustainable development.

24. We shall continue to pay special attention to the developmental needs of small island developing States and the least developed countries.

25. We reaffirm the vital role of the indigenous peoples in sustainable development.

26. We recognize that sustainable development requires a long-term perspective and broad-based participation in policy formulation, decision-making and implementation at all levels. As social partners, we will continue to work for stable partnerships with all major groups, respecting the independent, important roles of each of them.

27. We agree that in pursuit of its legitimate activities the private sector, including both large and small companies, has a duty to contribute to the evolution of equitable and sustainable communities and societies.

28. We also agree to provide assistance to increase income-generating employment opportunities, taking into account the Declaration on Fundamental Principles and Rights at Work of the International Labour Organization.[7]

29. We agree that there is a need for private-sector corporations to enforce corporate accountability, which should take place within a transparent and stable regulatory environment.

30. We undertake to strengthen and improve governance at all levels for the effective implementation of Agenda 21, the Millennium development goals and the Plan of Implementation of the Summit.

Multilateralism is the future

31. To achieve our goals of sustainable development, we need more effective, democratic and accountable international and multilateral institutions.
32. We reaffirm our commitment to the principles and purposes of the Charter of the United Nations and international law, as well as to the strengthening of multilateralism. We support the leadership role of the United Nations as the most universal and representative organization in the world, which is best placed to promote sustainable development.
33. We further commit ourselves to monitor progress at regular intervals towards the achievement of our sustainable development goals and objectives.

Making it happen!

34. We are in agreement that this must be an inclusive process, involving all the major groups and Governments that participated in the historic Johannesburg Summit.
35. We commit ourselves to act together, united by a common determination to save our planet, promote human development and achieve universal prosperity and peace.
36. We commit ourselves to the Plan of Implementation of the World Summit on Sustainable Development and to expediting the achievement of the time-bound, socio-economic and environmental targets contained therein.
37. From the African continent, the cradle of humankind, we solemnly pledge to the peoples of the world and the generations that will surely inherit this Earth that we are determined to ensure that our collective hope for sustainable development is realized.

Notes

* The text has been reproduced fully from the original UN document A/CONF.199/20. Please refer to http://www.un.org/esa/sustdev/ for full details of references cited.

1 *Report of the United Nations Conference on the Human Environment, Stockholm, 5–16 June 1972* (United Nations, publication, Sales No E.73.II.A.14 and corrigendum) chap 1

2 *Report of the United Nations Conference on Environment and Development, Rio de Janeiro, 3–14 June 1992* (United Nations, publication, Sales No E.93.I.8 and corrigenda) vol I–III

3 Ibid, vol I: *Resolutions adopted by the Conference*, resolution 1, annexes I and II

4 *Report of the International Conference on Financing for Development, Monterrey, Mexico, 18–22 March 2002* (United Nations, publication, Sales No E.02.II.A.7) chap I, resolution 1, annex

5 See A/C.2/56/7, annex

6   See General Assembly resolution 55/2

7   See *ILO Declaration on Fundamental Principles and Rights at Work and Its Follow-up Adopted by the International Labour Conference at its Eighty-sixth Session, Geneva, 18 June 1998*, ILO (Geneva International Labour Office, 1998)

Index

For Product Safety Concerns and Information please contact our EU
representative GPSR@taylorandfrancis.com Taylor & Francis Verlag GmbH,
Kaufingerstraße 24, 80331 München, Germany

Printed and bound by CPI Group (UK) Ltd, Croydon, CR0 4YY
08/05/2025
01864457-0007